JERASH AND THE DECAPOLIS

JERASH

AND THE DECAPOLIS

By

IAIN BROWNING

JORDAN DISTRIBUTION AGENCY, AMMAN
in association with
Chatto & Windus · London

Published by
Chatto & Windus Ltd
20 Vauxhall Bridge Road
London SW1V 2SA

First published in 1982
Reprinted 1985, 1988 and 1991

BRITISH LIBRARY CATALOGUING IN PUBLICATION DATA

Browning, Iain
Jerash and the Decapolis.
1. Jerash (Jordan) – Antiquities
I. Title
933   DS110.J/

ISBN 0 7011 2591 8

Printed in Great Britain by
Butler & Tanner Ltd,
Frome and London

To
His Majesty King Hussein I
by gracious permission

Contents

List of Illustrations   *page* 8

Chapter

1 FRIENDS IN NEED   11

2 'THE WILDERNESS WITH VOICE'   18

3 'NO MINOR EVENT'   59

4 FROM PILLAR TO IMPOST   77

5 JERASH TODAY   103

Glossary of Architectural Terms   217

Bibliography   218

Index   220

Illustrations

COLOUR PLATES

Between pages 112 and 113

1   Pillars of the Temple of Artemis
2   The North Colonnade Street
3   The south side of the Artemis Temenos
4a The Central Colonnade Street
4b Birketein

OTHER ILLUSTRATIONS

The monochrome illustrations may be found from the Index, where their page references are set in italics.

MAPS

1 The ancient kingdoms of Transjordan and Palestine   10
2 The Region of the Decapolis   14
3 Plan of Jerash   83
4 Birketein   214

All illustrations in this book are by the author except for the following which are reproduced with the kind permission of: Mr Peter Hooker, Fig. 69; The Palestine Exploration Fund, Figs. 2, 14, 15, 16, 19, 20, 44, 51, 59, 66, 70, 76, 89, 90, 103; Jordanian Department of Antiquities, Fig. 56.

Acknowledgements

First of all, I would like to express my gratitude to His Majesty King Hussein at whose instigation this book was written, and whose practical support, encouragement and interest have made it possible.

For the generous facilities throughout Jordan which enabled me to carry out the necessary site research, I am much indebted to His Excellency, Ma'an Abu Nowar, Minister of Tourism and Antiquities. His friendly help and attention have been delightfully reassuring. Likewise, my thanks also go to Dr Adnan Hadidi, Director of the Department of Antiquities, and his staff, who were ever-willing to give of their time and assistance. I should, in addition, like to thank Miss Ferial Bakri for the charming and uncomplaining way in which she coped with my ever-changing schedules, and Mr Adeb Dababneh, my driver, who patiently and in blissful safety drove me on all my journeys throughout Jordan. My friends in Amman have, as ever, been unstinting with their co-operation and hospitality, not least Mrs Crystal-M. Bennett, Director of the British Institute at Amman for Archaeology and History.

In the U.K. the assistance and forbearance of all my friends has been wonderful. The good offices of Mrs Mae Palmer-Hall in establishing contacts in Jordan are greatly appreciated. Similarly, Mr Geoffrey Wilkinson and Mr Stephen Crawley were ever-patient with my photographic problems. It is, however, with special pleasure that I acknowledge the help of Mr Barry Norman who read the proofs with me.

South Kensington,
London   IAIN B. BROWNING

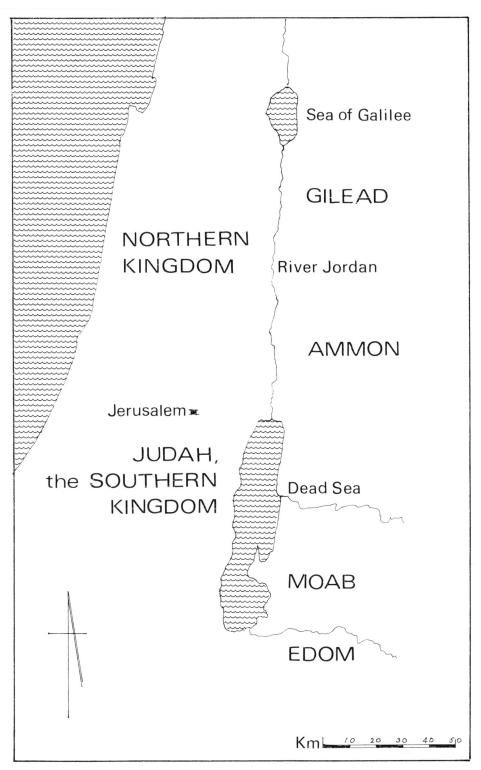

Map 1   The ancient kingdoms of Transjordan and Palestine.

CHAPTER ONE

Friends in need

JERASH is one of the three great classical city sites of the Near East. It is, however, altogether different from Petra and Palmyra. The grandeur of Jerash is tempered by a charm to which one can relate immediately. Here the gods of antiquity presided benignly over the everyday life of the people, and still one can feel this human measure. For above all, Jerash is typical of a prosperous provincial Roman town.

Set in a wide, fertile valley high in the Hills of Gilead, Jerash is also the best preserved of the cities of the Decapolis. Josephus tells us in his *Wars* that Scythopolis was the largest of the 'ten cities' but one can hardly believe that it was as magnificent as Gerasa, as ancient Jerash was called. During the first and second centuries A.D. all the cities of the Decapolis developed into grand metropolises adorned with many fine civic and religious buildings. According to tradition Gerasa, like Pella and Gadara, was founded by Alexander the Great. This proud claim was not strictly accurate. Certainly one can say that the history of all 'ten cities' started with Alexander because it was he who created the political and cultural environment in which they were conceived and in which they grew up. It was as though he set the stage for all subsequent events; but this is true not only of the 'ten cities' but of the whole of Palestine, Jordan and Coele-Syria.

What then was the Decapolis? All one can say with certainty is that the word 'Decapolis' means 'ten cities' and that these were of Hellenistic origin. Were they federated in any way or did they form some sort of league? At times they are clearly being referred to as a particular group, but how did it come about that people should consider these ten cities to be a distinct group – and why only these ten? The situation is complicated by the authors of the classical period who disagreed on which were the ten; the count-list can reach as many as eighteen.

There is no answer from antiquity on any of these questions, so it is no surprise that scholars vary considerably in their assessments. But when one reviews the history of the whole area, a general pattern appears which permits speculation.

For centuries Transjordan had been made up of three main kingdoms, Edom, Moab and Ammon (Map 1). All three were carrying on incessant wars, either independently or collectively, with the Jewish kingdoms. Invaders, be they

Assyrian, Neo-Babylonian, Egyptian or Persian, had torn their bellicose way across these lands and held them in subjugation. With the fall of Jerusalem in 587 B.C., a new pattern began to form. King Zedekiah of Judea was led away with all Jews of any consequence into captivity in Babylon, leaving Palestine severely depopulated. The Edomites moved westwards into the fertile lowlands across the Rift Valley, there to create the new state of Idumea. In time the Neo-Babylonians fell to the Persians who, in about 538 B.C., allowed some of the captives to return. The Persians had other peoples to think about – the Greeks.

Despite their almost constant bickerings the Greek cities presented the major obstacle to Persian supremacy, and a head-on conflict was inevitable. The Hellenic city-states woke up in time to the scale of the Persian threat and, abandoning their prejudices, joined arms and faced the Persians. However, the overwhelming Greek victory at Salamis in 480 B.C. did not remove the long-term threat of oriental domination, for the Persians continued to be a powerful and potentially crippling force.

Then Alexander appeared on the scene, larger than life, larger even than the heroes of the epics. Son of the brilliant Philip II of Macedon (359–336 B.C.) who had established himself as the dominant force in Hellas, he like all his countrymen was considered little better than a barbarian by the cognoscenti of the Hellenic states. But that hardly mattered because on his father's death Alexander took the reins of pan-Hellenic power firmly in his hands and turned it towards the Persian threat. A pupil of Aristotle and, through him and his father's court, steeped in Greek culture, he knew what was at stake. It was this awareness which lies behind his contest with Darius, the Persian.

The consequences of his campaigns were not only to secure the future independence of Greece but were to affect all the lands over which he and his armies strode; none more so than Syria, Palestine and Jordan. As Professor Nicholas Hammond has pointed out, 'It must have been clear to Alexander that if he succeeded in overthrowing Darius, a very important centre of his communications would be Syria; so he took all possible steps to strengthen the Macedonian control of that vital area.'* Control meant Hellenistic penetration of all aspects of life, from military and civil administration to cultural environment. This he achieved principally through the creation of Macedonian settlements across the length and breadth of the conquered lands. Satraps were also appointed, such as Andromachus who 'ruled' Coele-Syria (Hollow Syria) which probably comprised the lands of the Bekka, the area around and south of Damascus and the Jordan Rift Valley as far south as the Dead Sea.

By 332 B.C., Alexander had established settlements at strategic points in that

---

* N. G. L. Hammond, *Alexander the Great*.

area. Not that all these sites were new, for there is ample evidence in the majority of cases of occupation extending back many centuries. Nonetheless, the new settlements were overtly Hellenistic, peopled by the many wounded and disabled Macedonian soldiers who were one of the consequences of his campaigns. His methods, according to Professor Hammond, 'in contrast to those of Persia were calculated to win the native peoples to his side'. But it was not always so amicable, for it depended very much on how the 'native peoples' accepted the new arrivals with their alien ideas. An example of a less happy case is Samaria, where a revolt was overthrown in 331 B.C., and the entire defeated population was ruthlessly expelled and replaced by Macedonian stock.

A group of these settlements developed in time into the cities of the Decapolis. They had a common history: we know of their struggles with the Hasmonean dynasty in Jerusalem, of their 'liberation' by Pompey the Great, of their Golden Age, of their Byzantine period and of their final eclipse. But there is no contemporary evidence to tell us of their founding, and one must question whether each was formally founded as a *polis* (city) at this stage. The majority were established after Alexander's time, as strategic posts, vulnerably isolated in a land where there could be no certainty that the indigenous population would remain friendly. So the claim that Alexander founded Gerasa and Pella, made by Stephanos Byzantios in his treatise on cities, *Ethnica*, must be interpreted with caution. He was writing some eight hundred years after the event, about A.D. 535, and there is evident confusion in much of his material. Neither do we have any text from that time which mentions the word 'Decapolis'. All one can say is that during the early Hellenistic period a large number of principally Macedonian settlements were established in the region, some of which later – probably before Pompey – developed into the cities of the Decapolis (Map 2).

The first reference we have to the Decapolis is in St Mark's Gospel: 'And he went away and started to proclaim in the Decapolis all the things Jesus did for him; and all the people began to wonder.'* Later in the same Gospel the Decapolis is again mentioned: 'Now coming back out of the regions of Tyre He went through Sidon to the Sea of Galilee in the midst of the region of Decapolis.'† In neither of these is anything about the nature or character of the Decapolis revealed except for the word 'region'. St Matthew is equally unhelpful when he wrote '. . . consequently great crowds followed Him from Galilee and Decapolis and Jerusalem and Judea and from the other side of the Jordan.'‡ What is obvious from these references is that the Decapolis was an accepted territorial definition; that people recognised that a particular area was being referred to. But it does not tell us how this came about or what the Decapolis was.

* St Mark 5:20.   † St Mark 7:31.   ‡ St Matthew 4:25.

Map 2 The region of the Decapolis.

The first historical text which says anything specific about the Decapolis was written towards the end of the first century A.D. by Pliny, who gave a list of the cities. But he admits that even then historians disagreed as to which were the member cities:

> Adjoining Judea on the side of Syria is the region of the Decapolis, so called from the number of its towns, though not all writers agree to the same list; most however include Damascus, with its fertile water-meadows that drain

14

the river Chrysorrhoe, Philadelphia, Raphana (all these three withdrawn towards Arabia), Scythopolis (formerly Nysa, after Father Liber's nurse, whom he buried there) where a colony of Scythians are settled; Gadara past which the river Yarmuk flows; Hippo, Dion, Pella rich with its waters, Galasa and Canatha.*

Galasa is a misspelling of Gerasa.

Pliny, like St Mark, refers to the 'region' of the Decapolis. Dr S. T. Parker has pointed out that Pliny uses the word *regio* meaning 'region', 'territory' or 'district'; and not a term like *foedus* or *societas* which could be translated to mean a league. The choice of word is obviously intentional.

The only other Roman commentator of the first century whom one might expect to be interested in the Decapolis was Strabo. He refers to individual cities such as Gadara, Philadelphia and Scythopolis but of the group name there is no mention. This is surprising when one remembers his interest in the Lycian League, which was a 'federation of twenty-three cities in western Asia Minor organised and supervised by the Romans'.† He was also interested in the Tetrapolis in northern Syria which consisted of four cities founded by Seleucus I, Seleucia, Antioch, Apamea and Laodicea. There was no actual federation here; the word 'Tetrapolis' being only a generally recognised definition of the area controlled by these cities. Strabo's comment, however, that the four cities 'used to be called sisters, because of their accord with one another'‡ is surely important, for it is possible that the same sort of accord existed between the ten cities of the Decapolis, giving rise to the popular recognition of them as a group.

Also writing in the first century A.D. was Josephus, who mentions the Decapolis by name four times, but he tells us nothing to suggest a formal link.

Only in the second century is something of a constitution hinted at. Like Pliny, Claudius Ptolemy, the Geographer, gives a list of the cities of the Decapolis and Coele-Syria without distinguishing which was in which. It is evident that he was combining two lists. Whether this can be taken as an indication that the need for an organised Decapolis was declining is debatable. Times were more peaceful under the *Pax Romana*, so any mutual self-preservation pact there may have been would have lost much of its point. In A.D. 106, the Emperor Trajan had reshaped the east yet again, with the result that old loyalties faded into the background. On the other hand the inclusion of Coele-Syrian cities in Ptolemy's list could equally be taken to indicate that the old Decapolis had expanded far beyond its original conception – whatever that was. Ptolemy's list is, however, interesting: Heliopolis, Abila, Saana, Ina, Damascus, Samoulis, Abila of Lysanias, Hippos, Capitolias,

---

* Pliny the Elder, *Natural History*.   † S. T. Parker, *Journal of Biblical Literature*.   ‡ Strabo, *Geography*.

Gadara, Adra, Scythopolis, Gerasa, Pella, Dion, Gadora, Philadelphia and Canatha. Of these cities which correspond with Pliny's list only Raphana is not mentioned: some have identified this with present day er-Rafeh, but other scholars maintain that Capitolias is the same place by a different name. Pliny certainly does not mention Capitolias. To Pliny's list Ptolemy also adds Samoulis, Adra and Abila of Lysanias but it could be argued that Samoulis, Adra and Gadora were not in fact Decapolis cities (of the ten), only cities in the geographical area generally recognised as being called by that name. The same would apply to places like Arbila (present-day Irbid) which also claims to have been a Decapolis city. Heliopolis, Abila of Lysanias, Saana and Ina are clearly cities of Coele-Syria.

However, Ptolemy's work is suspect because, in the form in which we know it, it is a compilation of the tenth and eleventh centuries from texts now lost. Under such circumstances the possibilities of error are greatly increased.

Another writer who mentions the Decapolis is Eusebius who was writing his *Onomasticon* during the fourth century. He also uses the word *regio* and again provides no clue of a formal treaty. Epiphanius, also writing from the fourth century, refers to the Decapolis only in a regional sense. He says about an early heretical sect: 'This heresy is found in the vicinity of Beraea in Coele-Syria, in the Decapolis....'* The double 'in' – in Coele-Syria, in the Decapolis – might be interpreted that the Decapolis had expanded to include part, if not all, Coele-Syria. Or should it be read the other way, as a scaling-down from Coele-Syria to a part of it, to the Decapolis, and then to a particular city, for the text continues '...in the vicinity of Pella ...'; were this to be the case it would mean that the Decapolis had been absorbed into Coele-Syria and had lost its identity but as the name of a recognised geographical location.

And, indeed, a name is all we are left with. Still, in his *Historical Geography of the Holy Land*, G. A. Smith wrote in 1894 that the Decapolis was 'a league of Greek cities against the Semitic influences east and west of Jordan'. J. S. Buckingham in his *Travels etc.* published in 1821 was more circumspect when he wrote: 'and ten principal cities were built on the east of the Jordan, giving the name of Decapolis to the whole part of that portion of land over which they were spread'. But the idea of a formal grouping has stuck fast and has been slow to lose its grip, for even C. H. Kraeling in his outstanding *Gerasa: City of the Decapolis*, published in 1938, refers to a 'confederation of free cities'. But tempting as it is to place a formal structure behind the name, there is no evidence to support it. If one bases one's argument on textual sources alone, Dr Parker went as far as one legitimately can when he wrote '... we may safely assume only that the Decapolis was a geographical region in

* Epiphanius, *Treatise on Weights and Measures.*

southern Syria and north-eastern Palestine composed of the territories of member cities'.

That these cities had a common Hellenistic culture is not questioned. That there was 'fraternal sympathy' between them at times of trouble can hardly be doubted. And because the core of the group is closely located, this 'fraternal sympathy' would have been obvious to any contemporary observer even though there was no concerted effort which historians could record. Any cohesion behind the name 'Decapolis' is likely to have been forged during the Hasmonean period when these cities were 'up against it'. When he 'liberated' the cities in 64/63 B.C., Pompey did not band them together in a formal federation, he only re-established each as an independent city-state united only in their membership of his Province of Syria. The citizens were so grateful that they proclaimed a new Era, and henceforth everything, including their coinage, was dated from that event. This has led some numismatists to suggest that the Decapolis was conceived by Pompey. It is more likely that he inherited the situation. It is possible that Pompey may even have been opposed to any federation. However much the ruling-classes of Rome might admire Greek culture, they never quite trusted the Greeks. Was it not better, having freed them, to encourage them without providing a means by which they might pose a threat to Roman authority? The old principle of 'divide and rule'.

Less than a hundred and fifty years after Pompey, Trajan created the Province of Arabia, to which he annexed the Nabatean Empire and most of the cities of the Decapolis. In the process the cities became just provincial cities with Bosra as the capital. Professor Yadin has argued against Bosra being the first capital, contending that this was at Petra until A.D. 132, when it was transferred to Bosra. Father Spijkerman has, however, argued for Bosra from the start, basing his argument on the facts that the city's name was *Nea Traiane Bosra*, that it was at the head of the *Via Nova*, that it was the headquarters of the legions and that the city dates worked on yet another, Trajanic, Era.

The indications, therefore, are that there was never any confederation of the cities of the Decapolis. Each was independent of the others, but they shared a common heritage and common cause in which 'fraternal sympathy', or accord, to use Strabo's word, was a powerful and cohesive force. The word 'Decapolis' remained only the name by which the geographical region of the ten cities was known.

CHAPTER TWO

CHAPTER TWO

'The Wilderness with Voice'

ON ALEXANDER THE GREAT'S early death in 323 B.C., the vast Macedonian Empire was left without a leader of equal stature, and it began to break up almost immediately. It was split up amongst his 'Successors', the eastern part being divided between two of his generals, Ptolemy and Seleucus. Ptolemy took Egypt, to which he later added by conquest Palestine, Jordan, Coele-Syria, Cyprus and Cyrenaica. Into this sphere, therefore, the region of the future Decapolis initially fell. Seleucus, on the other hand, took the satrapy of Babylonia, to which he added the northern part of Syria, an area in which he was challenged by a rival 'Successor', Antigonus. Seleucus may not have been one of Alexander's most prominent generals but in the developing chaos he was able to reassemble most of the old empire in Asia. This alone marks him as one of the ablest of the Successors, both as a military commander and as a statesman. Having dealt successfully with Antigonus and secured northern Syria, he sought to bring some realistic and economic shape to his dangerously extended dominion and so moved south and occupied the ancient Jordanian kingdom of Ammon. This he did without meeting much opposition, for Ptolemy had his hands full consolidating his other gains. He was certainly not in a position to do anything about the invasion of Jordan.

His successor, Ptolemy II, did however, mount a campaign against the Seleucids, for he reconquered Ammon. After that, hostilities between the two rival Hellenistic empires dragged on for nearly another century, ending only when the Seleucid king, Antiochus III known as 'The Great', won the decisive Battle of Panias in 198 B.C. By a treaty, Syria, Jordan and Palestine became irrevocably a part of the Seleucid Empire.

But what of the Macedonian settlers, with their broad-brimmed hats, whilst all this was going on? They found themselves within one or other empire according to the swing of events but otherwise unaffected. Whichever way things went, they were as Hellenistic as the two antagonists.

The settlements were usually in commanding positions and, although they might well have had the appearance of an armed camp, they soon developed into small urban communites. This would have been an appropriate moment to confer some privilege of status, an action which was, in some cases, tantamount to 'founding' the city. The first documented 'founding' is during the Ptolemaic period when Philadelphia (present-day Amman) and Scythopolis (present-day Beisan) are recorded. These were far from being new sites, for the site of Philadelphia had been occupied from Pre-Pottery Neolithic times (as the extensive site currently being excavated just north of the city clearly demonstrates), with subsequent occupation during the Early Bronze Age (circa 3000–2000 B.C.), and during the Biblical period from 1200 B.C. onwards when it had been Rabbath Ammon, the capital of the Ammonite kings. However, Ptolemy II Philadelphos (285–247 B.C.) granted it the status of *polis*. Scythopolis was probably even older, dating back to Chalcolithic times (circa 4000–3000 B.C.), in fact, the site has one of the longest unbroken occupations in Palestine, with all ages represented archaeologically.

The sites of Gadara (Umm Qeis), Hippos (Qal'at Husn), Gerasa (Jerash), Abila (Tel Abil, otherwise called Quweilbeh), Dium (site not yet identified) and Capitolias (Beit Ras) are all pre-Hellenistic sites which may date from the Persian period, or even earlier.

However, they all became Hellenistic settlements which grew into urban communities and eventually into *poleis*. Father Spijkerman has written: 'Gadara, Abila, Gerasa are clearly Seleucid (for each in antiquity had the additional name Antiochia), which were founded following the Battle of Panias, when the region passed from Ptolemaic control to the Seleucids of Antioch.'* This does not preclude the possibility that there were Hellenistic settlements at these sites before the battle, it only demonstrates that these communities were promoted to *polis* status at a later date. The same applies to Hippos Antiochia.

The site of Dium is still unknown: geographically (taking Claudius Ptolemy the Geographer as one's indicator) it was likely to have been of Seleucid foundation also. Pella, on the other hand, presents a rather complex situation. The historian, Appian, writes in his *Roman History*: 'Seleucus [he refers to Seleucus I, Alexander's general and Successor] founded cities throughout his whole empire ... [some of these] he named after Greek or Macedonian cities, or after some achievement of his own, or in honour of King Alexander. Thus in Syria and the barbarous regions to the north many of the names of cities are Greek, and others Macedonian, namely Beroea, Edessa, Perinthus, Maronea, Callipolis, Achaia, Pella ...'. Appian almost certainly drew on Seleucid sources when he was writing, circa A.D. 165, but as Dr Robert H. Smith has pointed out, Appian's writings are a 'considerable simplification of the facts, since Seleucus only refounded and renamed some of the cities which Appian lists. ... it would be hasty ... to conclude that Seleucus I had anything to do with that city [Pella] or its name, for his empire did not extend so far south. The most satisfactory explanation is that the name of Pella was included

* A. Spijkerman, *Coins of the Decapolis etc.*

because Appian, or his sources, knew of the city and assumed that it must have had something to do with Alexander's birthplace. . . .'* Pella, at that time, was still in the control of the Ptolemies; it must, therefore, appear that it is a Ptolemaic foundation.

Canatha is also probably Ptolemaic. Like Damascus, it is isolated from the relatively close grouping of the other cities of the Decapolis. If its foundation as a *polis* is early Hellenistic it will be Ptolemaic, for at the division of the eastern part of the empire Ptolemy's domain extended as far north as that city. Damascus, however, is an ancient site with a long history which lies outside the scope of this work. In the early Hellenistic period, however, it fell into the Ptolemaic Empire and remained there with varying fortunes until the beginning of the second century B.C. when it passed with Syria, Jordan and Palestine into the Seleucid camp.

Of the main group there remains only Capitolias and Raphana, which some scholars maintain are the same place. The geographical position of Capitolias (Beit Ras) at the centre of a triangle formed by Abila, Gadara and Gerasa, all Seleucid foundations, would lead one to suspect that its foundation was in that period as well.

These, then, are the ten cities whose region was for ensuing centuries to be known as the Decapolis (Map 2). They were modelled on Greek municipalities in which there was an annually elected council, a *gerousia*, expressing the democratic concept of control through elected representatives. Republican in concept, each *polis* had its own particular laws and retained the right to judge its own citizens. Each sought to create typical Greek institutions such as schools in which the young (almost exclusively male) could receive both the physical and moral training, a *gymnasium* and an *ephebeion* respectively, that would prepare them as heirs to the Greek traditions. There was the ideal of *paieia* in which perfection was to be achieved through a 'complete' education in which physical, intellectual, religious and artistic attainment were of equal importance.

Anyone could be a Hellenist simply by attending a Greek school; admission was not restricted to Greeks alone. One may be precluded from being a 'citizen' (an honour reserved for the upper classes) but the implanting of a cosmopolitan frame of mind was open to anyone, along with all the advantages of Greek culture, technology and administration.

At community level this was a highly organised type of society. At the centre of it was the concept of the *polis* with its organised political, economic, administrative as well as philosophical and social implications. It was a fundamental concept which was to spread to all lands and peoples who were touched by Greek culture –

* R. H. Smith, *Pella of the Decapolis*.

even to Rome herself, for Pliny, writing in the first century A.D., records communities using the word *civitas* to describe them. It is generally accepted that, as Dr A. H. M. Jones writes, 'Pliny derived much of his geographical information from the statistical survey of the empire carried out by Marcus Agrippa and Augustus. The documents [which he used] were lists of cities in the strict sense of the term . . . that is, [they] were not places but communities.'* They were, however, all referred to as cities, some enjoying privileged status such as colonies, *municipia*, of Latin rights, federate or free cities.

Apart from their structure, there was one unifying factor, the Greek language. In Palestine, Syria and Jordan it superseded Aramaic and Hebrew as the *lingua franca*, a uniform means of communication in which local dialects were almost unknown. The Old Testament was translated into Greek, the Septuagint, and hundreds of Greek words found their way into Hebrew which was still used in rural areas and religious observances. In the towns and cities, however, Greek was universal, resisted only by the most conservative persons and communities.

Indeed it is true to say that Hellenism in the Near East started and developed as an essentially urban phenomenon and had little impact on the rural community. It was in the rural areas that the ancient Semitic values persisted; it says much for the strength of those values that they survived and remained potent enough to fuel the various revolts which in time were to tear the country apart.

Nonetheless, Hellenism had a great impact in the Near East, not least in Palestine and Jordan. Before Alexander, these lands had only had sporadic contact with Greek culture and ideas, these being carried principally by traders and merchants. With his conquests, Greek and eastern cultures were thrown together into much closer contact. Much in Greek culture was diametrically opposed to the traditional local values. In particular Hellenism taught that one was not just a citizen of a town or city, important though that was, one was a 'citizen of the world' sharing the common worldwide culture and fraternity of Hellenistic peoples which vaulted the narrow bounds of mere race or nationality. Such new ideas came to be accepted with enthusiasm, particularly by the upper classes of Jewish society. They adopted the new culture to such an extent that they came to regard their own customs and traditional values as out-of-date. In opposition to their ancestral belief in being the 'chosen people' they began looking upon themselves as 'citizens of the world'. In this respect Hellenism proved to be a corrupting force for the native population. The situation is summed up in the Latin verb *pergraecari* which strictly meant 'to become Hellenised' but which in common usage was understood to mean 'to lead a licentious life'. And this is what happened; it was only in the erstwhile Macedonian settlements, and those founded

---

* A. H. M. Jones, *Cities of the Eastern Roman Provinces.*

or fostered by either the Seleucids or Ptolemies, where Hellenism was a primary force that it did no harm.

The settlement of Palestine during the Hellenistic period had followed similar lines to that in Syria and Jordan. Settlements were established from which Greek culture and ideas attempted 'to deeply permeate the centuries old oriental milieu, so radically different both culturally and religiously'.* Under the Ptolemies there was complete religious freedom, and indeed the hereditary High Priest in Jerusalem, hereditary to the House of Zadok, continued as both religious and secular leader. Like all other 'local' rulers he was of course subject to the king in Alexandria to whom he paid taxes. The authorities in Alexandria encouraged friendly exchanges between the two cultures, Semitic and Greek, and this occurred on all urban levels from the nobles to the commercial classes. Naturally it was the higher strata of society which felt the impact most, for it was they who had closest contact.

Hellenism, however, presented an acute conflict of conscience, for it provided an attractive alternative to the ancient, indigenous culture of Judea. The old and immutable traditions were put at risk and the pious traditionalists were gravely concerned and, indeed, often violently resentful.

The innovation of democratic rule by elected representatives was seen as an attack on the old system because it cut across the existing hierarchical structure. The fears of the traditionalists were justified, for a pro-Hellenist High Priest later transferred the privilege of appointing succeeding High Priests to te Seleucid king: never before had the right of the House of Zadok been challenged. He also petitioned the king, Antiochus IV, to proclaim that the citizens of Jerusalem were citizens of Antioch, citizens of the capital and not just of a provincial city. This effectively transferred control of internal affairs to the rule of the *gerousia*, making even the Commandments of God subject to their approval. The *gerousia* was, of course, dominated by the pro-Hellenistic party. All this was done in order to create an ideal *polis* and thus bring Jerusalem into line with other Hellenistic cities.

But Hellenism was never aimed at the religious beliefs of conquered peoples. If anything it was, as the Maccabees were to recognise a century later, aimed at bringing an end to the exclusiveness of the Jews, only so that they would feel themselves free to be 'citizens of the world'. This was just what the traditionalists did not want, for it was diametrically opposed to the ancient teachings.

With the Seleucids things began to deteriorate: it was not that they were less tactful in their handling of subject peoples, only that the circumstances which had permitted a period of relative calm under the Ptolemies had changed drastically. The pro-Hellenist sector of the Judaic nobility had become by now so corrupted

* A. Spijkerman, *Coins of the Decapolis etc.*

that they were acting against the very foundations of their traditional heritage. They had taken to the 'sweet life' and were doing all they could to appear as 'citizens of the world', effectively denying their exclusiveness.

The ordinary people of Judea never became Hellenised, and more and more found themselves out of sympathy and out of touch with their ruling classes. Ultimately this led to a serious decline in national solidarity. The tide of anti-Hellenism was rising, and the concept of the *polis* came to be identified as the arch-symbol of all that was wrong in the state. This immediately put the Hellenistic settlements in their midst at risk.

In the third century B.C., Hellenism in Palestine seems to have been centred round the ancient noble family of the Tobiads: indeed they were the epitome of a pro-Hellenistic house. They were related to the priestly aristocracy and secular nobility in Jerusalem and enjoyed considerable influence. Since the end of the fifth century they had controlled estates in Ammon where, it has been suggested, they acted for the Persians as Governors of certain Ammonite lands. Towards the end of the third century they were still entrenched in Jordan, possibly as local Governors appointed now by the Ptolemies. However, at this time a Tobiah married the sister of the High Priest and had a son, Joseph, who became a 'tax farmer' (a collector of taxes from which the tribute was paid by the High Priest) in Palestine and Coele-Syria. Joseph's son, Hyrcanus, is important to us because he left to history what is probably the finest remaining example of large-scale Judeo/Hellenistic architecture in the whole area, even accepting the so-called 'Hellenistic Tower' at Samaria.

Hyrcanus quarrelled with his half-brother, and had to flee to family lands in the Wadi es-Syr in Jordan. There, in the first two decades of the second century, he established himself in what was tantamount to a petty state. Here he built a 'strong castle' which today is known as Araq el Amir – or, Caverns of the Prince.

The situation of the ruins is very fine. One approaches through tall trees and terraced water meadows set in the narrow wadi with high, bare hills above. The terrain eventually opens out onto a wide, level plateau overlooking the wadi as it plunges southwards to the distant Wadi Kefrain. Hills encircle and protect the place with a range of cliffs to the north-east. Almost in the middle of the plateau stands the QASR EL 'ABD (Fig. 1). In plan it is a huge rectangle with a pillared vestibule *in antis* at the north and south ends. These originally led into a large pillared central court (which may have been roofed) with chambers and a staircase in the corners. The flanking east and west walls are completely plain in their lower stages except for the panelling-out of each colossal stone. Above this, seven windows were evenly spaced between monolithic piers which were also panelled-out. A fine dentillated cornice went round the building tying the composition together, over which rose a tall frieze decorated with carved animals striding in

Fig. 1 Arak el Amir, the Qasr el Abd, 'the only Hellenistic ruin of great interest in Jordan'.

pairs towards each other. This was topped off by another, final, cornice.

The ruins are now filled with the debris of the original and later, Byzantine, walls. The site was first noted as early as 1817 (by Irby and Mangles); excavations, however, did not start until the late Dr Paul W. Lapp began digging in 1961. From subsequent seasons Dr Lapp was able to attribute 'the Qasr to Hyrcanus' building operations in the early second century B.C.'* Stylistically it is certainly early second century as has been shown by D. K. Hill in the *Bulletin of the American School of Oriental Research* (1963). Probably the most important decorative features were the two animal fountains discovered at the north ends of the east and west walls at ground level; both are carved from a single block of pink and white mottled local dolomite. They are marvellously alert and feline. Inside the building water channels have been discovered which came through the walls, allowing the water to spout through the animals' mouths.

* Nancy L. Lapp, *Annual of the Department of Antiquities*, 1979.

The principal piece of literary evidence is from Josephus, who records its building and the approximate date:

> [Hyrcanus] seated himself beyond Jordan, and was at perpetual war with the Arabians and slew many of them, and took many of them captive. He also erected a strong castle, and built it entirely of white stone to the very roof, and had animals of a prodigious magnitude engraven upon it. He also drew round it a great and deep moat of water. He also made caverns of many furlongs in length, by hollowing a rock that was over against him, and then he made large rooms in it, some for feasting, and some for sleeping and living in. He also introduced a vast quantity of waters which ran along it, and which were very delightful and ornamental in the court. But still he made the entrance at the mouth of the caves so narrow, that no more than one person could enter by them at once. And the reason why he built them after that manner was a good one; it was for his own preservation, lest he should be besieged by his brethren, and run the risk of being caught by them. Moreover, he built courts of greater magnitude than ordinary, which he adorned with vastly large gardens. And when he had brought the place to this state, he named it Tyros … and he ruled over these parts for seven years, even all the time that Seleucus [Seleucus IV] was king of Syria. But when he [Seleucus] was dead, his brother Antiochus . . . took the kingdom. . . . As for Hyrcanus, when he saw that Antiochus had a great army, and feared lest he should be caught by him, and brought to punishment for what he had done to the Arabians, he ended his life, and slew himself with his own hand; while Antiochus seized upon all his substance.'*

The caves to which Josephus refers are still there, and the description of the Qasr el 'Abd also still holds good except that it has weathered and, instead of being white, is a soft golden colour.

Dr Lapp, on the basis of his own excavations and those undertaken subsequently by the Department of Antiquities in conjunction with an expedition from the French Institute in Amman, has concluded that the Qasr el 'Abd is 'a unique, indigenous example of the old Syrian temple type in the Hellenistic Period, providing a link between the stair temples of Ugarit and Jerusalem and those characteristic of the Roman East.'†

The building was never completed, and much of the original internal arrangement was destroyed during the Byzantine period when redevelopment went below the Hellenistic floor level. In any case, before that the building had been substantially wrecked by an earthquake which shook the whole of Jordan in A.D. 365.

---

* Josephus, *Antiquities*.   † P. W. Lapp in *Encyclopedia of Archaeological Excavations in the Holy Land*.

The reason why the fugitive Hyrcanus should have laid out such a huge complex of temple, enclosures and caves is not fully understood. With him came numerous followers, some of whom saw him not only as a potentially successful soldier of fortune but as an exciting new prophet or High Priest destined to found a new Jerusalem in which Hellenism and Judaic traditions could be reconciled and synthesised; unless, as Butler wrote, 'a second Temple to Jehovah and a new Jerusalem were projected'.

Nonetheless, Hyrcanus has left us with what Rostovtzeff called 'the only Hellenistic ruin of great interest in Jordan'.* One might add it is the most significant Hellenistic ruin in the Near East. Above all it tells us something of the stylistic impact of Hellenism and of the pride, ambition and sense of splendour which it evoked in aristocratic pro-Hellenistic hearts.

Back in Jerusalem other proud, pro-Hellenistic hearts had similar visions of grandeur and sought to accumulate power and wealth to a degree never seen or contemplated before in Judaic society. Eventually the situation became so critical that internecine violence ensued. To the Seleucids such internal problems were properly the responsibility of the leaders of the local community, but when civil revolt broke out they felt they had to act. This was in 169 B.C., after the Tobiad family had supported the appointment of a non-Zadokite as High Priest. Antiochus IV was then preoccupied both by an increasing Roman threat and by dynastic troubles at home, and the civil cum religious commotion in Palestine must have seemed the last straw. He swept down on Jerusalem and savaged it. The Second Book of Maccabees tells us that he massacred eighty thousand people in three days, pillaging and desecrating the Temple, and carrying off something in the region of two million pounds worth of treasure. The blame was laid squarely on the heads of the traditionalists, and Antiochus decided to put an end to this troublesome faction. Religious persecution, which had never before been known in the Hellenistic world, ensued, culminating two years later in a total ban on Jewish religious observance.

Opposition hardened, and open revolution broke out in 167 B.C., bringing to the fore Judas Maccabeus. After a seesaw of events Maccabeus gained control of Palestine, neighbouring Ideumea, Galilee and the northern part of Jordan, and managed to wrest religious freedom and control of communal affairs from the Seleucids. But Judas Maccabeus wanted political autonomy as well. However, he now faced a strong new ruler in Antioch, Demetrius I Soter, and it was he, through his general, Bacchides, who finally defeated and killed Judas at the Battle of Elasa.

This revolt against Hellenism had been dangerous for the Greek *poleis*. The region of the Decapolis was directly affected, for Gerasa, Pella, Scythopolis, Dium,

---

* Rostovtzeff, *Social and Economic History of the Roman Empire*.

Gadara, Abila, Hippos and Capitolias all fell under Maccabean control, leaving only Philadelphia, Canatha and Damascus free of their domination. All Greek cities, not only those of the Decapolis, would have been identified as symbols of the *polis*, a concept which had done so much to undermine the traditional order. They, therefore, became a focus for the resentment of the Maccabees. They were only saved from cultural obliteration by the fact that, despite Judas Maccabeus's successes, the pro-Hellenistic party in Jerusalem was not crushed. The party was, however, seriously weakened and now had to be propped up by the Syrian authorities.

But Seleucid dynastic squabbling in 157 B.C., coupled with an increasingly powerful threat from the Parthians, made the authorities less able to maintain control of events in Jordan and Palestine. By the time John Hyrcanus (not to be confused with the Hyrcanus of Araq el Amir) came to the helm in Jerusalem (shortly after 135 B.C.) the pro-Hellenist party had lost all its political strength. As a social and cultural force, however, it continued, for right up to his death in 104 B.C. Hyrcanus's Hellenism brought him into serious conflict with his own traditionalists.

In 103 B.C., the Greek *poleis* came to face their severest threat, a forty-year period of ruthless domination. Alexander Jannaeus became ruler of Judea and almost immediately launched attacks on the *poleis*. These cities had frequently refused to acknowledge Hasmonean rule, not regarding themselves as anything other than independent Hellenistic city-states. Philadelphia at that time was ruled by the 'tyrant' Theodorus, or by his father Zeno Cotylas, who successfully resisted the Jannaean onslaught. But Canatha was under the grip of the Ituraeans, whose pro-Jewish sympathies made them almost 'comrades in arms' to Jannaeus. This left Damascus alone of the Decapolis cities in the crumbling purlieu of the Seleucids.

Those cities which refused to be Judaised were 'destroyed'. Josephus tells us that 'Alexander [Jannaeus] on his part, captured Pella and went against Gerasa [where] having surrounded the garrison with a triple barricade, he took the place without a battle.'* Twenty years later Josephus returned to the subject but inexplicably changed his report to say that Jannaeus 'marched on the city of Dium and took it. He also marched on Essa.'† (Essa can be taken as a scribal error for Gerasa because the offensive technique of the triple barricade is again mentioned.) Later in the same passage Scythopolis, Gadara and Pella are stated to have been conquered also, along with 'others among the leading cities of Syria which had been subdued'. Pella was referred to as having been 'destroyed because the inhabitants did not promise to change to the national customs of the Jews'†, but

---

* Josephus, *Wars*.   † Josephus, *Antiquities*.

the word 'destroyed' is open to interpretation. Dr R. H. Smith has suggested that this was probably more a case of being captured and looted, with the imposition of penal taxation, whilst others maintain that the city was indeed destroyed and depopulated, so that it lay all but deserted for the next forty years. The historian Georgios Synkellos, writing about A.D. 800, adds Abila, Hippos and Scythopolis to the list of cities similarly attacked.

Indeed, virtually the whole of the Decapolis was in Hasmonean hands at the time of Jannaeus's death in 76 B.C. But internal dissent in Judea soon broke into open civil war, with the Hasmoneans, the Pharisees and the Sadducees all fighting each other. So intent were they on their sectional programmes, each armed with the righteousness of their own cause, that they did not heed the impending doom which was purposefully conquering its way down from the north. The majesty of Rome in the person of Pompey the Great strode emphatically onto the stage.

II

Pompey set out after Aristobulus [the then High Priest], taking the Roman army and many auxiliaries from Syria. After marching past Pella and Scythopolis he reached Corea, from which point the territory of Judea begins as one ascends through the interior.'*

This passage does not say that Pompey actually visited Pella and Scythopolis, but one can be certain that the local inhabitants went down into the valley to welcome the man on whom they looked as a liberator. The passage does, however, probably indicate that there were a few inhabitants at least remaining or returned at Pella, for Josephus is likely to have been referring to the city in the classical sense, i.e. as a community rather than as a place. It is unlikely that he would include in his text a city with no population at all. Pompey, however, had no time to celebrate with them and pushed on southwards and, after the delay at Alexandrion, ascended 'through the interior' on his way towards Jerusalem.

All this happened in 63 B.C. Once things had settled down Pompey set about reorganising the government administration and redefining state borders. Judea was deprived of all the conquests and was reduced to being a small subject state. Even so, Pompey proved to be a far more impartial conqueror than the Persians or even the Seleucid, Antiochus IV, for complete religious freedom was established and there was no looting. For all his aptitude in statesmanship and his brilliance as a military commander, Pompey was a 'plain soldier', free of prejudices about the

* Josephus, *Wars*.

28

peoples he conquered. For him 'the Jews were just one of the many kingdoms throughout the East which had to be dealt with in a way conducive to Rome's interests. . . .'*

Rome's interests were also served when he liberated the Greek *poleis* and restored their local autonomy within the higher authority of his Province of Syria.

This far-reaching and fundamental reorganisation of the whole area was also recorded by Josephus:

> Divesting the Jewish nation also of the cities in Coele-Syria which they had taken, Pompey made them subject to a Roman governor appointed for that purpose, and confined them solely within their own boundaries. To please a certain Gadarene named Demetrius, one of his own freedmen, he also re-founded Gadara, which had been destroyed by the Jews. He liberated from them, moreover, those cities in the interior which they had not previously razed, namely Hippos, Scythopolis, Pella, Samaria. . . . Handing all of these cities over to their lawful inhabitants, he placed them in the Syrian Province. When he had entrusted that province and Judea, and indeed everything between Egypt and the Euphrates, to the supervision of Scaurus, with a resident force of two legions, he himself marched off by way of Cilicia to Rome.'†

It is interesting that in this text Josephus says that Pella had *not* been razed, contradicting his earlier statement in the same work. In the *Antiquities*, he added Dium to the list of liberated cities.

This meant a new start for the 'ten cities'. Indeed, the majority declared a new Era, taking 63 B.C. as the date from which all future events were to be dated, including the issue of coinage. Realising the value, both politically and from the point of view of security strategy, of a buffer group of free republican-minded city-states between Judea and the Ituraeans, Pompey effectively reinstated a barrier against their uniting and becoming again a powerful threat to his new Province of Syria. 'For however much he might trust a local dynast, he recognised much advantage in "free" communities which would tend to be good republican watch-dogs against the imperialist revivals of strong dynasties while avoiding the instability of weaker ones whose internal squabbles would require tiresome interventions by the nearest Roman governor.'* In such a context the cities of the Decapolis prepared to enter a new future full of promise.

In 64 B.C., Pompey had annexed Antioch, effectively bringing the Seleucid Empire to an end. His new Province of Syria took its place, but the affairs of the

---

* P. Greenhalgh, *Pompey, the Roman Alexander*.   †Josephus, *Wars*.

Near East were not yet stable enough to bring about prosperity. A new power was threatening Rome's supremacy – the Parthians. The Province of Syria was built by Pompey as a strong eastern frontier against their expansion. This led to protracted wars in the area, which only ended in 38 B.C., when Anthony's lieutenant finally denied Syria to the Parthians.

The *Pax Romana* heralded a period of stability and growth in which Pompey's reorganisation and administrative plans were continued by Aulus Gabinius, the pro-Consul of the Province. Although Josephus specifically refers to his activities in Judea when he wrote '... and whenever he came upon a ruined city, he gave directions for it to be rebuilt'*, Gabinius was active throughout his vast domain. Coins minted at Canatha suggest that he was operating even there. Indeed, throughout all the Hellenistic cities there must have been much feverish building as temples, civic and domestic structures sprang up; so much so that some of the cities were beginning to spill over into small suburbs.

Public and cultural life was also returning to normal, and an air of well-being sent spring-like shivers of pleasure and excitement through the inhabitants. Trade continued to expand. The independence of the cities remained intact until Augustus, who succeeded as Emperor in 30 B.C., gave Herod the cities of Gadara and Hippos in recognition of his having been a 'friend of Rome'. This involved little more than the cities having to pay a tribute or tax to Herod, who is unlikely to have attempted to disturb their essential character. On Herod's death they were returned to autonomy within the Province of Syria. A second change came when Abila was ceded to Agrippa II during the reign of Nero in A.D. 53. It also was returned at his death. Neither of these political stratagems disturbed the prosperity of the cities, which continued to develop happily along their own lines.

But strife, fuelled by resentment, still boiled under the surface of Palestine. Late in A.D. 66 it burst out in the form of the First Revolt, triggered off by the Caesarea incident in which it is said that twenty thousand Jews were slain in one hour. Outraged zealots from Judea, clearly inspired by racial and religious motives, savaged what they still saw as the cardinal enemy of the Judaic state – the *poleis*:

> The whole Jewish nation was enraged at the pogrom at Caesarea, and in separate bands they pillaged the villages of Syria, and nearby cities – Philadelphia, Heshbonitis, Gerasa, Pella and Scythopolis. Having fallen upon Gadara, Hippos and Ganlanitis, subduing some and burning others, they moved on.... Many villages around each of these cities were ravaged, and innumerable captive males were slain.*

This must have been profoundly disturbing to the *poleis*, for above all the Revolt

---

* Josephus, *Wars*.

held in question Rome's ability to control events. Josephus writes that certain cities were 'pillaged' but this is not confirmed; at Gerasa, for example, there is evidence of a huge building programme which does not seem to have suffered any particular set-back. In truth, it may only have been armed bands marauding initially in Transjordan and then in Judea, but they were on large enough a scale to precipitate Rome into ferocious action. Dr Smith has rightly asked 'where they obtained sufficient arms and military training to be effectual against the cities'.* But the crisis has the symptoms of a planned revolution which went off prematurely, triggered by the Caesarea incident. The Judeans bitterly resented the domination of Rome, their loss of autonomy as God's chosen people, as well as the continued existence of the alien *poleis* in their midst. With a full-scale revolution brewing, caches of arms would have been secretly stored, with military guerrilla training taking place in remote rural areas out of sight of the urban centred authorities. During the Revolt the XVth Legion of Vespasian was in winter quarters at Scythopolis, so the marauding bands must have been well enough organised and armed to be able to consider attacking the city.

The reaction within the cities was as violent as the Revolt itself; each had its Jewish community, and these became harried and persecuted in retaliation. It is unlikely that we shall ever know the full story of what proved to be a suicidal outburst; suicidal because Rome had to act.

Not all Jews felt inclined to follow their brothers into the field of war – the growing Christian community in Jerusalem in particular absented themselves. The evacuation of the Christians from Jerusalem in A.D. 66 brings us the first historical reference to a Decapolis city by an early Christian writer – apart from the Gospels. Eusebius, who was writing in the early fourth century relates:

> When the people of the Church in Jerusalem were instructed by an oracular revelation delivered to worthy men there to move away from the city and in a city of Peraea called Pella, the believers in Christ migrated from Jerusalem to that place. When holy men had completely abandoned the royal metropolis of the Jews and all the land of Judaea, the judgement of God thereupon overtook the Jews in the same measure as they had acted unjustly towards Christ and his apostles, utterly obliterating that impious generation from mankind. How many misfortunes at that time everywhere deluged the Jewish nation, the extent to which the inhabitants of Judaea were driven in suffering, the way that myriads of persons from youth upwards, including women and children, perished by the sword, famine and countless other forms of death, how many sieges the Jewish cities endured and what things took place – especially such

---

* R. H. Smith, *Pella of the Decapolis.*

31

terrible and worse than terrible things as those who fled to Jerusalem expecting an invincible metropolis saw, including the course of the entire war and above all the last things which happened in it, when at the end the 'abomination of desolation' which the prophets had proclaimed was set up in the once-renowned temple of God and it underwent complete destruction and final obliteration by fire – all these things one can learn in detail from the history written by Josephus.'*

No publisher today would allow a writer to get so carried away; and how strange that everyone thinks God is on his side and sees His hand in the downfall of the other. One wonders what God makes of it all. Whether it was on the advice of God – the oracular revelation – or just that the Christian community did not feel that they could share 'the suicidal political course of their nationalistic countrymen'† they, or at least the majority of them, fled to Pella. The heavy hand of Rome hit hard, for in A.D. 67 the army of Vespasian and his son, Titus, were in complete control of Galilee; four years later Jerusalem fell. The Revolt was savagely stamped out, culminating in the horrific massacre at Masada in A.D. 73. Josephus records in his *Wars* that in A.D. 68 Vespasian sent an expedition under Lucius Annius against Gerasa, which was stormed and plundered. This should probably be read as a mopping-up operation in Jewish villages in the Gerasa state rather than as an assault on the city itself. Certainly no archaeological evidence has come to light to support the idea that the city was attacked. One of the leaders of the Revolt, Simon bar Giora, was a Gerasene, but this is not to say that he came from the city itself. It could be that he came from one of Gerasa's Jewish villages. It may be this which focussed Annius's attention on Gerasa and led Josephus to state that Annius attacked the city.

The next reorganisation came when Trajan (A.D. 98–117) annexed the Nabatean Empire in A.D. 106, and incorporated it into his new Province of Arabia, to which he added Gerasa, Philadelphia, Dium and Canatha, leaving those in the Rift Valley in the Province of Syria. All lost their autonomy and became no more than provincial cities under Bosra, which the emperor founded as the capital of his new province.

The beneficial effects of Trajan's reorganisation cannot be doubted, for it marked the beginning of a new period of prosperity for the whole area. The release of the inland trade routes from the Nabatean monopoly placed the Hellenistic cities on the high Syrian/Jordanian plateau in a marvellously privileged economic position. The trade route north from Aqaba to Damascus, which had been jealously defended by the Nabateans, now poured its riches into the other cities along its

* Eusebius, *Ecclesiastical History*.   † Spijkerman, *Coins of the Decapolis etc.*

path. For such cities as Philadelphia and Gerasa it was a revitalising 'shot in the arm'. Central to this was the construction of the great new road, the *Via Nova*, which linked the provincial capital with the Gulf of Aqaba. Started by Trajan and completed by Hadrian, it was an immense undertaking; traces of it can still be seen.

Philadelphia soon developed into a fine city. The site is enclosed by seven steep-sided hills which drop down into a wide central valley. The floor of this valley is flat, and through it meandered a perennial stream called the Seil Amman (Fig. 2). Overlooking this, on the northern side, is the precipitous height of el Qal'ah, known as the Citadel. The ancient Ammonite capital was probably restricted to el Qal'ah, as might have been the later Hellenistic town. Mrs Crystal-M. Bennett, the Director of the British Institute at Amman, has in her excavations on the Citadel established a late Hellenistic/early Roman presence, but it is still too early to say whether the site was used for domestic occupation. But under the Romans the valley floor began to be developed leaving el Qal'ah, it has been suggested, as an acropolis. A colonnaded street was laid out beside the stream which was vaulted over for most of its length, and along this were located the main public buildings. A vast theatre was built into the side of a southern cliff by the Emperor Antoninus Pius between A.D. 138–161, which could accommodate about six thousand spectators (Fig. 3). In front of this was a large open space (possibly an Agora) which had a pillared portico round it, whilst to one side was an *Odeon* or small, roofed theatre designed for musical performances. The Romans re-walled el Qal'ah, leaving us with some of the finest ancient fortifications to survive in Jordan. This acropolis was approached from the city up a long flight of steps which passed through a propylaea reminiscent of the one to the Temple of Artemis at Gerasa: our knowledge of this ruin is largely from old photographs because little trace of it can now be seen. On the top of the acropolis was built a temple to Hercules which had a strong, uncompromisingly muscular design as befitted the hero. Beside the temple there was reputed to have stood a gigantic statue of Hercules: two fragments of this have been found – a piece of a hand and an elbow – and from these it has been calculated that the statue was some thirty feet tall.

Philadelphia, however, has all but vanished under the huge modern capital which has grown up on the site. Today there are few remains even of the later Byzantine city. We know that it was one of the nineteen Sees of Palestina Tertia, for a bishopric of Petra cum Philadelphia is recorded. On the acropolis there are the remains of a Byzantine church, and Mrs Bennett's excavations have revealed a considerable amount of building from that period.

The photograph shown in Fig. 2 was taken in 1867 when the site was still deserted. Since then the stream has again disappeared from view, not this time beneath a Roman vault but under an expanse of concrete.

Fig. 2 The ruins of Philadelphia, the site of present-day Amman, taken by Corporal Phillips in 1867. The fortress-like Nymphaeum overlooks a now vanished section of the Roman vaulting over the stream.

Fig. 3 The auditorium of the theatre at Amman.

The theatre, however, remains, substantially restored by the Department of Antiquities, and the *Odeon*. They alone demonstrate that Philadelphia was no backward, impecunious country town but a grand and sophisticated city whose citizens knew how to live and how to do things on the grand scale – and could afford it. North-east of the city is the Qasr el Nueijis, a fine late-Roman family tomb of handsome proportions and luxuriant carved detail. This beautifully constructed monument demonstrates probably more than any other in Amman, the scale and grandeur with which the wealthy citizens of the city could surround themselves – even in death.

Further north, Gerasa also blossomed into a spectacular city despite the reported attack on it during the First Revolt. The nucleus of the Hellenistic city is believed to have been on Camp Hill – the low, round hill on which now sits the Tourist Restaurant. This walled city was very small in scale, vastly different from the huge Roman city which was to develop later. After Pompey's reorganisation, it began to spill out into small suburbs. A new Temple of Zeus was going up across the shallow depression in which now is the Oval Piazza, during the first half of the first century, whilst on a high point to the north a group of shrines, one dedicated to Dionysus and the other to the 'ancestral' goddess Artemis, were receiving attention. An inscription records substantial gifts of money made towards the building works in A.D. 22/23 and A.D. 42/43 by Zabdion and Aristonas at the Zeus Sanctuary. It is evident that not only was much building in progress, but also there was the money to pay for it. This came from the trade which was flowing through the city on the Nabatean trade route.

The great trading empire of the Nabateans remained powerful despite Pompey's having restricted them to their heartland. It is no surprise, therefore, to find them exerting an influence on Gerasa. A great many coins have been found, as well as an important bilingual inscription, in Greek and Nabatean, which refers to the erection of a statue to King Aretas (probably Aretas IV, 9 B.C.–A.D. 40). Kraeling has seen in the archaeological evidence the possibility 'that the Nabatean community had special rights and privileges at Gerasa. . . . Perhaps it was incorporated as a separate *ethnos* in the organisation of the city.'* Be this as it may, the Nabateans would have been familiar in the city, and the worship of their gods would have been happily tolerated. Their deities appear to have been Pakidas, with Hera as his consort, and the 'Arabian God'; the latter can possibly be identified with Dusares, a deity prominent in the Petra pantheon. The majority of inscriptions relating to this Arabian God have been found in the area of the Cathedral where Crowfoot has suggested there was a temple to Dionysus. It is

* Kraeling, *Gerasa: City of the Decapolis.*

35

possible that there was a synthesis between Dusares and Dionysus, in which case the dedication should properly be to Dusares-Dionysus, but of this we cannot be sure.

Not enough archaeology has yet taken place for us to determine the extent of the Nabatean impact, but it can be said that their trading activities were an important factor in the city's commercial development and early prosperity.

The second half of the first century was a pivotal time for Gerasa. The First Revolt probably diverted inland some of the trade which would otherwise have used the Palestinian and Jordan Valley routes. At this time, also, security was strengthened when a Roman garrison was established in the city.

It was about A.D. 50 when the ambitious city plan was set out. This does not mean that the whole of Gerasa was built at that time, only that the street plan was laid down, affording a framework in which all subsequent developments took place. The last half of the first century saw the construction of the city walls: a ring of defences which was designed more as a protection against raiding desert nomads than as a fortification to withstand a siege.

Gerasa must have been the scene of feverish activity with work on the Temple of Zeus in progress, financed by gifts from devout citizens amongst whom Theon, son of Demetrius, seems to have been prominent. Besides the Sanctuary of Zeus, the South Theatre was taking shape. It had been started in the reign of Domitian (A.D. 81–96); again some of the finance came from the private sector for one Titus Flavius, son of Dionysus, donated a block of seats. Northwards, the old Temple of Artemis was given a portico and sacred pool; Diogenes, son of Leonidas, subscribed an altar whilst Sarapion, son of Apollonius, paid for the construction of an *andron*, the purpose and siting of which are still uncertain (see page 185). At this time also, Alexander, son of Apollas, grandson of Alexander, constructed a doorway to honour the 'ancestral Goddess, Artemis'. The area where the Cathedral now stands was also being developed. In A.D. 73/74, a separate temple to Hera was erected in the same area. All the time inscriptions tell us the names of those who were donating substantial amounts. Theon could lay out ten thousand drachmae as well as dedicating 'two sons and a daughter to the service of Zeus'*, Titus Flavius three thousand – these were large sums – whilst Agathocles, son of Aninus, was also digging into his purse.

There can be little doubt that the merchants and Roman officials were providing for themselves as well as for the good of their souls and the community. Little domestic building has been excavated (see page 140) but these would have been of the standard Roman type. As with even the poorer structures, the majority were built round an open courtyard which in the grand houses would have been a fine peristyle. Inside these there was a considerable degree of comfort and elegance.

* C. C. McCown, *Journal of the Palestine Oriental Society*, 1936.

Fine pottery and bronze utensils would have been in evidence along with Syrian glass. This glass was manufactured on the Levant coast: 'Between Acre and Tyre is a sandy beach, which produces the sand used in glass making.'*

The famous Oval Piazza (sometimes called the Oval Forum) (Fig. 4) was probably laid out toward the end of the first century along with the entire length of the Cardo, the main north/south Colonnaded Street. Originally its entire length was of the Ionic order: the southern and middle sections were later widened and given Corinthian columns (see page 50). The South Theatre was well advanced and the Temenos wall of the Sanctuary of Zeus would have been finished – also in the Ionic order (Fig. 5). By the end of the century the main streets were marked out.

These developments, exciting though they may have seemed, were but a prelude to what was to happen under Trajan (A.D. 98–117) and his successor, Hadrian (A.D. 117–138), culminating in a Golden Age under the Antonines. Both emperors were deeply interested in the eastern provinces, which they saw as a secure base for their fluid policy concerning frontiers. Of particular significance to Gerasa was Trajan's policy of expansion which led to the annexation of the Nabatean Empire in A.D. 106, and the creation of the Province of Arabia. Hitherto remote from the centre, Gerasa now found itself geographically close to the new provincial capital. To ensure security and ease of control, a system of fine roads was constructed, not only the huge *Via Nova* but also a road between Philadelphia and Gerasa, one connecting Gerasa with Dium and Bosra, and another linking Gerasa with Pella. This last, built under the direction of C. Claudius Severus, Legate of Trajan, opened the way for trade to pass through Gerasa en route to the coast. Gerasa suddenly found itself in a strategic position and soon began to reap the benefits which had made Petra so rich.

Trajan was looked upon as 'saviour and founder', an inscription on the North Gate tells us. The words demonstrate that the Gerasenes clearly understood who was responsible for their prosperity. The city felt very much a part of provincial affairs with the citizens cutting a figure in the world. One inscription is of particular importance, for it tells us of the inauguration of an annual contest, held in the South Theatre (Fig. 6), then the most splendid structure of its kind in the province, of the 'Sacred guild of the ecumenical, victorious, crowned artists in the service of Dionysus and of our Lord'. Such festivals had long been a feature of prominent cities across the Graeco-Roman world, and this guild contest made the Gerasenes feel they were truly 'citizens of the world'. Furthermore, it gave stimulus to the patronage of the arts, which was seen as a worthy activity.

Hadrian spent at least part of the winter of A.D. 129–30 in Gerasa. His prolonged

* Strabo, *Geography*.

Fig. 4 The Oval Piazza at Jerash, with the Cardo leading northwards from it through the ancient city. Camp Hill, the site of the Hellenistic settlement, lies behind the Piazza on the right.

visit must have been a 'shot in the arm' for civic pride. The city was for a short time the very centre of the Empire, and the streets were full of the huge retinue which followed the restless emperor on his travels. It was presumably he who elevated Gerasa to the honorific status of a 'holy and inviolate and autonomous' city. To honour him, a huge archway south of the city was constructed, which suggests that an extension of the city was envisaged. All very flattering for Hadrian who was keen on such civic expansions – one remembers his new quarter of Athens – but perhaps an over-confident gesture. But to have thought of such a massive project shows that Gerasa looked to a splendid future. Wisdom prevailed and no such development took place.

Over the hills and not all that far away lay the city of Pella. The site is a fine one (Fig. 7), a long spur, Tabaqat Fahl, in a wide, west-facing re-entrant in the hills overlooking the Jordan Valley. To the south, across the Wadi Jirm, with its abundant spring and sparkling stream, rise the steep slopes of a high, dome-topped hill called Tell el-Hosn. From both Tabaqat Fahl and Tell el-Hosn there are splendid views westwards over the Jordan Valley.

Fig. 5 A conjectural reconstruction of the Temenos of the Temple of Zeus in the first century A.D.

Fig. 6 The South Theatre at Jerash.

Fig. 7 The site of Pella. In the foreground are the excavations of the Temple overlooking the Civic Complex in the valley below. The long bare hill to the right of the Wadi is the Tell Tabaqat Fahl; an excavation trench down the side of the hill can be seen on the right.

The scarcity of Hellenistic evidence on Tabaqat Fahl, coupled with a considerable number of surface finds of pottery from that period in the saddle behind Tell el-Hosn, leads one to believe that the early Hellenistic settlers did not occupy the ancient tell of Fahl but chose instead the fine, naturally fortified Tell el-Hosn. Certainly there are remains of fortified walls on the steep slopes of that hill commanding its weakest point.

How much the city suffered during the First Revolt we do not at present know. During the first century it is obvious that the population had increased considerably and that the city was no longer confined within its Hellenistic walls. Civic developments were being undertaken in the Wadi Jirm, which, besides public halls, temples and the like, included a small theatre built right down on water level. At the same time a temple complex was built on the hillside to the east (Fig. 7). As with other expanding sites, groups of suburban villas and dwellings sprang up around the old walls and into the slopes nearby. Tabaqat Fahl does not, however, appear to have been built over during this period.

It was, perhaps, the migration of those Jerusalem Christians in A.D. 66 which has made Pella a subject of study for Christian scholars, resulting in its being probably the best researched site in the Decapolis. It was not only the writings of Eusebius which attracted attention, for scholars could also turn to Epiphanius who recorded the Nazoraean and Ebionite heresies being practised in the city. There is nothing like a good heresy for getting ecclesiastical scholars worked up.

Epiphanius also recorded that when Hadrian visited Jerusalem in about A.D. 130, he found the city a desolation after the destruction wrought by Titus.

> Thereupon Hadrian decided to rebuild the city, though not the Temple. So taking Aquila.... a relative by marriage..., he appointed him to supervise the projects connected with the rebuilding of the city. He bestowed on the city his own name and the benefit accruing therefrom; for as he was named Aelius Hadrian, thus he also named the city Aelia. Whilst living in Jerusalem, Aquila saw the disciples of the apostles flourishing in faith and performing great signs of healing and other marvels, for they had returned from the city of Pella to Jerusalem and were teaching.*

Apart from a survey made by Richmond in 1934, archaeological excavation only started in 1965 by Wooster College, Ohio. Work, however, had to be suspended during the June War. Since then it has been resumed, conducted as a joint expedition by Dr Robert Smith of Wooster College, and Dr Basil Hennessy of the University of Sydney, Australia: each team does a season of approximately two months in a year but works in its own area. It is still too early to discuss the full implications of all their results but Pella is evidently rich in potential and these excavations may well prove to be of great importance.

Across the valley stood the city of Scythopolis, set well back from the river into the embracing hills. This was the only city of the Decapolis to be situated west of the River Jordan. It too was blessed with a perennial supply of good water in the River Harod which flowed through the Wadi Jalud at the foot of the high hill, the Tell el Husn, on which the Hellenistic city stood. Under the Romans the city expanded down into the surrounding valleys and at its zenith the circuit of walls was two and a half miles long. Josephus referred to it as the 'chief' city of the Decapolis. Quite what is meant by 'chief' is not clear but he was writing towards the end of the first century and it is possible that the city was already a boom town due to its exceptional position on the main arterial road up the west bank.

The First Revolt seems hardly to have impeded progress, even though trade would have been affected for a while, but having the XVth Legion of Vespasian stationed there would have done much to reassure the citizens.

Tell el Husn was first excavated in 1921–33 by an expedition from the University of Pennsylvania Museum: 'In scope and in conception this was the pioneer excavation in the archaeology of Palestine.'† Despite the fact that few structures of the Hellenistic period survive, the Roman remains attest to a city of considerable grandeur. The theatre is particularly interesting in the unusual arrangement of

---

* Epiphanius, *Treatise on Weights and Measures.*

† F. James, in *Encyclopedia of Archaeological Excavations in the Holy Land.*

having the podium wall of the auditorium running right up to the front of the stage without any flanking *vomitoria* openings, creating a curious semi-circular well approached only down steps. Irby and Mangles were fascinated by this theatre (see page 67).

Further north, the Jordan Valley widens out to embrace the southern end of the Sea of Galilee. It is a rich, brilliantly coloured pastoral landscape, with flat fields and stands of trees stretching away to the foot of the high hills on either side and with the dark waters of the Sea to the north. The stillness, the silence and the playful, drenching sunlight belie the fact that history has tramped its often destructive way through this pleasant land. High above on its ridge to the east stands ancient Gadara, commanding a panoramic view of bewitching beauty.

'To please a certain Gadarene named Demetrius, one of his own freedmen, he [Pompey] also refounded Gadara, which had been destroyed by the Jews.'* This mark of favour can only have given a boost to the morale of the lately beleaguered citizens. Under settled conditions the city grew rich; indeed Josephus describes it as a wealthy place with 'villas and small cities round about it'. However, the impression one gets from both literary sources and from the architectural evidence on site, is of a city as much concerned with the affairs of the mind and of pleasure as with the cut and thrust of trade. There can be no doubt that the citizens took good care of the trade, for this provided the funds with which they could afford their other inclinations.

Josephus also records that during the First Revolt Gadara was subdued and burned. This may be an exaggeration: the attack may have been directed against outlying towns and villages in Gadarene territory. Interpretation is also required concerning the activities of Vespasian and his son Titus who put down the Revolt. Some modern writers, relying on ancient commentaries, have said that Vespasian was 'welcomed in Gadara, apparently as a liberator', whilst others, relying on other texts, have pointed out that 'Gadara was destroyed by Vespasian'. Is it perhaps a case of Jewish villages in Gadarene territory being destroyed, an act for which the city itself welcomed him as a liberator?

Excavations only started in 1974. The site is a long, flat-topped spur, with its lightly wooded sides sloping gently away before dropping precipitously. The ancient acropolis at the east end is at present covered by a stone-built village, beside which the main archaeological activity has taken place. The North Theatre and the East Gate by which one enters the site today are both very ruined, as is the long Colonnaded Street, although the German Evangelical Mission, under the direction of Dr Ute Lux and Dr E. Kruger, has excavated a short stretch of the street (Fig. 8). The whole area is scattered with ruins, including an extremely

* Josephus, *Wars*.

Fig. 8 A recently excavated section of the Colonnade Street at Umm Qeis, ancient Gadara.

impressive underground family tomb. This is of bold, simple design, the inner, double arcaded chamber being set behind a curiously 'baroque' approach down a flight of steps. It was discovered by accident in 1968 and was excavated the following year.

Close to a colonnaded precinct near the acropolis, in which stood a central-plan Byzantine church, a north/south side-street runs off to the West Theatre. Like most of the buildings of Gadara, this is built of black basalt, not especially attractive as a colour but very hardwearing, and when finely dressed it has a sharpness of cut and lustrous satin-like finish which is infinitely pleasing. Even in its present state one can appreciate the precision of its masonry and the refinement and elegance of the detailing. The plan of the auditorium was considerably more than the half-circle which removed it from the standard Roman type such as at Gerasa, Scythopolis and Philadelphia, and brought it nearer to the Greek ideal in which the *orchestra* was a complete circle. Also there was no podium wall or screen dividing players from spectators: all were involved in the action. The only visual break in the unity of actors and audience was the high-backed VIP seats – even today wonderfully comfortable – which formed the bottom row of seats. In plan, arrangement and detail it is a remarkable fusion of Greek styling and superb

Fig. 9 One of the vaulted passageways beneath the auditorium of the West Theatre at Umm Qeis.

Roman engineering. These details may be significant, for they suggest a continuing Hellenistic tradition.

The Roman engineering, nonetheless, reaches almost poetic power in the range of vaults and *vomitoria* which lie beneath the auditorium (Fig. 9). The beautifully tailored masonry is remarkable, powerful yet subtle, with the barrel vault depressed into an elegant 'carriage' arch.

The citizens of Gadara used to 'solace their leisure with plays performed in the theatres'* after having bathed in the thermal waters by the Yarmouk River at the

* G. Schumacher, *Abila of the Decapolis*.

44

bottom of the hill (present-day al Hammah). Strabo disliked the smell of the waters but the Gadarenes enjoyed its therapeutic benefits, even though they may have been less enthusiastic about the long climb back up to the cooler air of the city heights. Schumacher's mention of the theatres is important because the poets of Gadara have left the most enduring testimony of the cultural traditions of the city.

Menippos, the Cynic satirist, was born in Gadara towards the beginning of the third century B.C. All his written works have been lost, but his style is known to have combined poetry with verse and included the diatribe (the aspect of abusiveness is a modern influence in the word) and parody in which the Cynics 'clothed philosophy in motley' (Eratosthenes, scholar and scientist, born c. 275 B.C.). Varro and Lucian were deeply influenced by him.

Philodemos, by contrast, was an Epicurean philosopher and epigrammatic poet born in Gadara in the first century B.C. Of the Roman poets, Virgil was one of his pupils during his stay in Rome and Herculaneum: it was his writings which were uncovered in the famous library, having been buried for centuries after the eruption of Vesuvius. His writings covered a wide variety of subjects which were treated with a sensual, often erotic, enjoyment and lightness of touch truly in accord with the School's dictate about pleasure, the practice of virtue being the highest good.

Meleager, also born in Gadara in the first century B.C., wrote mainly brief elegiac epigrams which dealt with love and death. He is remembered also for his anthology of verses by various poets, including himself, entitled the *Garland*. This work is full of charm and poetic conceits like comparing each of the forty-one poets he quotes with plants or flowers. It is, however, his epigrams which have stood as his greatest testament. There is a lyrical, sun-drenched quality about them in which nature and Man are seen as allies:

> Noisy cicada, drunk with dew drops, thou singest thy rustic ditty that fills the wilderness with voice, and seated on the edge of the leaves, striking with saw-like legs thy sunburnt skin thou shrillest music like the lyre's. But sing, dear, some new tune to gladden the woodland nymphs, strike up some strain responsive to Pan's pipe, that I may escape from Love and snatch a little midday sleep, reclining here beneath the shady plane-tree.

Towards the end of his life this immensely human poet returned in memory to his home, Gadara, and affirmed with humour his being a 'citizen of the world' – indeed, the oneness of Mankind:

> Island Tyre was my nurse, and Gadara, which is Attic, but lies in Syria, gave me birth. From Eucrates I sprang, Meleager, who first by the help of the Muses ran abreast of the Graces of Menippos. If I am a Syrian, what wonder?

Stranger, we dwell in one country, the world; one chaos gave birth to all mortals. In my old age I wrote these lines in my tablets before my burial; for eld and death are near neighbours. Speak a word to wish me, the loquacious old man, well, and mayst thou reach a loquacious old age thyself.*

Gadara may be seen as the intellectual – possibly even the cultural – heart of the Decapolis, a city where the precepts of Hellenistic traditions were cherished and fostered. Small wonder then that it was viewed with ferocity by the Judaic zealots.

To the north, overlooking the Sea of Galilee from its hill-top site on the eastern shore, was Hippos. It had a particular rival in the city of Tiberias across the bright waters; indeed it was not so much rivalry as a sworn hostility. The city's natural defences were strengthened by a defensive wall of which sections, with their towers, survive. The main reason, however, for its small size throughout much of its early history was the shortage of water. The natural supply within the city was not enough to support a large population, and it was only when an aquaduct was built across the saddle to the spring at Fiq, some four kilometres away, that Hippos could develop beyond the walled confines of the Hellenistic city. This aquaduct was very much a liberating factor, equally important in its own way as the city's liberation by Pompey.

The city was substantially rebuilt after Pompey, and a long colonnaded street, paved with black basalt, was laid along the ridge with a gate on the south-eastern end facing into the saddle. There are few remains of the Hellenistic period but remarkably a Nabatean presence has been established. An inscription mentioning Dusares has been found. As Asher Ovadiah has pointed out, 'The surprising thing about this discovery is that until now, Nabatean remains had not been found in the region of the Sea of Galilee which was outside the sphere of the Nabatean kingdom.'† The Roman remains are considerable and they suggest a city graced with many fine structures.

Small-scale excavations were mounted in 1951 and 1955, which revealed some impressive Byzantine structures. The city plan has been established by aerial photography. It is an interesting and beautiful site with spectacular views.

Damascus was so far away that there is no apparent reason why it should have been included in the Decapolis. For centuries it had been a major city and an outstandingly prosperous trading emporium. Indeed Strabo's comment acknowledges this: 'The city Damascus is also a noteworthy city, having been, I might almost say, even the most famous of the cities in that part of the world in the time of the Persian empire ...' Damascus does present a problem in the context of the Decapolis, simply because of its geographical isolation.

---

* *Greek Anthology*, Book 7.   † Asher Ovadiah, *P.E.Q.*, 1981.

The same might be said of Canatha. But was its very isolation the reason for its inclusion in the group? Dr Jones has pointed out that it was the only city in the area for nearly three hundred years. This alone is perhaps enough for an 'accord' or 'fraternal sympathy' to develop between the cities of the central core and isolated Canatha.

Canatha is today identified with the ruins at Kanawat in Syria. It is an extensive site on the northern slopes of the Jebel Hauran. The city was small in size compared with Gerasa, but during the Roman period it acquired all the civic attributes one has come to expect, such as a paved street with colonnades along which were set the public spaces. The high part of the town forms an acropolis. The city was walled, and stretches of these defences with their towers still exist. Architecturally, and in sculptural work, one feels the influence of Palmyra, and of the Nabateans. Neither of these is surprising, but the Parthian influence from Palmyra is particularly evident in the 'frontality' of figurative sculpture (a lintel showing the Judgement of Paris is an example). Yet Canatha was an important emporium in a virtual no-man's-land and would have been open to a wide range of influences. The Hellenistic settlers were in a beleaguered location, and their descendants had to cope with Ituraean hostility until the solution of the Near East by Pompey. From then on it kept aloof from the Ituraeans; indeed, as Dr Jones has shown, 'its superiority is shown by its contributing separate cohorts of the Canathenes to the Roman army and not allowing its citizens to be merged in the cohorts of the Ituraeans.'* Its supremacy in the area was only challenged when Philip the Arab (A.D. 244–249) raised the nearby village of his birth to *colonia* status, giving it the name of Philippopolis, and when Diocletian (A.D. 284–305) raised the adjacent village of Saccaea to the status of *colonia* also, naming it Maximianopolis. The important factor about all three of these cities, however, is that they were, in respect of the territory they controlled, very small. Canatha's territorial limits were little more than a few miles around the city walls; this is not to say that her influence over the steppe was not considerable. She can, therefore, be seen as the only city of the Decapolis to have retained its original frontier outpost character: unlike the others she did not expand to control a large city-state.

Butler waxed lyrical about the site, noting the brilliance of effect of black basalt against the bright green vegetation and the beauty of the trees. Yet, even today, for all its natural beauty, it has a feeling of isolation and a sense of introspection: one comes almost from nowhere upon it, and nowhere exists beyond it.

Neither Raphana nor Dium have been conclusively identified. There are four suggested sites for Dium, the most persistently quoted being Tell el-Husn, just south of Irbid. Others are Kefer Abil, near Pella; Edun, also near Irbid; and,

* A. H. M. Jones, *Cities of the Eastern Roman Provinces.*

probably more promising, Tel el Ash'ari, near the town of Dera'a just over the present border with Syria.

There have been no excavations at the site of Abila, even though the hypogea nearby have been studied. It is still a virgin site but this will soon change, for in 1980 the site was surveyed by a team from the Covenant Theological Seminary of St Louis, Missouri, and proposals are being considered for excavations in 1982. The site is set in rolling, moor-like landscape with high plateaux and deep coombes. But for a few houses in the village of Harta (birthplace of the notable Jordanian historian, Suleiman Mousa) on the western horizon, there is not a building in sight, and in consequence there is a magical rural silence disturbed only by the sound of the stream and the minute intimacies of the wildlife. It is a place of singular beauty; there are no signs of life, and the wind creeps mysteriously amongst the trees in the valley and about the dense patches of thistle in which hide the shattered stones and fallen columns of the ruined city.

The remains on the hill, which might be referred to as the acropolis, called Tell Abil, probably mark the site of the Hellenistic town. There are traces of defensive walls all round this acropolis, whilst to the east more walls run across the slope, with a short section of arched construction, which may represent a phase of urban expansion. This two-part town may be all that there was to Abila until Pompey revivified the Decapolis. However, with 'liberation' the city expanded to the south. A Roman theatre was built into the side of the opposite hill, the Umm el Amad (Fig. 10) with a huge temple(?) complex with vaults and courtyard below. On the top of Umm el Amad are scattered ruins, whilst in the valley below there are the remains of a basalt-paved colonnaded street running up from the stream. At the foot of the slopes on the other side of the Wadi Queilbeh are a series of important hypogea, most of which have exquisite, if damaged, wall paintings and some huge, empty, sarcophagi.

It is to be hoped that the Jordanian Government will declare this site an 'archaeological zone' and thus prevent the uncontrolled building which has marred the environs of Jerash. The environment of Abila is exceptionally fine, a place of outstanding natural beauty, and one can only pray that it will be protected, for the setting of any site is just as important as its archaeological interest.

Capitolias must have felt particularly grateful to Trajan, for the city determined a new Era from A.D. 98, the year of his succession. Hardly anything of the ancient city is now visible, the whole site being covered by the village of Beit Ras. Nonetheless, there are architectural fragments to be seen built into modern houses. There are also traces of a city wall, a vast number of natural and man-made cisterns and some interesting hypogea – one with a noteworthy painted interior.

Fig. 10 The unexcavated site of ancient Abila from the hill on which was the Hellenistic settlement. The shadowed area on the right marks the position of the Roman theatre.

Capitolias could never have been very large, and probably never extended much beyond its original acropolis. The main reason for this was probably the absence of fresh water within the city – even today water has to be piped in. The citizens had, therefore, to rely on the extensive system of cisterns and caves in the limestone bedrock for storage of rain water. Some of these chains of caves were artificially linked so that one system fed the next and eventually filled a huge man-made reservoir in a dammed-up wadi. The lack of water can be seen as an inhibiting factor and despite its dignity as a *polis*, and later as a See, Capitolias was evidently a poor relation – or at least a country cousin – to the grand city of Gerasa.

Trajan and Hadrian had been men of great gifts and tireless energy, and the stability they wrought created for the majority of the Decapolis cities a vision of endless prosperity. The Antonine Period which followed was to see the Golden Age for Gerasa; it was all too good to be true. Antoninus Pius (A.D. 138–161) virtually marked time but Rome could afford a respite. Marcus Aurelius's reign (A.D. 161–180) was, on the other hand, one of almost incessant wars and the reign of Commodus (A.D. 180–192) saw the beginning of despotism which was to lead to instability. But at Gerasa and in the Decapolis generally, these ructions seemed very far away and the warning was hardly sensed: the vision of a glorious future continued, supported by vast wealth lavished on splendid embellishments. It was the most energetic complacency the city had ever known.

Building projects were undertaken on the grandest scale. A new temple to the

49

Fig. 11 A conjectural reconstruction of the South Tetrakionia before the creation of the Circular Piazza (*compare with Fig. 73*).

patron deity, Artemis, was begun, with its huge propylaea, built by Attidius Cornelianus, Legate of Antoninus Pius, being dedicated in A.D. 150. The Cardo itself was widened from the Oval Piazza to the North Tetrapylon, and the order changed from Ionic to Corinthian. A great drain beneath the pavement was inserted. At the junction of the Cardo and the South Decumanus four pylons – or a tetrakionia – were raised at the four angles of the crossing (Fig. 11). The Temple of Dionysus was given a propylaea and monumental flight of steps, and in A.D. 191 the Nymphaeum was built. As though to compensate Zeus for having been outshone by his daughter, Artemis, he was given a splendid new temple about A.D. 163. To this period can also be attributed the North Theatre complex, whilst an inscription indicates that there was a stoa built by the Proedros Symmachus. Kraeling suggests that the West Baths are of this time also. To the north of the city were the Temple of Nemesis and the Temple of Zeus Epicarpius (the fruit-bearer), the latter being paid for by the centurion, Germanus, probably the same whose exquisite tomb is to be seen at Birketein. A further inscription tells us that there was a Temple of Zeus Helios Sarapis, Isis and the 'Younger Goddess' near the south-west gate. McCown has, however, pointed out: 'The evidence seems to indicate that this strongly Greek city was slow to accept the mystery religions. . . .'*

* C. C. McCown, *Journal of the Palestine Oriental Society*, 1936.

Everything speaks of fabulous wealth and a confident view of the future. The city had arrived and knew it: her pride in herself as a Roman metropolis was unbounded. The dark clouds seem hardly to have been heeded, but as the third century dawned, they began to spread and a chill wind blew through the Empire. Instead of the creative rule of Trajan and Hadrian there was megalomania, repression and tyranny. Even before the turn of the century, at the end of the Antonine dynasty, civil disorders at Rome were weakening the central authority. A feeling of instability crept in which was only exacerbated by increased taxation to help pay for the army and by the depreciation of the value of capital. To make things worse, the rise of a new power, the Sassanians, was threatening the eastern frontier. With the death of Severus Alexander in A.D. 235, the centre of power crumbled and control of the far flung empire began to disintegrate. Rome for forty years was a jungle of intrigue, blood and uncertainty, as one short-lived emperor followed another. The rule of law and order was a shadow and a pretence. The Sassanians pushed westwards, smashing Valerian at Edessa in A.D. 260, leaving his son, Gallienus, to cope with a desperate situation made all the more difficult by uprisings all over the Empire.

Trade was seriously affected and this precipitated Gerasa into a decline. A gesture of reassurance was perhaps thought necessary and this may be the reason why Caracalla (A.D. 211–217) decided to raise the city to the status of a colony, giving it the name Colonia Aurelia Antoniniana. Even so there can be no doubt that the Gerasenes began to question the brightness of their future and to tighten their belts drastically. This is obvious from the drop in the number of civic projects undertaken during the period of the Severan dynasty. The cut-back in public works and the devaluation of money would have hit the artisan and working classes hardest, putting many out of work and reducing others to near poverty. This would have led to large sections of the population becoming restive. The construction of the East Baths may, therefore, be seen as a scheme to provide employment in an effort to placate the populus.

The North Tetrapylon and the Festival Theatre at Birketein were also built at this time, but compared with what had been constructed during the Golden Age, these were almost dispiritingly inconsequential. During the middle of the third century nothing, as far as we know, was built in Gerasa.

Whereas the third century had been one of continual downhill slide, the beginning of the fourth marked at least a levelling out if not an actual up-turn in the fortunes of the city. Diocletian (A.D. 284–305) reorganised the Empire's internal affairs as well as its army, which he greatly increased in size. He devised a network of garrisoned defences with fast-moving strike-forces which could be rushed to any trouble spot. Raging inflation, which had so devalued money, was brought under control by the institution of a prices and wages control. But the most fundamental of all his imperial measures was to separate the administration of the Empire into east and west zones, each with its own ruling 'Augustus' supported by an assistant emperor called a 'Caesar'. From A.D. 286, Diocletian ruled the eastern zone as Augustus with his centre at Nicomedia close to the Black Sea: Maximian ruled as Augustus in the west. Diocletian's rule was autocratic and he surrounded himself with a court and panoply which was to foreshadow that of the Byzantine emperors.

For all the cities of the Decapolis – indeed all the cities of the Near East – Diocletian was important because he re-established order and some security along the eastern frontier. The Sassanians were held at bay and trade picked up again. The only major building in Gerasa from this period is the creation of the circular piazza round the South Tetrakionia. The picture of life in Gerasa is a depressing one. There was a lot of patching up and making do with what was already there. The spirit had gone out of the city and it lay waiting for a new stimulus.

A bloody and debilitating internal conflict followed Diocletian's abdication, from which emerged Constantine the Great (A.D. 312–337). A man of tireless energy and breadth of vision, he reformed the monetary system, he reformed the Senate, disbanded the Praetorian Guard, but above all he decided to build a new eastern capital on the site of the ancient Greek colony of Byzantium. In A.D. 324 he began building his new Rome – Constantinople.

Constantine the Great was the link between two epochs, between the past and the future: to preserve the past he created the future. In A.D. 314 he gave official toleration to Christianity, ten years later making it the official religion of the Empire: 'His new capital was to be a thoroughly Christian city, in which the temple would give way to the church.'* The new stimulus had arrived.

III

Pilate's wife could not have known just how right she was. By the middle of the first century there were Christian congregations in many cities in the eastern part of the Empire – and indeed, in Rome itself. Initially Christianity was viewed as yet another saviour cult such as those centred on Mithras, on the Great Mother or on Isis. These were tolerated because they were personal deities which did not conflict with the official public worship of the Emperor's Divine Majesty. Nero only turned on the Christians in Rome in A.D. 64 because he needed a scapegoat and not because he had any fear of them.

Emperors and officialdom were, however, nervous about secret societies in case they were politically motivated. Because of their refusal to worship the Emperor's

---

* Jack Holland, *Imperium Romanum*.

Divine Majesty the Christians had soon self-segregated themselves and so created the impression of a secret society; thus they became suspect.

The situation is well illustrated by a letter to Trajan written by Pliny the Younger (born A.D. 62) when he was provincial magistrate in Bythinia. He was unsure how to treat Christianity, what charges should be brought against Christians or what punishment was appropriate: '... whether it is the mere name of Christian which is punishable, even if innocent of crime, or rather the crimes associated with the name.' His picture of Christian ritual was hazy: they meet to 'chant verses' and later to partake of an 'ordinary, harmless kind' of meal. He then, immediately mentions the edict 'which banned all political societies'. He had to know exactly what went on so 'This made me decide it was all the more necessary to extract by torture the truth from two slave-women, whom they call deaconesses. I found nothing but a degenerate sort of cult carried to extravagant lengths.' Rome's attitude towards Christianity was based on the fear that it was a subversive political movement. Trajan's reply was curt but friendly; 'These people must not be hunted out' but he went on to say that Pliny had 'followed the right course of procedure. But pamphlets circulated anonymously must play no part in any accusation. They create the worst sort of precedent and are quite out of keeping with the spirit of our age.'*

We know from Epiphanius that Hadrian was aware of the Christians in Jerusalem (see page 41), but he does not seem to have taken any action against them. However, when the Empire declined into a state of crisis in the third century it was inevitable that any movement which refused to submit to the worship of the Emperor's Divine Majesty was seen as a threat to security. Persecutions under Trajan Decius (A.D. 249–251) and Valerian (A.D. 253–260) followed, culminating in the horrors of Diocletian's reign.

Constantine undoubtedly hoped to find in Christianity a force which would reunite the fractured Empire. To a certain extent his hopes were fulfilled but in the east certain 'heresies' had long become established, notably the Ebionite ('poor' in Hebrew). These rival interpretations had arisen because there was no established rule on doctrinal matters: the history of the early Church is marred by the most bitter quarrels. Eventually the crisis was tackled by a series of Councils at which the Early Fathers tried to resolve the conflicts of doctrine and practice.

The second half of the second century has been suggested as the time when Christianity became established in Gerasa. Certainly by A.D. 359, Bishop Exeresius of Gerasa attended the Council of Seleucia, and Bishop Placcus was at the Council of Chalcedon in A.D. 451. Nearby Pella quite early became a notable

---

* Pliny the Younger, *Letters.*

Christian centre but it is possible that the brethren there were 'heretics' such as the Ebionites or the Elchasaites. During the middle of the second century the city saw the writing of an important Christian work, Aristo's *Disputation*, a discussion between Jason (a Christian) and Papiscus (a Jew) on the truth of the claims made for Christ. By the fifth century Pella had its bishop: Bishop Zebennos was a signatory of the Latrocinium Council of Ephesus in A.D. 449, he also attended the Council of Chalcedon. Subsequent bishops such as Paulos and Zacharias are also recorded. It was, in fact, during the Byzantine period that the city reached its zenith. At this time there must have been much building activity, not only in the domestic sector but also at the many churches and monasteries which were springing up. The West Church, excavated during the initial seasons of the Wooster College expedition, has proved to be one of the largest in the Levant: other churches of this size have usually been cathedrals, and it may be that this structure, which has been attributed to the sixth century, was the cathedral of Pella. To the west of it was an atrium which was probably colonnaded on all four sides. This, however, was only one adjunct to the church which was surrounded by an extensive complex or *domus ecclesiae*.

The Byzantine period is the one of which there is most architectural evidence at Scythopolis. Literary sources refer to the city as a flourishing Christian centre; 'a city of saints, and scholars, churches and monasteries'.* Scythopolis was the metropolitan See in the ecclesiastical district of Palestina Secunda: the records of the Council of Chalcedon give four of the provinces and the names of their bishops: Severianos of Scythopolis, Annianos of Capitolias, Zebennos of Pella, Johannes of Gadara.

Being the metropolitan See would have attracted great importance to the city, and there is ample evidence to suggest that the city was a flourishing place, not only for trade but as an administrative centre.

Each city has the remains of some Byzantine building of interest, and the round church at Scythopolis is no exception. Its interest lies in that it appears to have had an unusual ambulatory round an open court. Dr FitzGerald of Pennsylvania University, who excavated there from 1930–33, dated the church to the early fifth century, which means that it must have been known to Bishop Severianos.

Capitolias has little of consequence to show except for some Byzantine architectural fragments. There is, however, a body of literature concerning the See and its incumbents. The city had its own saint, St Peter of Capitolias.

Gadara also had its martyrs, St Zachary and St Alpheus of Eleutheropolis who were decapitated during the pogroms of Diocletian in A.D. 303. Excavations by the German Evangelical Mission have brought to light a large and impressive

* F. James, in *Encyclopedia of Archaeological Excavations in the Holy Land*.

Fig. 12   The recently excavated ruins of the Byzantine church at Umm Qeis, with the distant view to the Sea of Galilee and the Golan Heights.

octagonal church. This was built into an existing Roman colonnaded space (the purpose of which is uncertain) which was then pressed into service as an atrium. The church has pillars of black basalt which contrast strongly with the white limestone columns of the atrium (Fig. 12). The plan is a centralised octagon within a square, the corners occupied by exedra.

Hippos was also a See within Palestina Secunda, and during the Byzantine period there was much church and other building taking place. Five churches have been found, excavated between 1951–55, including a large structure which was probably the cathedral. This also consisted of a basilica surrounded by dependencies, the most interesting of which was the Baptistry dedicated to St Cosmas and St Damian, which is a small church in itself. Construction can be dated to A.D. 591. That it had a separate dedication from the main church is very unusual, for this was usually done only in Mother Churches when Baptistries were annexes within a *domus ecclesiae*.

Canatha had a fine cathedral complex in which two churches shared the same atrium. The architecture is more strained, tight-skinned and assertive, bringing it more in line with Syrian Hauran Byzantine concepts than with those of Palestine/ Jordan.

Southwards, in Palestina Tertia, Philadelphia also had its fair share of martyrs, St Julian, St Theodore, St Eubulus, St Malkamon, St Mokimos and St Salomon.

The little church on the Citadel was dedicated to St Elianus, also martyred, and there was a church dedicated to St George. Bishop Cirius was present at the Council of Nice (Nicaea?), whilst Bishop Eulogius attended the Council of Chalcedon. As with the remains of earlier periods, much of the evidence of Byzantine Philadelphia now lies buried beneath the modern city of Amman. However, Mrs Bennett's excavations on the Citadel have revealed 'a complex of Byzantine buildings of some importance'.*

There is, however, always a dispiriting element in provincial Byzantine remains: the vast majority of projects were put up at the expense of earlier works in that the construction was usually attended by the wholesale quarrying of some pagan work. A very obvious example of this is the re-use of a section of the architrave from the peristyle of the Temple of Artemis as the lintel to the main west doorway of the Basilica of St Theodore at Jerash. Pillars re-used in a new composition are sometimes of different heights, giving a disturbing botched-up appearance. Building methods also frequently left much to be desired, so that it is today no surprise that few walls remain. There was also much in-building into older structures, a spirit of make-shift and make-do. Byzantine building at its best has thrilling spatial relationships and an intensely spiritual atmosphere; at its worst it is insensitive and crude. But the spirit of the age of the Byzantines was as different from that of the Romans as the Romans had been from that of the Greeks: new ideals call for new ideas.

Nonetheless, as Krautheimer has pointed out, 'The churches of Gerasa are extraordinarily impressive – through their size, through their number, and through their tendency to group several structures within one precinct.' These churches are in the main fifth- and sixth-century work and represent the revival in the city's affairs at that time, a revival for which Justinian (A.D. 527–565) was in no small measure responsible. It was his reforms and reorganisations which consolidated the revival. Trade and commerce had been picking up since the middle of the fifth century, allowing once more a degree of public and private wealth. Spending on public and religious works was resumed. This is reflected in a series of splendid churches of the late fifth and sixth centuries together with their associated complexes.

Many of the clergy were men of substance or came from well-to-do families, and from their own pockets, or through their persuasion, gifts and donations poured into the churches' coffers. They created a scene of some brilliance and richness of effect, in which architectural harmony and decorative dazzle found an answer in lavish, sonorous ritual.

But like the political and economic fabric, the walls and domes behind the

* Mrs C.-M. Bennett, *Annual of the Department of Antiquities*, 1978.

shining glass mosaics were crumbling from within. Workmanship was shoddy and maintenance was minimal: even the city water supply failed through lack of attention. At the beginning of the seventh century, the heady ritual of the Church was being conducted in gorgeous palaces of faith set in what was almost a slum. Decay was rampant, and the city fell more and more into decline. The Persian invasion of A.D. 614 was the first of two shocks which were eventually to bring it to its knees. The Persians occupied the crumbling town until A.D. 628, leaving as a testimonial only their adaptation of the Hippodrome into a polo field.

All the cities of the Decapolis were affected by this conquest, but it is questionable whether one can really talk about the Decapolis as such by this date. Whatever their connection with one another, it had no significance whatever by the end of the Byzantine period in Gerasa, and probably by a date several centuries before that. The cities survived the Persian invasion but, whilst still reeling from the shock of it, the next violent change was launched upon them.

IV

The first clash between the Byzantines and the Moslems was at Motah, near Kerak, in A.D. 629, when the Moslems were defeated and their three leaders killed. What was left of their army was led back to Medina by one of the greatest figures in the annals of early Islam, Khalid ibn al Walid. Four years later he was back with another large army and this time with much greater success. The Byzantine, Sergius, was defeated and much of the country over-run; only Jerusalem, Caesarea and a few other cities held out expecting relief. The Emperor Heraclinus marched south with an army of fifty thousand. The opposing forces joined battle not far from Abila on 20th August, A.D. 636, at a point where the River Yarmouk is joined by a tributary, the Ruqqad. The place is called Yaqusah. Al Walid achieved a resounding victory, and Byzantine control of Palestine and Jordan came to an end. Abila was not the only city in the erstwhile Decapolis to feature in the campaign, for Pella was once more in the firing line. The great Battle of Fahl was fought nearby in the Jordan Valley: with the Moslem victory, Scythopolis returned to the name of Beth-Shan, and Pella to the name of Fahl.

It is generally held that after the Moslem conquests Jordan sank into a state of poverty and was only kept going because it lay on the route between Damascus and the Holy Cities of Medina and Mecca. Certainly no grandiose building projects were undertaken, and there was little social or economic development comparable with the Roman period. But present researches are beginning to show that the land was not left neglected nor under-nourished. Indications at Jerash are that, although the population had shrunk, the city was far from deserted or inactive. The discovery in 1981 of an Ummayyad mosque (see page 165) clearly indicates urban activity, possibly sustained by and catering for pilgrims on their way south from Damascus to the Holy Cities of Arabia. A clear picture of early Moslem life in these ancient lands cannot, however, yet be drawn.

The shift of the centre of authority from Damascus to Baghdad was a blow from which only Damascus survived. For the other cities of the late Decapolis it was a twilight period slipping into the darkness of abandonment. The corruption of time was aided by a series of savage earthquakes which rocked the whole area and brought down mighty works into the accumulating sands of neglect. The great earthquake of A.D. 747, which destroyed the Church of the Holy Sepulchre, wrought terrible damage in tottering Gerasa, sending the few remaining inhabitants fleeing from the unsafe ruins to build their hovels in the Oval Piazza and round the ruins of the South Tetrakionia.

Eventually even the survivors departed, leaving the wilderness without voice save for that of Meleager's cicadas. Sand blew in and thistles clutched at defenceless columns; the sun beat down on a motionless landscape of slow, triumphant destruction. Ruined pomp stood stiffly in an intimidating and unheeding silence, broken only by the occasional sickening thud as yet another lintel or column grew too weary to stand. Time passed, having no beginning and no ending.

CHAPTER THREE

'No Minor Event'

FOR CENTURIES the ancient Biblical lands east of the Jordan lay derelict and deserted. In A.D. 1122, the crusader William of Tyre noted that Jerash was reduced to a mass of ruins. A terrible torpor had settled on this almost forgotten land which persisted right up to the beginning of the nineteenth century. It was a place as remote and as dangerous as the surface of the moon.

European interest was only awakened when a French expeditionary force swept up the Palestine coast in 1799 in an attempt to reach, and capture, Constantinople. This was stopped by the Ottoman Governor of Akko, Ahmed Jazzar, known as 'the Butcher', with the aid of the British Fleet under Sir Sydney Smith. Sir Sydney's involvement did not, however, stop there, for in 1801 he made a sudden march in strength with his Marines on Jerusalem and Bethlehem as a demonstration of support for the Christians whom 'the Butcher' now accused of complicity with the defeated French.

This was the age of exploration in which the world was opened up; and the Holy Land was as little known as the heart of Africa. Palestine and the lands east of the Jordan had the particular attraction of being the land of the Scriptures. Travel there was hazardous, to say the least, with very little in the way of comfort and a lot in the way of danger. The local Bedouin were warring amongst themselves, and most of them had never seen a European. In the tense atmosphere they were nervous of anything that moved and suspicious of strangers in particular. The early travellers in this area were, in consequence, an intrepid band, and what they achieved is amazing. They brought home the first factual information and descriptions of an unknown world.

The first man to set foot upon the lands of the Decapolis was a German, Ulrich Jasper Seetzen. Even as a young man he had shown a remarkably resolute character, combining great powers of concentration with clarity of thought, perception with receptivity, courage with caution – and an iron constitution. His interests were wide-ranging, from zoology to architecture, botany to Greek, mineralology to antiquities. He pursued each assiduously. His formal education was completed at Göttingen University, where he came under the influence of the great scholar, Johann F. Blumenbach, who instilled in him an orderly, 'scientific' approach to everything which caught his highly-tuned faculties. Seetzen was also an avid traveller with seemingly inexhaustible energy.

In 1802 he set out for Constantinople with the intention of exploring the East and Africa. Initially he had very little money but with commendable entrepreneurial instinct he arranged to send antiquities back to the museum at Gotha along with any other archaeological information he could acquire, including transcripts of newly found inscriptions. In this he was singularly successful, and he was soon despatching antiquities not only to the museum but to the Duke of Saxe-Gotha and a rapidly increasing number of princely patrons, including the Tsar of Russia. The Tsar took the very practical step of giving him the Civil Service rank of Ambassadorial Councillor to help him in his relic- and antiquity-hunting.

But for Seetzen exploration was a 'scientific' exercise which required its proper preparation; thus he made a point of learning Arabic and studying Islamic law, religion and custom. He dressed as an Arab and absorbed all that he could. He soon moved to Aleppo where, during his long stay, he perfected his Arabic whilst continuing to collect antiquities and manuscripts which he despatched back to Europe.

The beginning of 1806 found him on his way south from Damascus to Tiberias on the Sea of Galilee. His extensive reading of Biblical and ancient authors had prepared him, for he was well aware that to the south and east lay 'the region of the Decapolis'. In a letter to the Court at Gotha he wrote: 'I thought it would be rendering service to science, if I became competent to give the public certain intelligence of the present state of Decapolis, its antiquities, plants, minerals &c. ...' Having passed round the southern end of the Sea, he climbed the 'considerable eminence' and explored the ruins on the top. These he took to be ancient Gamala, but in all probability he was standing on Qal'at el Husn, the site of ancient Hippos: if this was so, how sad that he should write 'I could not obtain any information concerning Hippos'. One of his main troubles was that he was relying to some extent on extremely inaccurate maps which had no scientific basis. Thus Capitolias, Gadara, Pella and Gerasa were all wildly misplaced. This again made him despondent, for he 'was equally unsuccessful respecting Capitolias and Pella' which, according to his map, could not have been far away.

The misplacement of Gadara on the map did not, however, deceive him: 'we set off the next morning for M'kess (Umm Qeis). This town is situated in an angle of a high mountain. . . . It was formerly a large and opulent town, proofs of which are still visible in remnants of marble columns, and of large buildings, in great numbers of sarcophaguses, ornamented with bas-reliefs. I thought there was reason to believe that M'kess was the ancient Gadara, a town of the second rank among the decapolitan cities. . . .' This was the first of his identifications but he wanted to check his deduction against associated topographical features. 'I set myself to seek, in the environs of M'kess, for some hot springs, which were formerly near Gadara, and I discovered them on the northern side, at a league's distance from the foot of a mountain on which M'kess stands . . .'

He had considerable trouble in getting to Abila but made it in the end. 'The town is situated in the angle of a mountain, formed by the two bases . . . [it] is completely in ruins and deserted. There is not even one single building standing; but the ruins, and the remnants attest its ancient splendour, some beautiful remains of the ancient walls are to be discovered, together with a number of arches, and columns of marble, basalt and grey granite . . .' The magical thing about Abila is that it is still exactly as Seetzen found it.

He stayed at the village of Beit Ras, 'situated on a moderate elevation, . . . and which from some ancient remains of architecture appears to have been once a considerable town.' Little did he realise that he was sheltering amid the very ruins of Capitolias about which he had sought information.

'The next day I had the satisfaction of seeing the important ruins of Jerrash . . . which ruins may be compared to those of Palmyra, or of Balbek. It is impossible to explain how this place, formerly of such manifest celebrity, can have so long escaped the notice of all lovers of antiquity.' How right he was, for had Jerash had its Wood and Dawkins it would have been as celebrated. Doubtless it was the great difficulty in getting there which prevented this – though Wood and Dawkins managed to get to Palmyra – but also, by the time Seetzen's description was published in London in 1810, the whole mood of the Neo-Classical Movement had changed and the passionate pursuit of the antique had cooled.

Nonetheless, his brief description of the ruins, despite its lack of detail, amounted to what one might call a 'rave review':

It is situated in an open and tolerably fertile plain, through which a river runs. The walls of the town are mouldered away, but one may yet trace their whole extent. Not a single private house remains entire. But on the other hand I observed, several public buildings, which were distinguished by a very beautiful style of architecture. I found two superb ampitheatres, solidly built of marble, with columns, niches &c., the whole in good preservation. I also found some palaces, and three temples, one of which had a peristyle of twelve grand columns of the Corinthian order, eleven of which were still upright [the Temple of Artemis – Fig. 13]. In another of these temples, I saw a column on the ground of the most beautiful polished Egyptian granite. I also found a handsome gate of the city, well preserved, formed of three arches, and ornamented with pilasters.

The most beautiful thing I discovered was a long street crossed by another, and ornamented on both sides with rows of marble columns, of the Corinthian

Fig. 13   The ruins of the Temple of Artemis at Jerash from a nineteenth-century engraving.

order, and one of whose extremities terminated in a semicircle that was set round with sixty pillars of the Ionic order. At the point where the two streets cross, in each of the four angles, a large pedestal of hewn stones is visible, on which probably statues were formerly set [the South Tetrakionia]. A part of the pavement still remains, formed of hewn stones.

To speak generally, I counted about two hundred columns, which yet partly support their entablatures but the number of those thrown down is infinitely more considerable; I saw indeed but half the extent of the town, and a person would probably still find in the other half, on the opposite side of the river, a quantity of remarkable curiosities.

Jerrash can be no other than the ancient Gerasa, one of the decapolitan towns.... He had got it in one.

This description of the discovery of Jerash was, however, more than just pictures in words, for Seetzen also arrived correctly at the period when the main structures had been built. 'From a fragment of a Greek inscription, which I copied, I am led to conclude, that several of the buildings of this town were erected under the Emperor Marcus Aurelius Antonninus.... It is at all events certain, that the edifices of this town, are of the age of the most beautiful Roman architecture.'

Lacking in detail though these first descriptions are, they have an enthusiasm and warmth which create a vivid mental picture of this 'Pompeii of the East'. Almost as a bonus, he went on to visit and describe the ruins of Philadelphia: 'I found there some remarkable ruins, which attest its ancient splendour. I could only spare a short time to the examination of these objects – and I hope that any other traveller who may visit the ruins of Jarrash, will not forget those of Amman.'*

All his observations were written down by Seetzen in a diary which became a valuable record for his reports to Europe. He can properly be called the pioneer of travel and study in the Biblical lands east of the Jordan. And yet he is, even to this day, far less well-known than his contemporaries, Burckhart and Buckingham. To some extent this is because he undertook his explorations on his own initiative and not at the behest of one of the influential exploration societies which were springing up in educated circles all over northern Europe. The Palestine Association, founded in London in 1804, certainly took great interest in his Holy Land travels and, indeed, published a considerable extract from a letter he had sent to the Grand Marshal of the Court of Saxe-Gotha, in which he briefly described where he had been. But his diaries were not published until half a century later, in 1854, by which time several other reports were already on the market. Through his Palestine Association publication, however, the results of his explorations were known in England, for J. S. Buckingham, who travelled over much of the same ground in 1816, refers to Seetzen's discovery and identification of Gadara.

Six years after Seetzen's exploration, John Lewis Burckhart set out from Tripoli, Syria, on his way overland to Cairo. Unlike his predecessor, he had been retained by an exploration society in London, the Association for Promoting the Discovery of the Interior Parts of Africa. The Association had commissioned him to explore for the source of the River Niger but it was decided that he should first gain complete fluency in Arabic and the Moslem way of life. Thus, after a prolonged stay in Malta, he went to Antioch and then, like Seetzen, to Aleppo. Much of his time there was spent studying Koranic law and the Traditions, in which he became so fluent that questions of exegesis and doctrine were brought to him for explanation and interpretation. In a way it is sad that he and Seetzen never met. For by chance, Burckhart had also studied under Blumenbach at Göttingen, where his restless zeal was given direction and organisation. When he arrived in London in 1806, it is hardly surprising that this serious but energetic young man was snapped up by the Association which was so concerned about those 'Interior Parts of Africa'.

By 1812 he felt ready to face the 'Interior Parts' and set off for Cairo, from where he planned to mount his expedition in search of the source of the Niger. From

* U. J. Seetzen, *A Brief Account etc.*

Tripoli he went south, dressed as an Arab, over the high, rolling hills. At Abila he found that 'neither buildings nor columns remain standing' and 'at Om Keis [Umm Qeis] the remains of antiquity are very mutilated'. He missed the way to Beit Ras from 'Erbad' [Irbid] but reports that he 'was told that the ruins were of large extent'.

On 2nd May he reached Jerash but was only able to spend about four hours there although he was evidently fascinated by the place: 'but my guides were so tired of waiting, that they positively refused to expose their persons longer to danger, and walked off, leaving me the alternative of remaining alone in this desolate spot, or of abandoning the hope of correcting my notes by a second examination of the ruins'. However, during the four hours his guides were skulking under a bush by the wadi side, he managed to see a remarkable amount of the ruins and make sense of them. Above all it was the Temple of Artemis which impressed him, particularly the mighty stand of splendid pillars which to this day are one of the grandest sights in Jerash (Fig. 96). 'Their style of architecture is much superior to that of the Grand Colonnade . . . and seems to belong to the best period of the Corinthian order, their capitals being beautifully ornamented with acanthus leaves. The whole edifice seems to have been superior in taste and magnificence to every public building of its kind in Syria. . . .' High praise from one whose descriptions were usually so sober.

His brief, matter of fact, account of the ruins of Amman have often been taken to imply that he was not impressed with them. Reading the account, it is clear that this is not so; his brevity was due to his being yet again pressed by his guides. 'I am sensible that the . . . description of Amman, though it notices all the principal remains, is still very imperfect; but a traveller who is not accompanied with an armed force can never hope to give very satisfactory accounts of the antiquities of these deserted countries. My guides had observed some fresh horse-dung near the water's side, which greatly alarmed them, as it was a proof that some Bedouin were hovering about. They insisted upon my returning immediately, and refused to wait for me a moment, rode off while I was still occupied in writing a few notes upon the theatre.'*

Burckhart's great triumph was yet to come for, later, in August, he discovered Petra locked away in its mountain fastness.

Throughout all his journeys he kept a diary which, like Seetzen, he wrote up in great secrecy. The Syrian diary was eventually published, five years after his untimely death, in 1822: he never reached those 'Interior Parts'.

Four years after Burckhart, in 1816, an Englishman appeared on the scene, James Silk Buckingham. As a traveller and observer he did not enjoy Seetzen's or

---

* J. L. Burckhart, *Travels etc.*

Burckhart's orderly scientific method of enquiry. Nonetheless he was not unlearned, as the marshalling of lengthy discussions and quotations of ancient sources clearly shows. But through his writings one senses a strange, neurotic unease of personality, as though he were exploring as much himself as the Holy Land. There is a constant undercurrent of the need to impress, of the mistaken need to disagree. In consequence he has had his ardent admirers and equally ardent detractors, though neither would deny his arrogance and vanity, or that his published travels contain much of great value and fine perception.

He visited Jerash in 1816, and the description he gave of the ruins was the lengthiest and most detailed to that date. After a brief general description, he went on to describe in much greater detail each monument in turn. Sometimes he got things horribly wrong, for he took the Propylaea of the Temple of Artemis to be 'a noble palace, probably the residence of the Governor', not appreciating its architectural relationship to 'a beautiful Corinthian temple ... behind, in right lines with it....' Had he had a more scholarly turn of mind, he might have understood the relationship. He did, however, make some important observations such as the fact that the Hadrianic Arch 'stood quite unconnected with any wall' (see page 105). He also realised, and was the first to record, that there was a formal plan to the city which had been conceived as a whole: 'The general plan of the whole was evidently the work of one founder, and must have been sketched out before the Roman city, as we now see it in its ruins, began to be built.'

He was enthusiastic about the ruins and worked himself, and his text, 'to such romantic heights whilst we attend to the descriptions of ancient temples; it was the prodigious number of columns they were enriched with, that enchanted us.' Wherever he turned there was something to get excited about: 'There were also other edifices scattered in different parts of the city, which will be seen in examining the plan [he, again, was the first to publish a rudimentary map of the city] but the whole was remarkable for the regularity and taste of its design, no less than for its able and perfect execution' (Fig. 14). Coming down from the heights of euphoria with a bump, he was bitterly disappointed by the plain interior of the Temple of Artemis, which he found 'to consist simply of one square cella, without any subdivisions of basilica, adytum, penetrale, or sacrarium'.*

The next two visitors made no pretence at being anything other than well-read amateurs. In March 1818, two of the most entertaining and engaging of travellers, both Commanders of the Royal Navy, crossed the Yarmouk and 'ascended the mountains by a very steep road, and before sunset arrived at Om Keis....' The Hon. C. L. Irby and Mr J. Mangles had arrived in the Decapolis. Their travels had started in August 1816, when they left England to tour the Continent, but they

---

* J. S. Buckingham, *Travels etc.*

Fig. 14 The South Colonnade Street, taken by Garstang in 1927, before clearance had begun, showing the ruins of the Temple of Zeus in the distance.

became so impressed by classical antiquities that they decided to extend their trip. Between 1817 and 1818 they spent a great deal of time travelling about the Near East and became involved in all sorts of adventures. They were well educated and versed in the classics and architecture. They were also tough, hardy and brave. Visitors in the backwoods of the Near East were still a great rarity, and those who did venture forth were really quite intrepid. Dressed as Arabs (or rather, their romantic notion of what an Arab should look like), these two redoubtable sea captains braved the considerable risks of travel in the area. On their return to England in 1820, they were persuaded to publish a compilation of the letters they had sent home to their families. This they did for private circulation but the little book was passed around and became so popular that they eventually, in 1844, allowed a general publication which became a run-away best-seller.

In March 1818, they explored the remains of ancient Gadara, and with great glee noted that 'the pavement of the city is still very perfect; and the traces of the chariot wheels are visible on the stones'. Why is it that when looking at a Roman road, even today, people always expect to find the tracks of chariots, indeed, feel cheated if they don't, as if the Romans spent all their time rushing about in chariots? They examined several underground sepulchres and made an observation which can still be made by visitors touring in the area: 'the doors [to these tombs] are very impressive, being cut out of immense blocks of stone ... the hinge is nothing but a part of the stone left projecting at each end, and let into a socket cut in the rock; the face of the doors are cut in the shape of panels'. They also went down to el Hammah, where they found 'several sick persons at these springs who had come to use the waters'.

Six days later they were at Beishan, where they spent a day inspecting the ruins of Scythopolis. Again their knowledge of the history of architecture came in handy: 'The most interesting [ruin] is the theatre ... and is remarkable as having those oval recesses half way up the theatre, mentioned by Vitruvius as being constructed to contain the brass sounding tubes. We had never seen these in any other ancient theatre, and were, at the time, quite at a loss to conjecture to what use they were applied. There are seven of these cells, and Vitruvius mentions, that even in his day very few theatres had them. We were very careful to take a correct plan of this theatre, attending to every minute particular.'

Two days later they forded the Jordan and visited the ruins at 'Tabathat Fahkil'. They were delighted by the beauty of its situation but were concerned that no one seemed to know of which ancient city these were the remains: 'As this place appears to be as ancient as Scythopolis, and full two-thirds of its size, it seems unaccountable that history should not mention a town so near "the principal city of the Decapolis", as this is.' It was to be another thirty years before this was recognised as the site of Pella. Irby and Mangles were, however, the first Europeans to record the ruins.

Within five days they were at Jerash, where they spent a week busying themselves with measuring the ruins, whilst their companion, Mr Bankes, was 'drawing and copying inscriptions etc. . . . .' But, as usual, they were having terrible trouble with their guides and guards, who were forever asking for more money. As they saw it, everyone was jumping on the bandwagon of fleecing the Frank travellers 'since Lady Hester Stanhope *spoiled the market* by over-paying them when she went to Palmyra'.

Perhaps in answer to Seetzen's cry that Jerash had 'so long escaped the notice of all lovers of antiquity' they were set on recording the architectural splendours that stood before them. 'We were very anxious to finish the plan of Djerash, nothing having ever been published regarding these antiquities; indeed they were unknown to Europeans until Mr Seetzen discovered them in 1806. I believe Mr Bankes, Sir W. Chatterton, Mr Leslie, Sheikh Ibrahim [Burckhart's Arabic pseudonym], and Mr Buckingham are the only Europeans who have seen them.'

Usually they were super-critical of the architecture they found in the east – their disgust at Palmyra and Petra is well known – but at Jerash they went almost overboard with praise. 'It has been a splendid city'. They raved about the Colonnade Street and found the pavement exceedingly good, and, excitement reaching near fever pitch, 'the marks of chariot wheels are visible in many parts of the street'. Apart from the splendour of the temples (they were the first to note the unusual vault below the Temple of Artemis) and the intriguing 'magnificent Ionic oval space' (Fig. 15), they thought 'the scene of the large theatre ... singularly perfect' (Fig. 16).

They were also the first to record the great reservoir at Birketein: 'To the north-east ... are a very large reservoir for water and a picturesque tomb fronted by four Corinthian columns' (Fig. 142). They did not, however, mention the Festival Theatre.

Some of their text is weighed down with lengthy discussions of ancient sources, and they went astray when they concluded 'that the ruins of Djerash are those of Pella rather than of Gerasa', despite the earlier identification by Seetzen which they certainly knew about. Nonetheless, their enjoyment of the ruins is evident, for they agreed that 'on the whole, we consider Djerash to be a much finer mass of ruins than Palmyra'.*

The next visitor was Monsieur le Marquis, Léon de Laborde (Fig. 17), who likewise came wrapped up in turbans and cloaks with a dagger in his belt: it is inconceivable, however, that this nobleman, who was to become Director-General of the Archives of France and a member of the Académie Française, would have travelled barefoot. With him, in 1826, came the engraver, Linant, who was to do the first professional drawings of Jerash: de Laborde's text, however, contributed very little to our knowledge of the site.

1838 is a crucial date in the study of ancient sites in the Holy Land. The Reverend Edward Robinson (Fig. 18), an American Biblical scholar and virtual founder of Biblical archaeology, arrived for an extended tour of the Holy Land where, Bible in hand, he successfully identified a large number of sites that had hitherto been only names. That he was able to demonstrate that place-names in the Bible were actual sites gave birth to the desire for a more scholarly investigation of the area. The result of his travels that year, in the company of Eli Smith, a scholar and former missionary in Beirut, was *Biblical Researches in Palestine, Sinai, Arabia, Petraea and Adjacent Regions*, published in London in 1841. It was widely acclaimed.

However, Robinson regarded this first trip as only a beginning to his task of revealing the truth about the Land of the Scriptures. In the Preface to Seetzen's 1810 publication, the publisher wrote: 'Whilst a new world beyond the Atlantic has been frequently described and delineated in authentic maps; whilst the unproductive regions of Siberia, and the deserts of Africa, have been penetrated by modern hardihood and curiosity; the land which *might* be called the oldest portion

---

* Irby and Mangles, *Travels etc.*

Fig. 15   The ruins of the Oval Piazza at Jerash in 1867, taken by Corporal Phillips.

Fig. 16   Garstang's photograph of the Oval Piazza with the clearance of the South Theatre taking place in the background.

of the globe, or concerning which at least the oldest authentic history exists; where the seeds of Christianity were first sown, and where the author of our religion lived, and taught, is comparatively neglected and unknown.' Robinson sought, as a Christian Biblical scholar, to put this neglect and obscurity to rights. In 1852 he

Fig. 17 Léon de Laborde, one of the early travellers who wore Arab dress.

Fig. 18 Edward Robinson, the father of Biblical archaeology.

returned for another visit. His place in this narrative is focussed on 14th May of that year when he tramped all over the site of 'the ruins called Tubukat Fahil, described by Irby and Mangles'. He had long suspected that this was the site of ancient Pella but wanted to check. 'After completing our examination of the remains, in view of these considerations, I ventured to express to my companions on the spot the opinion, in which they concurred, that we were standing amid the ruins of the long lost and long sought Pella. It is at such moments that the traveller has his reward.'* Only the meanest of men would deny him his pleasure and that tingling thrill of excitement – and how gratifying it would have been for the sea captains had they known that it was they who had drawn his attention to the site.

It was not, however, until 1865 that the first of the great learned societies came into being with the purpose of serious study of Palestine and its neighbouring Biblical lands. This was the Palestine Exploration Fund, which is still one of the most important agencies concerned with these studies. The Palestine Association, which had published Seetzen's 1810 Report, had foundered in 1834 when its effects were transferred to the Royal Geographical Society. The new Fund, under the patronage of Queen Victoria, enjoyed immediate popularity and support. Captain Charles Wilson, who had already mapped and reported on Jerusalem, immediately put forward proposals for a small-scale survey of parts of western Palestine. The expedition was made up of men from the Royal Engineers, initiating the long association between the PEF and the Royal Corps. This initial survey was completed in 1866, and the following year another Royal Engineer, Lieutenant Charles Warren, then only twenty-seven years old, began excavations in Jerusalem with another team of Engineers. Having set the work smoothly in motion, Warren went off in July and August on two reconnaissance surveys, the first to the Dead Sea, and the second, which followed without a break, to the country east of the Jordan. Among other places visited on the second survey were Amman and Jerash. The party spent nearly three days at Jerash and 'were at work from sunrise to sunset'. Warren greatly regretted not having copies of the works of Burckhart and Buckingham with him, because their plans and descriptions would have helped him identify many of the 'distinguished ruins which no doubt are very much more damaged than they were fifty years ago'. Warren wrote a report of the expedition for the PEF which they published in their *Quarterly Statement* of 1869. Though the party was small and its objectives limited, the results are not unimportant because on this survey some of the earliest photographs of Jerash were taken (Figs. 15, 59, 70, 76, 89 and 103). Fig. 2, of Amman, was also taken at this time, as was Fig. 19, probably at, or near, es Salt.

The group in Fig. 19 presents a problem, for the records in the archives of the

* E. Robinson, *Later Researches in Palestine etc.*

71

Fig. 19 Captain Warren's exploration party of 1867.

PEF are contradictory as to who these people are: are they the party which went to the Dead Sea on the first phase of the survey, or are they the party who went east of the Jordan? Warren himself numbered this photograph No. 341 at the end of a long run of shots of Jerash and two of es Salt, the latter being numbers 339 and 340 – all taken on the second, Transjordan survey. Yet in the catalogue those shown are referred to by the names of the members of the first, Dead Sea, party. However, the Dead Sea party numbered only five; the later party had six. The group shows five people, but someone had to be taking the photograph and this was not a job they would have entrusted to one of their local staff. This seems to indicate that this is the second party which consisted of Warren (by now a Captain), The Reverend W. Baily (who joined the party on 5th August just before they arrived in Jerash), Edward Hanour, Corporal Birtles, the photographer, Corporal Phillips, his photographic assistant, and Jerius, their dragoman. Captain Warren can be identified on the left, relaxed and confident, determination and intelligence showing clearly in his face; in the middle right sits the Rev. Baily, as though clothed in mitre and full canonicals, staff in hand as though on some pious pilgrimage; on the

72

right Mr Hanour, watching keenly the scientific operation being performed before him; on the ground is probably Corporal Birtles who was ill with dysentery at the time but who had struggled on bravely; whilst Jerius, the dragoman, stands behind in his fancy buttoned shirt. This photograph was in all probability taken by Corporal Phillips who on the expedition had done most of the photographic work due to Birtles's illness. Unfortunately we do not know what Phillips looked like, and he remains a rather misty figure about whom one would like to know more, for he was one of the pioneers of Near-Eastern photography. His work was to be vital in years to come, for, as W. F. Stinespring has acknowledged, these pictures are 'invaluable to the modern interpreter as an indication of what was once to be seen'.* It was only some thirty years since Fox-Talbot had taken the first photograph at Lacock Abbey, and the difficulties which Phillips had to cope with were considerable. Indeed, Warren reported that 'Corporal Phillips experienced great difficulty in his work on account of the heat which caused his bath to split up: he lost one day's work through this.'† Corporal Phillips's photographs were eventually shown in 1873 at the Dudley Gallery Exhibition, when the general public were able to applaud and recognise his work and talent.

During the second half of the last century the Palestine Exploration Fund played a leading role in the surveying, mapping and archaeology of the Holy Land. In its wake, the American Palestine Exploration Society was founded in 1870, only to be disbanded fourteen years later. Then came the German Orient Company, the British School of Archaeology, the American School of Archaeology, the French Biblical School and School of Archaeology, and many others. These societies and schools, or their successors, are still among the main front-line forces in Biblical archaeology and research, now working in conjunction with the Departments of Antiquities in the lands concerned.

Jerash has probably had more effusive language lavished on it than most ancient sites: 'This is indeed a wonderful and magnificent ruin. . . . At every turn are picturesque subjects for sketches, at every corner food for reflection . . . it is glorious and striking – a glorious ruin, a striking desolation. . . . The tide of civilised life had ebbed, rolled back, and left Gerash stranded on its shore.' So waxed the Rev. A. E. Northey when he reported to the PEF *Quarterly Statement* on his *Expedition to the East of the Jordan* in 1871.

'At last it can be said with truth that the age of relic-hunting has ceased, and the era of exploration has fairly begun. The English and American societies have already achieved commendable results.' That was written by Selah Merrill, archaeologist of the American Palestine Exploration Society, after his extended survey travels in 1875, which he wrote up and published in popular form as *East of*

---

* W. F. Stinespring, Introduction to Kraeling's *Gerasa*.   † C. Warren, *PEFQS*, 1869.

the Jordan in 1881. Merrill is interesting as a link between the romantics and the scientific archaeologists. 'Walking about this ancient city by day, and especially by night, the silence, the desolation, the mystery connected with its origin, and its past, fill the mind with sensations which cannot be imparted to another. It is no minor event in one's life to visit a ruined and deserted city, where over three hundred columns are still standing amid fallen temples and other splendid monuments of a former prosperous age.' Even so his surveys were arduous, hard working and productive. In one report he writes that 'Every fountain, stream, and ruin, and almost every wadi, in the valley and hills immediately east of the Jordan, from the north end of the Sea of Galilee to the Dead Sea, has been visited.' He did little digging, or 'dirt' archaeology as it is called, for he rightly held that 'the field of surface archaeology ... has not yet been thoroughly gleaned; enough has been found, however, to awaken the profoundest interest in the subject.'

By this time the massive *Survey of Western Palestine*, undertaken by the PEF in conjunction with the War Office, was nearing its successful completion, and Merrill was looking forward to taking part in the survey of eastern Palestine, i.e. Transjordan, which was going to be conducted by the American Palestine Exploration Society. 'One of the most important features of this work of exploration is the identification of Biblical sites. Lieutenant Conder (who had led the Western Survey) reports that of the six hundred and twenty-two Biblical (place) names in Western Palestine, four hundred and thirty-four are now identified with reasonable certainty, and of the latter number one hundred and seventy-two are discoveries of the British survey party. It should be stated that Lieutenant Conder was connected with the survey for more than six years, a large portion of which period he spent in the field, going over the ground square mile by square mile, and often acre by acre, and hence his opinion on all topographical and archaeological questions merits unusual consideration.'

Unfortunately the American Eastern Survey never came about, for the Society was disbanded in 1884, but the work Merrill had already done for the Society had been of great service. With charming modesty, this most genial and attractive of men bowed out of the archaeological scene with the words: 'It is admitted by all that the work of exploring the land where the Bible had its origins is one of the most important that has been undertaken during the present century, and it affords me special satisfaction that I have had even a slight share of carrying it on.'*

The Western Survey had been such an unqualified success that the PEF decided to pick up the mantle the Americans had put down and turn their attentions to a survey of eastern Palestine. In 1880 Lieutenant Conder was again put in command and given the assistance of another Royal Engineers team. By the beginning of

* S. Merrill, *East of the Jordan*.

74

June 1881 everything was ready, but the Turkish authorities refused to allow the survey to start. The party did cross into Jordan and surveyed a small area – including Amman – but the political tide was against them and the job was never completed. Conder went himself to Constantinople to plead the cause but to no avail.

Back in Jerusalem by March 1882, Conder suddenly got a last chance to visit Jordan. Their Royal Highnesses Prince Albert Victor and Prince George (later to become George V), sons of the Prince of Wales (Edward VII), made a tour of the Holy Land and Conder was asked to accompany the party. The maps and reports of the curtailed eastern survey were being prepared in Jerusalem at that time, and Conder saw in the royal visit an opportunity. His persistence is wonderful, for he wrote in an appendix to the one and only volume of the *Survey of Eastern Palestine* to be published by the PEF: 'Opportunity was taken of this tour to clear up various points which had arisen during the course of the office-work in Jerusalem.' Right under the nose of the Turkish authorities and the cloak of the royal tour, Conder was back on the job.

The royal tour was a great success and was duly reported upon in the PEF *Quarterly Statement*: 'Jerash, which is one of the finest [ruins] in Syria . . . was visited on 13th April, and several Greek inscriptions, which do not appear to have been copied by any previous explorer, were found by the Princes. . . .' Being a royal visit, correspondents did the right sort of research, and we are told that 'The last Royal personage who appears to have journeyed to Jerash was the Crusading King Baldwin II. . . .'*

After this things settled down in the area, and eventually the PEF was able to employ Gottlieb Schumacher to continue surface exploration in the eastern region. His works published by the Fund and in the journal of the Deutscher Palästinaverein became for long the standard sources of reference for researchers. Jerash, by then, had been settled by a community of refugee Circassians who were put there by the Turkish Government in 1878. Their settlement was on the east bank of the stream; their town was to alter irrevocably the appearance of the site from what the early travellers had known.

Since then scholars, archaeologists and historians from many lands have worked amid the ruins of the Decapolis, and contributed to our knowledge of them. Brünnow and Domaszewski and the German team working on their monumental *Die Provincia Arabia* should be mentioned, as well as Professor John Garstang, Director of the British School of Archaeology in Jerusalem and first Director of the Department of Antiquities in Jordan at its inception in 1920, who did so much to open up the archaeological site of Jerash and to care for monuments throughout

* *PEFQS*, 1882.

the country. His car journeys across the length and breadth of the land, over virtually non-existent roads, are the stuff of which legends are made (Fig. 20).

The important contribution made by American archaeologists should also be recorded. A joint expedition in 1928 to Jerash was mounted by Yale University and the British School of Archaeology in Jerusalem. Professor B. W. Bacon from Yale was overall director, with J. W. Crowfoot of the British School overseeing all work on site. One of Crowfoot's first objectives was the Christian churches, and over the next three years all these were cleared and excavated. In 1930 the British School had to retire from the project, and the Americans under the direction of Professor Bacon and the great Professor Rostovtzeff assumed the whole work-load. Site-digging was then under the direction of Dr C. S. Fisher and Dr C. C. McCown of the American School in Jerusalem.

One cannot overstate the importance of the work they did in Jerash between 1928–34. In 1938 a vast compendium of all the results was published by the American Schools of Oriental Research, New Haven, under the editorship of Professor Carl H. Kraeling: this magisterial work *Gerasa: City of the Decapolis*, has become a standard work on the site, a kind of researchers' Bible, notable for its depth of learning and cautious yet imaginative perception.

Fig. 20   Garstang's photograph of his car in which he travelled throughout Jordan inspecting antiquities.

CHAPTER FOUR

From Pillar to Impost

'JARASH ... is a typical Roman provincial town, both in its plan and its architecture, and is perhaps the best and most completely preserved example of such in the Middle East.'* The architecture itself is neither particularly original nor innovative, being of a character which one finds frequently throughout the major, and many minor, centres in Roman Syria and Asia Minor. The end of Nabatean influence on the affairs of the city in A.D. 106 threw it into the mainstream of Syro-Roman architectural thought and practice, of which it is now an outstanding example. The language of that tradition is familiar and presents no problems to the understanding of the West: it is probably why such critical visitors as Irby and Mangles could find nothing but praise for the ruins, in contrast to their opprobrium of Palmyra and Petra where alien influences were at work on the architecture. Much of the detailing and richness of effect in Jerash has its roots in the Hellenistic tradition which, in Syria, never became wholly obliterated by the Roman tradition. Thus the unusual, but decorative, inverted bell of acanthus leaves immediately above the base moulding of the half-columns of the Hadrianic Arch (Fig. 21) and the South Gate probably have their origins in Ptolemaic Egypt; the volute pediments to the niches of the *scaenae frons* in the South Theatre (Fig. 22) can be related to similar features in the Nymphaeum at Miletus and were popular in the eastern part of the Empire (they appear also in Augustan Rome); whilst the so-called 'Syrian niches', in which the recess is framed by small columns carrying a broken pediment with a recessed centre, are a decorative feature which appears to have developed in late Hellenistic Syria. None of these features are, in themselves, exceptional, they are just part of the almost prodigal lavishness of the East.

But it should be seen that this lavishness is always highly disciplined, being concentrated on critical features in a design, such as a capital, a niche, a cornice or frieze, and is never allowed to proliferate aimlessly. The broken pediment of the Gate to the Cathedral (Fig. 23) is an excellent example of this control. Here the pulvinated frieze is carved with the 'palm-tree' pattern, whilst the cornice and pediment have every facet decorated, giving a luxuriant effect. This is off-set by the

---

* G. L. Harding, *Antiquities of Jordan.*

Fig. 21 Acanthus 'bells' at the bases of the pilasters on the Hadrianic Arch. Note also the carving of the capitals from which springs the side arch.

Fig. 22 Detail of the *scaenae frons* of the South Theatre. Note the carved decoration of the doorway and the scroll pediment of the pillared niche.

Fig. 23 Detail of the Propylaea to what is believed to have been the Temple of Dionysus.

plain moulded architrave, unrelieved tympanum, and smooth wall surfaces on either side. There is always space surrounding a concentration of detail, as though allowing it, and the viewer, to breathe. Also, all detail, whether architectural or decorative, is subordinate to the over-all design and is never allowed to over-assert itself. It is the persistent sense of order and control of the parts, however richly they may individually be handled, which in the end creates the splendour and excitement of effect. The Syro-Roman architects of the second and third centuries knew this lesson by heart.

As Dr Margaret Lyttelton has pointed out, it was 'in the sphere of town planning and the organisation of space ... that Jerash seems to have made her most interesting and original contribution to architectural history'.* One is tempted to suspect that the great first-century city plan was as much dictated by the natural topography as by the devising hand of Man: but certainly in the shaping of that plan to fit the natural character of the site and in the organisation of spatial effects within it, one must heartily agree. Quite rightly Buckingham had deduced that the plan was 'ohe work of one founder', but that is not the whole story.

* M. Lyttelton, *Baroque Architecture in Classical Antiquity*.

The walled Hellenistic city was restricted to Camp Hill (Fig. 4) which originally overlooked a depression in the ground to the south, on the other side of which stood the independently sited Sanctuary of Zeus. This juxtaposition had to be integrated into the southern end of the plan for the new city. However, the new plan was a grid which was to lie, due to the topography, on a north/south axis: the axis between Camp Hill and the Zeus Sanctuary was approximately north-east/south-west. The way in which these two axes were related was a brilliantly original stroke, the creation of a roughly oval piazza in the depression which acted both as a visual 'lead-up' to the Sanctuary and as a prelude to the formal layout of the new plan.

It is possible that the temenos wall of the Sanctuary, which terminated in a tower on its north-eastern corner, provided the closing feature on the south side, making the piazza stirrup-shaped rather than oval: it is unlikely that there was a colonnade on this side. Certainly there is a line in the paving stones (Fig. 24) which marks a change from the concentric laying of the flags of the piazza (Fig. 68) to the stones set square and roughly aligned in front of the temenos wall.

At the north end of the piazza stood a triple archway joining the two curved colonnades and providing both a sense of enclosure in the piazza itself and a ceremonial entry from it into the Cardo, which was the spine of the formal layout of the new plan beyond.

The Oval Piazza thus achieves several objectives and can be seen as a remarkable and unique piece of planning: unique because there is no other example in antiquity close to this arrangement.

The creation of urban landscape vistas, with principal buildings sited at strategic points, was a development which achieved spectacular results in Asia Minor and the Near East. The dramatic effects to be had by laying out a site to the best visual, as well as practical, advantage were fully appreciated. This is strikingly displayed at several points in Jerash, not least at the Oval Piazza. Here the siting of the Temple of Zeus, high upon its hill, was a critical factor. The vista down the last leg of the Cardo was terminated by the triple archway with the temple seen at an angle and in the distance above it. Thus the temple indicated that there was something beyond the archway and attracted one towards it. It is difficult for us today to realise just how much shade there would have been in the street, particularly under the porticos on either side. This would have helped to emphasise not only the architecture but also the sense of enclosure (Fig. 25). On passing through the archway, one was suddenly released from the confines of the street into a wide open area full of light and space: the effect was a fine piece of theatre. And yet this piazza was also contained by colonnaded porticos curving away on either side, drawing one towards the temenos wall on the south side. The eastern colonnade led irrevocably towards the entrance to the temenos, with the temple itself on its hill above seen head-on. This eastern colonnade is, in fact, a masterly

Fig. 24 The junction of the concentric paving of the Oval Piazza and the area in front of the Temenos of Zeus.

Fig. 25 A reconstruction of the South Colonnade Street, looking towards the archway into the Oval Piazza.

Fig. 26 Reconstruction of the Oval Piazza, looking towards the Temenos of the Sanctuary of Zeus.

way of conducting one from the axis of the Cardo to that of the Temple of Zeus. The western colonnade played a secondary role in this scheme, one of fixing the end of the sanctuary visually, and of completing a spatial composition (Fig. 26).

A reverse procedure was also served by these sweeping arcs of pillars. Anyone entering the city by the South Gate would have gone up the South Street with the high wall of the temenos on the left. Ahead was the broad flight of steps at the entrance to the temenos, with a distant view of the far colonnade of the piazza beyond: the piazza itself was hidden. On reaching the steps, however, the piazza would have been suddenly revealed. The eye was then drawn by the colonnades on both sides towards the archway at the entrance to the Cardo. This, visually, forced one to accept the new axis and drew one forward into the city. In both directions the piazza helped to achieve a change in axis without effort and without any interruption of the senses, for this is pure processional architecture and planning where one's path is not only laid out but one is conducted along it. Fig. 4 shows how both colonnades converge and lead one into the Cardo: the only missing element is the triple archway which linked the two colonnades.

At the archway one entered the new plan which was laid out on a Roman adaptation of the Hippodamian grid, in which the main street, the Cardo, was crossed at right angles by two *decumani* or principal secondary streets (Map 3). The

82

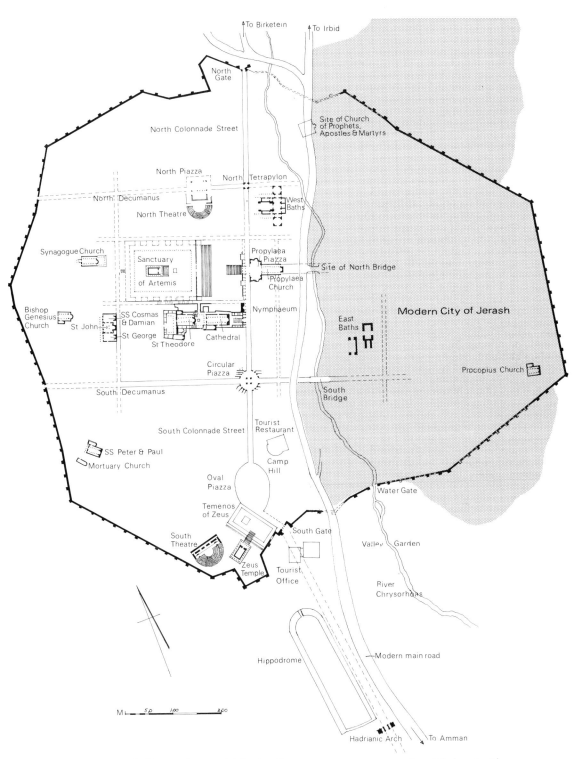

To Birketein

To Irbid

North Gate

North Colonnade Street

Site of Church of Prophets, Apostles & Martyrs

North Piazza

North Tetrapylon

North Decumanus

West Baths

North Theatre

Synagogue Church

Sanctuary of Artemis

Propylaea Piazza

Site of North Bridge

Propylaea Church

Bishop Genesius Church

St John

SS Cosmas & Damian

Nymphaeum

East Baths

Modern City of Jerash

St George

St Theodore

Cathedral

Circular Piazza

South Decumanus

South Bridge

Procopius Church

South Colonnade Street

Tourist Restaurant

Camp Hill

SS Peter & Paul

Mortuary Church

Oval Piazza

Temenos of Zeus

Water Gate

South Theatre

South Gate

Valley Garden

Zeus Temple

Tourist Office

River Chrysorhoas

Modern main road

Hippodrome

M 50 100 200

Hadrianic Arch

To Amman

Map 3   Plan of Jerash. Streets shown with broken lines are as yet unexcavated and their extent is, therefore, at present conjectural.

topography helped, for the Cardo is laid up a natural terrace along the eastern side of the hill overlooking the river, and the *decumani* are located in natural depressions which crossed the terrace at right angles.

Having gone through the triple archway, one was confronted by the long gentle rise of the colonnaded street creating an almost irresistible invitation to go along its route. Such colonnade streets became a popular feature of towns in the Eastern provinces; there are fine examples at Palmyra and Apamaea and, indeed, at Petra and Jerusalem. As Dr Lyttleton has pointed out, these streets 'revolutionised the aspect of these towns by replacing the purely utilitarian, undecorated streets, often running between blind walls, with highly decorated monumental colonnades, so that the street became instead of a mere means of communication an independent monumental feature'.

Along the Cardo were the principal civic and religious buildings whose street façades were part of the overall scheme, however much they may individually be given particular emphasis. Half-way up the southern section there is a case in point where the four pillars of a portico to an important building rise almost a fifth above those of the street colonnade. The entablature of the street colonnade is carried on a bracket on the sides of the outer columns of this portico (Fig. 71). Crowned probably by a pediment, this portico emphasised the individual building behind without interrupting the line of the street colonnade. It also created variety in the scene because a long unbroken run of columns all of the same height can be monotonous; this sort of punctuation mark in the steady rhythm of the colonnades created incident and interest in the overall design.

Long vistas require some feature at the end to resolve the composition; also there need to be checks along the route to break it up into comprehensible sections without destroying the vista. At Jerash the opportunity was taken at the crossing of the Cardo and the two *decumani* to create visual pauses by means of localised points of interest. Where the South Decumanus crossed the Cardo, a circular piazza was laid out with a towering Tetrakionia in the middle (Fig. 73). The date at which this piazza was conceived is still subject to debate; Kraeling argues for a fourth-century date, whilst Lyttleton places it in the early third century. In the present discussion, however, the date is immaterial, for here we are dealing only with the visual effect of the piazza and its tetrakionia within the urban landscape.

At the intersection one's attention would have been arrested by the four 'towers' of the tetrakionia. One would still have been able to see the next section of the Cardo, but the architectural composition in front of one would seem to bar the way. Although it was always possible to go straight ahead through the centre of the monument, the natural inclination would have been, indeed still is even in its ruined state, to go round it. The circular shape of the piazza created both a greater sense of space in contrast to the confined feeling of the street, and at the same time conducted one round to the next street, be it Cardo or *decumanus*, which then suddenly appeared as a new, exciting vista. The height and architectural treatment of the four quadrant buildings complemented the vertical emphasis of the tetrakionia and created a strictly ordered sense of enclosure in which the spiral of movement was controlled.

The intersection of the North Decumanus and the Cardo was treated in an altogether different way. At this point a four-way arch with a circular and domed interior was built, with an arch giving at right angles into the four converging thoroughfares (Fig. 101). This was a happy solution to a tricky problem, because the Cardo north of this intersection was narrower than the section to the south and the *decumanus* was again of a different width. As originally laid out in the first century, the Cardo was of the narrower 'gauge', but in the middle of the second century the middle and south sections were widened and given a more splendid Corinthian treatment. The North Tetrapylon masks this rather awkward junction. Had there been even an open-plan feature similar to the South Tetrakionia, it would have been much more difficult to conceal the change in width and in the architectural order. The solid mass of the North Tetrapylon managed successfully to curtail the overall view without breaking the fundamental axial sense, for it was always possible to see through the monument. Internally the circular plan was fundamental, for it carried one round in such a way that one was able to adjust to the new dimension and change in style.

The North Gate also presents an adroit piece of planning, for the two main façades faced squarely onto the streets which approached them, despite the fact that there is an 18° angle between the two axes. The plan (Fig. 104), it must be admitted, does not have the same masterly sophistication of the Trapezoidal Arch at Palmyra, but the effect is just as satisfactory. Angling the façades and slanting the entry passage had the effect of bringing those who arrived at the city straight up against a monumental gate, through which they found themselves facing square-on down the north section of the Cardo. The sense of ceremony can only have impressed visitors.

And indeed this desire to impress cannot be discounted as a strong motive for the creation of such public devices. The citizens enjoyed their architecture and revelled in its inventiveness, but at the back of their minds there may have been the thought of 'seeing ourselves as others see us'. In the ceremonial approach to the Sanctuary of Artemis, this reached a significant high-point. Whether out of civic pride or a desire to impress, or simply out of devotion, the Gerasenes achieved here one of the most impressive architectural schemes ever devised in the ancient Near East. There may be parallels here with other places, but at Jerash the arrangement is so dazzling, and indeed at times original, that it must stand as one of the major pieces of architectural inspiration in the whole of ancient Syria.

Fig. 27 The Central Colonnade Street.

The Propylaea held the dominant position on the crest of the hill in the central section of the Cardo. The four majestic columns of its portico towered above their neighbours (Fig. 27), their advent being announced by the four columns of the Nymphaeum just to the south. Here we have, however, an example of an urban vista not provided with a focal, eye-catching point. The approach from the Circular Piazza is a gentle rise to the Propylaea, and one is automatically drawn forward to investigate. The sense of mounting drama culminates in the colossal portico. But one is aware of a strong cross-axis, for this portico is facing into an open space on the other side of the street. This unseen, but very obvious, cross-axis is as much an eye-catcher as any tetrakionia. Today the feeling of the cross-axis is, however, not so compelling, for the Propylaea is incomplete, with assorted architectural fragments cluttering the small piazza.

The cross-axis had started away on the east bank of the river, and at the Cardo one is only half way through the sequence; it culminated in the Temple of Artemis high up to the left on the western side. The ground on the eastern bank is more level than on the west, and for this reason it is believed that the main residential quarter of ancient Gerasa was located here. A substantial bridge, the North Bridge, carried

Fig. 28 The ruins of the Propylaea Church; the apse inserted into the ruins of an archway which previously stood on this site. Note the almost buried vaults in the bottom right-hand corner.

the approach system to the Temple of Artemis across the river: only the abutments of this are now remaining on the western side. At the end of the bridge a flight of steps led up to a triple gateway, the central opening of which was arched whilst the flanking ones had lintels, traces of which can still be seen (Fig. 28) on the remaining side walls. This gateway led immediately into a short colonnaded street, the Bridge Street, which during the Byzantine period was roofed over and converted into a church. In this process the central opening of the gate was destroyed and an apsidal end built in its stead; it is this apse which we see today. Unfortunately it destroys completely the sense of process from the bridge into the street. Likewise, a wall that was built across the end of the street at the point where it entered a small, raised piazza breaks the sense of forward movement: the Byzantines created an atrium to the church in this small piazza. Consequently it is necessary to ignore the Byzantine developments of the area when considering the long system of approach to the Temple of Artemis. Having arrived at the gateway there would originally have been an uninterrupted vista down the Bridge Street and up into the small, raised piazza.

This piazza had a highly inventive shape and is one of the most exciting and

Fig. 29 The ruins of the Propylaea Piazza and the Propylaea Church.

original elements in the whole composition: as indeed it is in the whole output of Syrian architecture of the Roman period.

The colonnades of the Bridge Street terminated against a pair of massive columns on high plinths on either side of the opening into the piazza; one of them can be seen in Fig. 29. Four steps led up from the Bridge Street into the piazza which was of roughly trapezoidal shape (Fig. 83). However, the design was much more complicated than that because the sides of the trapeze were not straight but cut back into a rounded corner before encountering a pillar-framed exedra in which was set a fountain. On the other side of the exedras the walls tucked again into rounded corners before coming to an emphatic halt at free-standing columns on either side of the opening onto the Cardo, an opening which was almost twice as wide as that opening into the Bridge Street (Fig. 30). The shape of this piazza was first investigated by Kraeling and, whilst appreciating its almost 'baroque' character, he drew a plan which was rather simpler than that presented here. This revision of the plan is due to the work of Roberto Parapetti for the *Centro Scavi di Torino per il Medio Oriente e l'Asia*, who has made a detailed study of the whole approach system. The author is particularly grateful to Mr Parapetti for much helpful discussion on the subject and for having allowed him to draw on as yet unpublished material relating to it.

At the wider opening of this Propylaea Piazza there were four steps down into

Fig. 30 A reconstruction of what the view in Fig. 29 would have looked like at the end of the second century A.D.

the Cardo. Immediately opposite loomed the portico of the Propylaea. Thus the whole system of approach from the bridge (Fig. 31) was a build-up of visual excitement culminating, at this stage, in the portico of the Propylaea. Being on what amounted to a raised platform in the Propylaea Piazza greatly enhanced the spectacle of the view, particularly as the portico was also set on four steps on the other side of the street.

Remarkable though this exercise in planning and processional architecture is, it is by no means the end of the story. The temple stood high on a hill above the Cardo and a substantial retaining wall was built up against this, into which the Propylaea was set. Under the portico was a deep porch within which was a screen wall with a huge central doorway flanked by two smaller ones with highly ornate niches above them, between which were free-standing columns. Through these doorways one was suddenly presented with a view of a vast flight of steps climbing seemingly into the sky. Just visible at the top of the steps, as though to tell you that there was more to come, was the long pillared façade of the Temenos wall acting as yet another propylaea: not the view of the portico of the temple which we get today (Fig. 32). Rightly has Dr Lyttleton claimed that 'the monumental Gateway to the Temple of Artemis shows an ingenuity and inventiveness which marks it among the major surviving monuments of the baroque style in antiquity'.

Having climbed these seven flights of seven steps one came out into the middle of

89

Fig. 31 A reconstruction of the Propylaea of the Temple of Artemis.

Fig. 32 The Propylaea of the
Temple of Artemis. The rough stone
wall behind the pillars is a recent
construction to facilitate restoration.

Fig. 33 The Altar and Terrace of the Temple of Artemis.

a vast U-shaped terrace which acted as a forecourt to the Temenos. Wide though the staircase is, it feels enclosed because of the high flanking walls of finely laid and unadorned masonry, so emerging at the top onto the terrace creates the impression of coming up into the light and air: a feeling one still gets today. Immediately ahead, at the top of the stairs, was a large altar on a platform (Fig. 33) set with other smaller altars and votive pedestals. Behind this stood the long, colonnaded front of the eastern wall of the Temenos which probably had a small tower at each end (Fig. 92).

A further three flights of steps, in a slightly different location to those reinstated we see today, took one up to this façade and through a triple doorway into the Temenos or sacred enclosure, in which, at last, the temple stood (Fig. 94). The Temenos was lined on all four sides with porticos of majestic Corinthian columns.

The whole system of approach was one of mounting interest and excitement, in which one was conducted from one incident to the next, with the final view of the temple being held until the very last moment. The architectural orchestration was brilliant, with one feature or shape after another creating a constantly varying accompaniment as one climbed up and up to the eventual goal – the temple.

Within the Temenos there would have been an extraordinary sensation of delineated space, of light and of being on the level. After all those steps, to find so vast an area that was absolutely flat would have been a powerful sensation: to a considerable extent this can still be experienced. It would have helped to concentrate one's attention on the temple, which seems curiously remote and aloof in this huge courtyard. There is some truth in what Dr Lyttleton has written: 'In criticism of the complex of the Temple of Artemis it might be said that the temple itself seems rather insignificant, and appears as something of an anticlimax in relation to its vast system of approaches. It is too small and too orthodox compared with the splendours of the Propylaea and the monumental size of the steps which lead up to it.' This is certainly so but anything very much larger would have tended to swamp its surroundings in rather the same way that the Temple of Jupiter at Baalbek must have been inclined to do. But the Temple of Artemis is an altogether different spatial concept; it is a temple surrounded by its precinct and not one, as at Baalbek, overlooking its temenos. Here the space about the temple related to it in a wholly different way, and it probably dominated its temenos because of its very isolation in it.

Second only to the Artemis Propylaea, the Nymphaeum is the most impressive single structure remaining in Jerash. It was an extraordinarily grandiloquent and lively design, full of 'movement' and rich in dramatic effect (Fig. 81). Also, whilst acting as a punctuation mark in the continuity of the colonnades of the Cardo, it was an independent incident of the grandest kind.

The Temple of Dionysus, which was later redeveloped as the Cathedral, also had a fine propylaea, succeeded by a monumental flight of steps up to the temple, but on a much smaller scale and not having the same greatly extended approach system (Fig. 110). The portal under the portico was flanked by a pair of columns tucked into a slight recess. This made it look rather cramped and squashed into an uncomfortably restricted space. The columns supported a 'Syrian niche' type of entablature. This created a rich concentration of detail and 'movement' within a very small area, which acted as a contrast to the grand flight of steps within. These steps were probably framed by high finely dressed walls in very much the same way as behind the Artemis Propylaea. Due to the redevelopment of the site during the Byzantine period, we do not know exactly what the Roman arrangement was like, but there might well have been the same U-shaped terrace at the top, with the temple standing on the central axis of the stairs.

Before going on to consider briefly the Byzantine contribution to the architecture of Jerash, a further word should be said about the city plan, for this was the context in which all developments took place – even the Byzantine ones.

The plan was a strong and rational layout which was remarkably simple in its conception. It consisted of a central spine, the Cardo, running north and south, crossed by two *decumani* at approximately equal intervals. Between these there was a network of minor streets fitted round the great civic and religious monuments, providing communication across the city. About these we today know very little. Roberto Parapetti, however, has suggested that there was probably a minor street running parallel to the Cardo some distance down the slope towards the river, which, like the Cardo, would have intersected with and crossed the South Decumanus and the east-west street which served the northern side of the Artemis Temenos and the southern side of the West Baths. When this street encountered the Bridge Street, however, it was presented with an insuperable obstacle. It has long been noted that the eastern end of the Bridge Street was carried on a wide vault which went under the whole street from north to south. Mr Parapetti has suggested that this vault is nothing more than a bridge over the lower street constructed when the temple approaches were aggrandised in the second century. This relates to evidence further up the hill in what is now the Propylaea Piazza. It will be seen in Fig. 29 that there is a line of well-laid paving running down the middle of the piazza, on either side of which are areas of rougher surface. This middle strip may in fact be an earlier street which was covered over when the piazza was raised: likewise it was exposed by the Byzantines when they turned the piazza into the atrium of their street church; the rougher surface is their paving-over of the remaining area within the piazza shape. Originally the ancient street would have gone more gently down the hill to cross the lower road before it descended to cross the river by an earlier, and smaller bridge. This road up the slope from the river was of course buried when the Bridge Street and the North Bridge were constructed. This implies that even before the huge development of the Artemis approaches there was a much simpler, though nonetheless axial, road leading from the east bank across the river and up to the predecessor of the present propylaea. The system we see today may therefore be considerably older than the present architectural and planned arrangement.

The Byzantine period made a totally different, but yet major contribution to the architectural history and importance of much of Jerash. Although they were using the same classical architectural vocabulary, they were speaking a substantially different language, particularly in the development of plans and of surface decoration.

The Imperial Court at Constantinople continued throughout the fifth century to subsidise church building in the Holy Land. This was to have an indelible effect on the architecture for, as Krautheimer has pointed out, 'Through these Imperial enterprises the architectural concepts of the Aegean coastlands gained a firm hold.'* These concepts, such as polygonal apses, rich and elaborate geometric and

* R. Krautheimer, *Early Christian and Byzantine Architecture*.

figurative mosaics on floors and walls, and basilical form as well as cross-plans, are all magnificently represented at Jerash. But at Jerash, as in most other sites in Palestine and Jordan, the local Syrian tradition of building remained strong, so that we see a fusion of the two architectural themes. By A.D. 500, the Syrian tradition had become dominant after a long period of development and synthesis. This was a period which saw a boom in church building in inland areas, with the structures becoming more and yet more lavishly decorated and with the main structure becoming supplemented by attached but separate sacristies, martyria, chapels, baptistries and clergy and congregational complexes – the *domus ecclesiae*. Previously the apse of the church was usually flanked by small rooms, but now these were replaced by side apses terminating the aisles of the basilical design. Much of the building material was 'robbed' from older structures, so that it is quite possible to find a handsome set of first- or second-century columns in a fifth- or sixth-century church. These churches were always preceded by an atrium (an open pillared courtyard) or a narthex (an enclosed room which led straight into the body of the church).

However, by the sixth century, narthexes began to replace atria, as the churches accumulated a complex of supplementary buildings about them. Again as Krautheimer has pointed out, 'The churches of Gerasa are extraordinarily impressive – through their size, through their number, and through their tendency to group several structures within one precinct.' This grouping is demonstrated with great clarity in two distinguished examples; the early Cathedral and the somewhat later Basilica of St Theodore and their attendant clergy establishments, and the linked churches of SS. Cosmas and Damian, St John the Baptist, and St George.

The Cathedral, which is the oldest remaining church in Jerash (circa A.D. 365), was built on what is believed to have been the site of the Temple of Dionysus and employed the ancient propylaea to the temple as its Gate. The massive flight of steps within was re-graded and relaid, the flanking walls built with re-used pillars placed on top, and a complex of rooms above the erstwhile U-shaped terrace. Over the Gate they were supported by four large, re-used Corinthian columns of unequal height, placed rather awkwardly on the lower flights of steps below. There would have been in this arrangement (Fig. 109) a fine sense of theatre, but it was one in which the forward directional sense was negated by the blank outside wall of the apse. It is evident in all the Byzantine buildings that the old penchant for both stately approaches and handsome exteriors has gone, for the outsides of buildings were kept extremely plain and there is no case of a carefully devised and orchestrated approach system: one just arrived at church, one was not conducted there by architectural enticement or a sense of mounting excitement.

Internally the Cathedral had a simple plan (Fig. 111) in which two rows of re-used Corinthian columns without bases supported a straight re-used stepped

Fig. 34 A reconstruction of the interior of the Cathedral.

architrave, dividing the church into a central nave/chancel with an aisle on either side. The walls of the aisles and the apse were originally revetted with coloured marble, whilst the floor was paved with beautiful pink limestone. Above the pillars there rose high, plain walls into which were set small arched windows beneath an open timber-frame roof. These walls were covered with dazzling glass mosaics, as was the semi-dome of the apse which terminated the central aisle (Fig. 34). True to its comparatively early date, the aisles terminated in small rectangular rooms.

About one hundred and thirty years later, in A.D. 496, the Basilica of St Theodore was built on the higher ground immediately to the west. Three doors led from its atrium (Fig. 35) into the church, the centre one going into the nave and the other two into the flanking aisles. Two rows of seven re-used Corinthian columns divided the church into its three parallel sections, the centre one of which terminated in an apse.

St Theodore's marks a development from the Cathedral design, for here the straight lintel over the columns is replaced by arches except in the first and last bays. Above rose high, plain walls into which were set a row of small round-headed windows below the open-frame timber roof. The walls above the arcades may have

Fig. 35 The eastern side of the atrium of St Theodore's Church.

been plain-surfaced but they were far from being undecorated, for they were covered with a glittering glass mosaic. We do not know what was depicted on these walls but the scheme of decoration might well have had the overall impact one still feels in St Apollinare Nuovo at Ravenna (circa A.D. 490) or in St Sabina in Rome (circa A.D. 430). The floor was also more elaborate than the Cathedral's, having been paved in geometric designs in coloured marbles and hard limestones (Fig. 36).

Clustered round the basilica were other chapels and rooms, including a baptistry. This had the effect of placing the church itself, perhaps symbolically, within and at the heart of a 'community' of buildings: they did not stand alone, isolated in architectural splendour, as did the classical temples. The richness of Byzantine churches was within, and little conscious design was lavished on the exterior: frequently there was a fascinating and confused perspective of roofs but this was accidental rather than contrived.

Standing chronologically between the Cathedral and St Theodore's was the Church of the Prophets, Apostles and Martyrs (A.D. 465), a building of the greatest interest because of its plan (Fig. 37). This was the only example in Jerash of a cross-plan set in a square, an Aegean type which in the west was to have a long and remarkable development but which in the east is only an early phenomenon and even then a rare occurrence in Jordan and Palestine. The plan was probably derived from Constantine's Apostoleion via the Church of St John at Ephesus. Apart from the interest of its exceptional plan, this church had a fragment of a fine

Fig. 36 A reconstruction of the interior of St Theodore's Church.

Fig. 37 Plan of the now destroyed Church of the Prophets, Apostles and Martyrs (*after C. S. Fisher*).

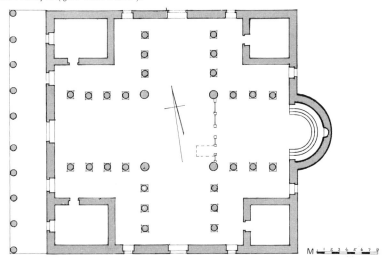

Fig. 38 A section of mosaic flooring from St John the Baptist's Church, showing the city of Alexandria.

Fig. 39 'Inhabited' acanthus rinceau border of the mosaic floor in St John the Baptist's Church.

geometric floor mosaic. It is fortunate that when the Americans carried out a partial excavation in 1929/30 a photograph was taken of this, for the remains of the church have since been destroyed to make way for a new road. This is a tragic loss not only because of the mosaic but because this Aegean plan is so rare in Jordan, and in Jerash it was unique.

The other important grouping in Jerash comprises the church of St John the Baptist flanked, and communicating with, that of SS. Cosmas and Damian to the north, and St George to the south; a complex which dates from A.D. 529–533. All three shared a common atrium and were conceived as one unit, not as isolated entities which happened by chance to be contiguous. The central church of St John is unique in Jerash, and a rarity at the best of times, because of its circular plan (Fig. 120); a circle, in fact, set in a square with deep, horse-shoe exedras in the four corners and a spacious apse to the east. In the middle, four large re-used Corinthian columns carried a lantern above the sloping roof, from which light came into the interior. An obvious parallel for this plan can be found in the colossal Cathedral at Bosra which was built twenty years before. The internal walls were revetted with marble, the exedras and the apse being covered with glass mosaics. The floor was covered with an exceedingly interesting pictorial mosaic, of which regrettably only fragments now remain. There is enough, however, for the whole scheme to be plotted. In the central square beneath the lantern were personifications of the months of the year and of the four seasons, all contained within a border. Outside this were three interconnected segments covered with a 'free' design in which there were representations of cities or shrines which had significance for Christians (Fig. 38); they were held together in a continuous composition by a river scene in which the flowing water was well stocked with a variety of fish, whilst ducks, storks, herons and other fowl either stood or flapped about on the banks which were bedecked with flowers and spindly plants. The only other example of this kind of composition in Jerash is to be found in the Church of SS. Peter and Paul: although this latter church is slightly later than St John's, it is probable that both mosaics were laid by the same group of craftsmen. The 'free' composition was tied together by a rich acanthusrinceau border, populated again by animals and birds (Fig. 39). This border went right round the whole church, even into the exedras, and would have been a strong unifying factor which emphasised the plan of the church.

The Church of SS. Cosmas and Damian lay to the north and could be entered from St John's through two large doorways in addition to its own western doors into the atrium. Like the majority of churches in Jerash, it had a basilical plan, but in this case solid piers were used instead of pillars. Once again it is the mosaics which were the main, indeed almost only form of internal decoration, and a large proportion of those on the floor have survived superbly intact. Within a border

Fig. 40 A section of the mosaic floor of SS. Cosmas and Damian's Church.

Fig. 41 Part of the mosaic floor in the north aisle of the Church of St George.

which alternated a swastika with panels, the main body of the mosaic was a spectacular geometric display in which a pattern of connecting squares and diamonds frame 'box perspectives', birds, animals, brilliantly imaginative geometric designs, and humans (Fig. 40). Just in front of the chancel steps is a *tabula ansata* which contains the dedication inscription, flanked by mosaic portraits

100

of the donors, Theodore, the *paramonarius* (priest and sacrist who was in charge of a church building) and his wife, Georgia.

The Church of St George, which lay to the south and was also approached through two doors from St John's in addition to its own west doors, was identical in all its principal features to SS. Cosmas and Damien. The decoration here was also along similar lines, including the reliance upon mosaics. The floor mosaic of the central aisle was a most sophisticated geometric composition of elongated hexagons and octagons tied together by a series of strands which knotted into swastikas in groups of four around the mathematical progression of octagons (Fig. 126). Within each of these octagons were figurative representations providing a lively contrast to the strict precision of the geometric design. The north and south aisles, however, had an independent design, or series of designs (Fig. 41), more in accord with the scheme in SS. Cosmas and Damian.

The Byzantine architecture in Jerash represents a span of two hundred and fifty years of building. Within this are displayed examples of the main characteristics of development throughout that period. The buildings themselves have never been altered or adapted, extended or enlarged after the end of the eighth century, a fate which has so complicated the study of ecclesiastical architecture elsewhere in the Holy Land. In consequence, it is possible at Jerash to examine the various types in their unadulterated state, and this is half their importance.

After the Roman period there was a gradual decline in the skills of architectural decoration giving rise to, and evidenced by, the considerable re-use of older materials. This decline was not matched in the production of mosaics; indeed the opposite is true, that there was an increasing technical and artistic skill so that during the middle of the sixth century pavements of the highest artistic quality were being laid. The great majority of these can be dated with uncommon accuracy and 'form a series which ... is unique in East Christian art. Beginning with the earliest examples in the fourth century, there is a constant increase both in the number of pavements, and in their richness and variety'.*

The study of mosaics is a huge field in itself, and although individual examples in Jerash will be discussed briefly in the next chapter, it is neither possible nor appropriate to investigate it at length in this work. However, the mosaics at Jerash do form a remarkable corpus and are generally of such good quality, both artistically and technically, that they should not be ignored. They deserve to be better known and better cared for. In Jordan, Madeba and Mount Nebo are justly celebrated for their mosaics, and they draw people from all over the world. It may well be that in time the Byzantine mosaics of Jerash will become equally celebrated.

* C. Kraeling, *Gerasa.*

Inevitably, it is the architecture of the second century which is the dominant element in the present ruins, not only by virtue of its quality but also by its sheer quantity and the state of its preservation. These classical ruins form a fascinating and often 'romantic' spectacle which provides endless interest for the scholar and delight to the visitor. But it should be borne in mind that the architectural heritage of Jerash spans six centuries covering Syro-Roman and Byzantine development, and that the various phases can be detected and studied with unusual clarity. In so many other sites, one period has been built upon another, creating often an almost unintelligible jumble. Of course, there are instances of this in Jerash, but in the main each monument relates to a particular period. To a great extent this was possible due to the size and overriding logic of the city plan, which permitted and accommodated a long and uninterrupted period of development in new, virgin areas. It is, indeed, the city plan which comes down to us as the finest achievement of ancient Gerasa.

CHAPTER FIVE

Jerash Today

THE ANCIENT CITY at Jerash is slow to reveal itself as one approaches from the south. Right up to the last moment there is no suggestion that one is coming upon a ruined city justly celebrated for its forests of columns. The long, gentle climb into the Hills of Gilead brings one into a land of high, rounded uplands and deep, green valleys with splashing streams. The road snakes round the hillsides until suddenly, between the trees, there is a glimpse of an ancient archway heralding the city beyond. Away on the skyline are the lofty contours of the hills folding gently down to form the elevated valley in which the ancient and modern cities lie.

With regret, it has to be admitted that the immediate approaches to Jerash are being spoiled. In recent years development in the suburbs has affected what was once one of the most charming and delightful settings to any city of antiquity. No one would deny that both the ancient and modern cities have a right to survive, but the environment of both is not well served by letting things look after themselves. Archaeologically this is such a treasured site that not only the ruins but the whole valley in which they, and the new city, are set should be protected, because this would benefit all concerned. The interests of the city of the living are not necessarily in conflict with those of the past.

There is a project planned to divert the main road eastwards round the city on a new bypass which will help enormously. But there also needs to be strict control on any kind of development if the total environment is to be saved.

Apart from the Petra/Jerash Project, there is a Five Year Plan, initiated in 1981, for a massive programme of excavation in the ancient city. The scale of the undertaking is colossal, far beyond the resources of the Department of Antiquities alone. Realising this, and therefore the need for international co-operation, archaeological teams from across the world are being invited to work in Jerash, each being allocated a particular sector of the ruins. This far-sighted and generous attitude will have profound repercussions, for very fast – by archaeological standards – the riches of ancient Gerasa will be uncovered and our knowledge of this precious site greatly increased. The future augurs well, and it is to be hoped that Jerash is on the threshold of another Golden Age.

Fig. 42 The Hadrianic Arch seen as one approaches from the south.

Ancient Jerash has a quiet, gentle, seductive beauty in which the clear mountain light plays an important part. The lie of the land over which it is spread means that it does not disclose everything at once; there is a constant change of view, a slow unfolding, so that one is kept enthralled in a sequence of delights. Tracks wind across the undulating ground, and everywhere there are pillars, some standing erect, others rearing up suddenly from the thickets of scrub and grass without the ordered purpose of science. Much remains to be excavated, and often there is the impression, particularly in the northern part, of walking through an eighteenth-century print with nature embowering the ruins with an unconscious artistry.

The exploration of the ruins which follows is divided into zones so that the logic of the site may be grasped, as well as serving those who seek information on a particular area.

ZONE I

The Hadrianic Arch, the Hippodrome, the South Walls, the Tourist Centre, the South Gate, the Sanctuary of Zeus, the South Theatre and the Oval Piazza.

The HADRIANIC ARCH, built in A.D. 129/30 in honour of Hadrian, stands boldly on the crest of a hill, silhouetted against the sky (Fig. 42). It was built well

104

outside the city, but the fact that the side walls were left untrimmed in such a way as to take the junction of walls, indicates that there may well have been a proposal to enclose a huge new extension to the metropolis. This never came about and the Arch was left rather marooned far to the south. It was not, however, without context because its through axis is parallel to that of the Hippodrome. There is an obvious relationship between the two monuments.

This was a triple archway, with a wide central opening nearly eleven metres high, flanked by two narrower and lower ones each just over five metres high: the proportions are the same in all three arches. These arches originally had massive wooden doors. McCown has pointed out that the inscription says that the Archway was built 'with a triumph', a phrase which Rostovtzeff interpreted to mean 'with a triumphal statue'.* Framing the arches were four engaged half-columns on high pedestals, carrying a complete entablature with a pediment over the central opening. Above the individual half-columns the entablature broke forward. Rising from the main cornice was a two-storey attic divided by an 'isolated' string course (one that is on the main façades only, and not carried round the entire superstructure), the whole composition being finished off by a top cornice, richly carved, on all four sides. The attic walls, the string courses and the top cornice all, likewise, broke forward over the half-columns, thus creating a strong vertical emphasis in what was otherwise a very wide composition.

The side pavilions were later additions constructed to buttress the Arch, which was structurally rather top heavy. Not part of the main architectural scheme, they had their own superimposed pilasters on either side of semi-circular niches on the ground floor level, and square, plain-pedimented niches above. Their restraint must have greatly emphasised the rich detailing of the main part. This richness was concentrated on the main architectural features such as the capitals on the half-columns, the entablature, which had a stepped architrave, pulvinated acanthus-scroll frieze, and lavish cornice. The niches above the side arches were also elaborate both in their design and in their decoration, with the square recesses flanked by pilasters, outside which were taller free-standing columnettes on wedge-shaped brackets, and supporting a broken pediment. Little of this is now in place, but what does remain gives a clear impression of the forceful quality of the carving (Fig. 43). The square impost capitals on which rested the actual arches had flutes faced with upright acanthus leaves, over which was a capping moulding (see also Fig. 21). The eastern side archway has been restored but the western retains its original carving. The most unusual feature is the inverted bell of acanthus leaves round the bottom of the shafts of the half-columns. The same feature also occurs on the South Gate.

* C. C. McCown, *Journal of the Palestine Oriental Society*, 1936.

Fig. 43 The Hadrianic Arch, showing the three entrances.

Both the north and south façades were substantially the same, but it is evident that the inner, the northern, face was intended to be the important one. On this side the dedicatory inscription was located, whereas the *tabula ansata* on the southern side was left blank.

The repair and conservation of the monuments at Jerash started in 1920. Later in 1925, the technical side of this was entrusted to Mr George Horsfield ('Mr Horse' as he was affectionately called) who was faced with a colossal job, for much was on the verge of collapse. It is thanks to his efforts that the tide of destruction was turned, thus enabling later scholars to study the remains and making possible eventual restoration. Much of his work may seem rudimentary (Fig. 44) but it was effective, and just in time. This opened the way for the studies by the American Expedition, not least at the Hadrianic Arch, of which Detweiler has written: 'Because of the fact that it can be dated so precisely and restored with such confidence, the Triumphal Arch ... becomes one of the most important monuments of its type in the Near East.... it provides criteria for the date of architectural features and design as no other arch in the East does.'* During their work between 1931 and 1934, the American Expedition discovered the dedicatory inscription along with almost every important element of the design, and thus it

* A. H. Detweiler, ex Kraeling's *Gerasa*.

was possible to produced a remarkably accurate reconstruction of the monument, at least on paper. The reconstruction worked out at that time by Detweiler has been modified slightly in view of Dr Lyttelton's discussion of the niches above the side arches (Fig. 45).

The HIPPODROME, which runs north for just over two hundred and sixty metres from the north-west corner of the Arch, has suffered badly over the years. The outline of the eastern wall is still quite traceable, as is the curved northern end. The slightly canted curve of the southern end is less well preserved. Except for the northern end, the western side has all but vanished. This is due to the Hippodrome having been built into a shallow, south-sloping depression. The eastern wall stands on bed-rock which is very close to the surface, but the western wall had to be constructed upon a deep substructure. Then, with immense labour, filling material was brought into the depression so that the arena could be made level. At some stage the foundations of the southern part of the west wall collapsed, perhaps due to seepage of water over a long period which undermined the footings. The result was that the in-fill began to be washed out, thus returning the depression almost to its original state. This rendered the Hippodrome useless in its entirety as a race-track, but the northern part, a little over a third, was still usable for athletic and other games. Eventually, probably during the Persian period (A.D. 614–628) as E. B. Müller suggests, a roughly semi-circular wall was built across the arena, thus enclosing the northern part. Fragmentary remains of this wall can still be seen. This has, in the past, led to the claim that the southern end was a *Naumachia*, or theatre for the staging of mock naval battles. Nothing could be further from the truth: Horsfield, indeed, pointed out that very few Gerasenes had probably ever seen the sea, and 'a taste for sham sea fights' amongst them would seem improbable. That was in 1938, but in 1912 the *Naumachia* theory was in full flood, and the Baedeker Guide to Palestine and Syria of that date waxed eloquent, pointing out to visitors that 'The South retaining-wall of this ... is still visible, with four sluice-gates for the admission of the water.' The northern half was considered to be the Circus for the staging of gladiatorial combats. It made a good story, and visitors love a bloodthirsty Roman; but it was all untrue. The northern half was nothing more nor less than a polo field, a sport the Persians loved passionately. But when they came to build their enclosing wall across the ancient arena, they found that their pitch had lost its levelness and so additional soil was excavated from the now derelict southern part of the depression to a point below the remaining foundations of the southern part of the west wall, which then disintegrated completely. Most of the new in-fill, however, probably came from the centre which, as Horsfield points out, explains why the centre is deeper than any other part of the depression.

The Hippodrome is smaller than the vast Imperial structures in Rome and Constantinople but it must, nevertheless, have been an attractive adjunct to the

Fig. 44 The Hadrianic Arch during remedial work carried out by Horsfield in 1929.

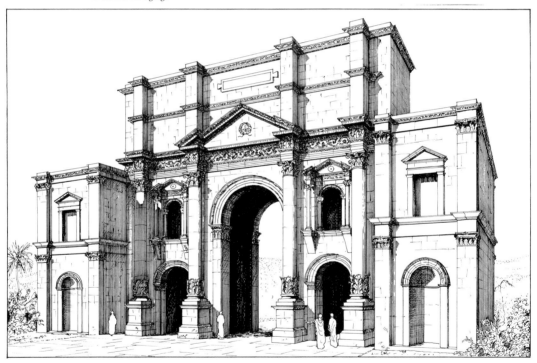

Fig. 45 A reconstruction of the Hadrianic Arch.

sporting life of the Gerasenes. Racing their camels and horses must have been a popular sport, and Horsfield is right to point out the significance in this regard of two inscriptions from the Propylaea to the Temple of Artemis, which record 'victorious athletes and horse-breeders in contests of various sorts. . . .'*

* G. Horsfield, ex Kraeling's *Gerasa*.

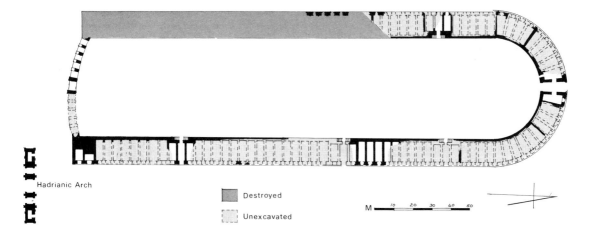

Fig. 46 Plan of the Hippodrome (*After E. B. Müller and A. H. Detweiler*).

The two scholars, Müller and Horsfield, disagreed about the date of the monument. The former argued for a date at the end of the second, or early third century, whilst the latter contended that it was planned and built before the Arch. Of importance in Horsfield's argument is the through axis of the Arch, which, had the Hippodrome not existed, would reasonably have been oriented on the South Gate. The Arch is, however, not aligned on the Gate but follows an axis down the side of the Hippodrome. In Horsfield's view the Hippodrome is, therefore, earlier than the Arch by as much as sixty or seventy years. The debate remains unresolved.

Partial excavations undertaken by the American Expedition, shortly after 1931, revealed enough to determine its plan (Fig. 46) and general scheme of construction. The arena was approximately fifty metres wide and two hundred and forty-four metres long, overlooked by sixteen or seventeen rows of seats resting on a system of rising arches comparable to the *vomitoria* in the South Theatre (Fig. 63). Thus it has been calculated that approximately fifteen thousand spectators could have been accommodated. The seats were reached by entering one of six doors in the outer walls, three on each side (Fig. 47), which led through into the arena. Side steps then took one onto the top of the podium wall, upon which the mounting rows of seats were set. Chambers below the seats were used as shops, store-rooms, etc. At the southern end there were ten stalls, five on either side of a central doorway, but little of this now remains. There was a corresponding entrance at the semi-circular northern end which contained a ramp leading down into the arena. Here there are several stretches of the podium wall still at their original height (Fig. 48). From these it will be seen that there was virtually no enrichment, the only decorative carving being a moulded base and capping to the podium wall. It has been argued that there was no *spina* down the centre of the arena.

It is now a rather deserted area, the depression making it look not a little forlorn.

Fig. 47 The eastern external wall of the Hippodrome, showing one of the entrances which led through into the arena.

Fig. 48 The podium at the northern end of the Hippodrome. Above this rose the tiers of seats for spectators.

Fig. 49 The southern City Walls.

Occasionally some children will kick a ball in the arena, but their shrill cries are but a mocking echo of the roars of excitement as fifteen thousand voices rose deafeningly into the ancient air.

The main road into Jerash runs alongside the Hippodrome until, shortly past the northern end, it tips down a slight hill, at the bottom of which is the new Tourist Centre. This is part of the facilities being created by the Petra/Jerash Project, a Government agency which has the responsibility of preparing the two ancient sites to receive future tourism whilst protecting the archaeological interest. There is an inevitable conflict of interests between scholarship and tourism in a place such as Jerash, but it is equally inevitable that the two are going to have to live together. It is to be hoped that a reconciliation can be worked out whereby the full tourist potential can be achieved without any damage to the site. This Tourist Centre is a much-needed facility and, being placed adjacent to the South Gate, is in an ideal position to serve visitors. Archaeologically it is less happy, for the large restaurant wing stands on the line of the ancient road and thus prevents any future examination or reinstatement of the area. Before building started, representations were made to the architects and the Petra/Jerash Project about the poor siting of this restaurant, but to no avail. As serious, however, was the destruction by bulldozer of a set of rock-cut tombs without any record having been taken of them or any archaeological investigation having been carried out. To these tombs should be related a collection of Iron Age I pottery, a period otherwise unknown in Jerash, which was retrieved from a bulldozer cut.

A short flight of steps to the right of the Tourist Centre leads to an elevated terrace, from which there is a good view of the ancient city's SOUTH WALL (Fig. 49); certainly the best preserved section of the entire circuit. When this terrace is finally landscaped it will provide an attractive prelude to the ruins; there is plenty of greenery to contrast with the crisp, hard line of the wall with its projecting towers. It should be remembered, however, that this present arrangement is very different from the original layout, for it has been suggested that a small piazza existed in front of the South Gate in which the axes of the road from the Hadrianic Arch and that through the South Gate crossed.

Almost the entire circuit of the city walls can be traced (Map 3). It is over three thousand four hundred and fifty metres in length, enclosing a total area of about two hundred and ten acres; this includes both the present-day ruins on the western bank of the Chrysorhoas and the modern city on the eastern bank. It was all started about the middle of the first century A.D. and probably completed about A.D. 75, the date ascribed to the North-west Gate which was never subsequently redeveloped. The North and South Gates, however, which we see today are later remodellings, and these involved minor adjustments and rebuildings of the adjacent walls at that time. The southern flank of the Zeus Temenos wall was also incoporated into Byzantine defences in A.D. 390. The city wall was consistently just under ten feet thick and had along its line a series of square towers, each about six metres square. These towers, which were spaced at intervals of seventeen to twenty-two metres apart, are integrated into the main fabric. The western sections are now very ruinous, as indeed are those on the north of the city. The long sections on the east are better preserved, and there are excellent proposals to restore them and set them in a 'green belt' round the new city. The south section, close to the South Gate, is now admirably cared for.

The South Wall is pierced by the SOUTH GATE, the grander of the two principal entries into the city. The present Gate replaced an earlier structure, which probably had only a single archway. The similarity between the present Gate and the Hadrianic Arch is inescapable and, although no dated inscription has been found, it is almost certainly coeval with the Arch. It has been suggested

Colour plates 1 Pillars of the Temple of Artemis. 2 The North Colonnade Street.
3 The south side of the Artemis Temenos. 4a The Central Colonnade Street. 4b Birketein.

Fig. 50   The ruins of the South Gate.

that when the city was honouring Hadrian with the Arch, the Emperor reciprocated by giving this fine new South Gate to the city. If the supposition that Hadrian had encouraged a vast urban expansion, with the Arch as its main, southern, entry, the South Gate would seem a logical concomitant: it is the story of Athens's urban expansion under Hadrian all over again (see page 38).

The present Gate is set back slightly from the line of the wall in a recess between two towers. Like the Arch, it had a triple archway with a tall central opening flanked by lower ones. Framing the three archways were four Corinthian half-columns standing on high pedestals (Fig. 50) with the same acanthus bells at the foot of each shaft. There are the same pilaster caps for the arches, stiff acanthus leaves in front of flutes, although only those of the western side arch are still *in situ*. Quite enough of the architectural elements have been found to determine the appearance of the lower sections of the Gate, but the character of the superstructure remains unknown: its treatment would, perhaps, have been consistently similar to that of the Arch. The flanking pavilions were integrated into the design and had simple niches on the south façade; on the north there were doorways which admitted into the guard chambers. These austere pavilions had the effect of removing the architectural elaboration of the three-arched centrepiece away from the two flanking towers, thus giving the gateway itself much greater prominence and effect.

The sculptural detail of the South Gate is generally finer in quality than that on

113

the Arch and, because of its more modest scale, suggests a finesse and deftness of touch which is somehow lacking in the great bulk of the Arch. Much of this is helped by the Gate's having a setting between two bastions which provide it with a sense of location, the absence of which is so much to the disadvantage of the Arch.

The orderly way in which whole sections of the Gate were found lying as they had fallen indicates collapse due to an earthquake. A series of these is recorded about A.D. 550–555. When the Gate was repaired, the side passages were blocked up and the central opening was reduced in width: the in-building of this can still be seen. There are indications also that the eastern bastion needed substantial repair, because fallen architectural elements were incorporated without any regard for their original logic. An example of this can be seen on the left of Fig. 49, where a piece of stepped architrave has been used on the corner at the bottom of this tower.

There is a suggestion that the South Gate should be rebuilt as a tourist entry into the ruins of the city. A careful consolidation of the monument, with judicious reinstatement of fallen elements, would be welcomed, but it is to be hoped that a full-scale re-build will be avoided because this could only invalidate the historical integrity of the monument.

Through the Gate one faces up a gentle slope of the South Street, at the end of which is the famous Oval Piazza. Excavations are still going on in the street (1982) in an attempt to establish its character, and it is not, therefore, possible to say much about it. Certainly, however, it must lie on a very ancient track, the one which passed between the Hellenistic *polis* on Camp Hill on the right, and its independently sited Sanctuary of Zeus to the left. Below the present level there are probably many other earlier levels, dating back to the days before the depression on which the Oval Piazza now stands was filled in.

A short distance up the street on the left stands the huge SANCTUARY OF ZEUS, an area of great complexity and importance. The temple we see today crowning the hill (Fig. 51) was dedicated in A.D. 166, but this was not the first temple. It replaced an earlier one constructed during the first half of the first century A.D., which probably replaced an even earlier one dating back to the days of the Hellenistic settlement. The site, therefore, can be taken as a traditional one which was for long the principal shrine of the town. The first-century temple possessed the right of asylum, which seems to imply that these rights had been held by its predecessors; certainly during the Jannaean Revolts the 'tyrant' of Philadelphia had entrusted his treasure to the Temple of Zeus at Gerasa, rather than to his own temples. It is not recorded when the site was first dedicated to Zeus Olympius but Kraeling has argued for the reign of Antiochus IV. No trace, at present, remains of anything previous to the first-century A.D. work, and it is with this, therefore, that one must start. This was the temple towards the building of which prominent citizens such as Demetrius, Zabdion and Aristonas contributed so

Fig. 51   The Temple of Zeus. Although this photograph was taken by Garstang in 1927, the view is substantially the same today.

lavishly. The whole site was redeveloped on the grandest scale, with the creation of a large temenos as well as a fine temple. This temple may, in fact, have taken the form of a monumental altar, constituting a cultic High Place in the ancient Semitic tradition. As Dr Fawzi Zayadine has pointed out, 'Similar altars were common in religious Nabatean architecture and are widespread in the Mount Lebanon. They are generally dated to the same Early Roman Period.'* The Temenos was surrounded on all four sides by wide barrel-vaulted corridors (Fig. 52). The south-western corridor was built into the hillside (a section of the ruined vault can be seen in Garstang's 1925 photograph – Fig. 51), as was a short leg on the north-western side. This latter still stands and is used by the Department of Antiquities as a store-room. The north-eastern corridor, due to the continued fall of the ground, was raised upon the top of a sub-vault so that the same floor level could be achieved in all four passages. This sub-vault (Fig. 53) is still completely intact and is one of the best survivals in the whole of Jerash. The quality of the masonry is excellent, as are the harmonious proportions and simple, strong architectural treatment. A bold cornice is the only decorative feature, from which springs the

* F. Zayadine, *Annual of the Department of Antiquities*, 1981.

115

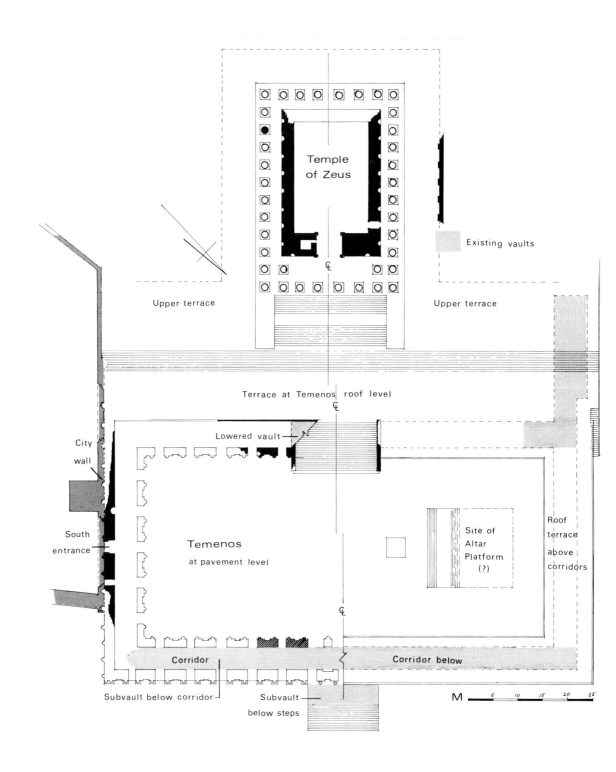

Temple
of Zeus

Existing vaults

Upper terrace

Upper terrace

Terrace at Temenos roof level

City
wall

Lowered vault

South
entrance

Temenos
at pavement level

Site of
Altar
Platform
(?)

Roof
terrace
above
corridors

Corridor

Corridor below

Subvault below corridor

Subvault
below steps

M

5   10   15   20   25

Fig. 52   Preliminary plan of the Sanctuary of Zeus. The left hand half of the Temenos is shown at pavement level, whilst on the right the level of the terrace on the roof of the corridors is depicted.

116

Fig. 53   The sub-vault of the Temenos of Zeus.

vaulted ceiling. To view this stern space is a satisfying experience, with the light splashing in at intervals across the silent passage, creating an extraordinary sense of depth and mystery within the tightly controlled architectural statement.

The north-eastern corridor above must have been very much like this sub-vault, except more lofty and lit on both sides by arched openings in the walls. A short section of the inner wall, that facing into the Temenos, has been reassembled recently from fallen members, and shows how all four façades might have looked (Fig. 54). Engaged half-columns established a steady rhythm along the façade, between which were alternating blind and open archways admitting into the corridor behind. Immediately above was a continuous entablature which included the present frieze of triglyphs and metopes (as reassembled, there is no architrave,

Fig. 54 The inner wall of the Zeus Temenos re-erected recently from fallen fragments.

a questionable piece of restoration for which there is no evidence) (Fig. 5).
Although the scale on which all this was carried out was very grand, it has to be
admitted that the carved architectural and decorative detail is decidedly crude.
The triglyphs and metopes are little more than roughly done, whilst the design of
the metopes themselves is basic to a degree, with little or no undercutting or
subtlety. The Ionic capitals are almost naif in their simplicity (Fig. 60): the volutes
are boldly conceived but the spirals are more channelled than carved into the face,
and they do not tie together over the top but individually terminate in little 'lotus'
style wings. The whole effect is rather amateur, and perhaps demonstrates none
too sure a knowledge of the canons of the order. And yet, there is about them a
curiously Hellenistic feel, as though a long remembered tradition were being
recalled by craftsmen who had been culturally beleaguered for a long time and
who had just been called upon to undertake a work of unprecedented
magnificence. The engineering expertise, however, must command unreserved

118

Fig. 55 The original South Doorway into the Temenos of Zeus. This was closed up when the City Wall was built against the southern side of the Temenos.

admiration, for behind these walls were high-vaulted corridors carrying a paved terrace on the roof above.

When this Temenos was being laid out, the Sanctuary was independently sited outside the walled city on Camp Hill. From an inscription we know that work was in progress in the Sanctuary in A.D. 22/23. A short section of this original Temenos wall, including its south doorway (Fig. 55), was revealed when part of the Byzantine defensive South Wall, built in A.D. 390, collapsed. From this we know that the exterior wall was also dressed with engaged half-columns similar to those on the internal walls: it is probable that all three exposed exterior walls were similarly treated. The doorway originally led into the south-eastern corridor, from which there must have been a corresponding opening into the courtyard. This immediately raises a problem of orientation, for to enter the Temenos and then have to turn a full right-angle to the left in order to face the temple on the hill would have been unacceptable.

In A.D. 161, a start was made on the TEMPLE OF ZEUS OLYMPIUS that we now see. It took five years to build. It was conceived on a large scale and, although

119

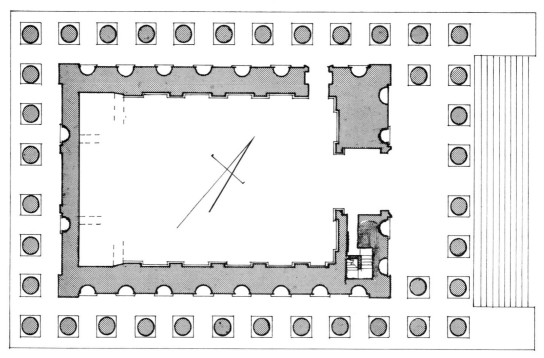

Fig. 56   Plan of the Temple of Zeus (*after A. Labrousse*).

it is fairly orthodox in design, the quality of the masonry and the carved detailing is exceptionally fine. It stood on a podium some forty metres by twenty-eight, which on the front, facing into the Temenos, broke forward into two plinths which embraced a flight of steps up to the main entrance. Giant Corinthian columns, fifteen metres high, surrounded the cella on all four sides, twelve on the long sides and eight across the front and rear; the space beneath the portico being two intercolumnations deep (Fig. 56). The capitals were deeply cut and drilled, producing an effect of great richness. The entrance wall within the peristyle was built very thick so that a staircase to the roof could be accommodated in its thickness. The doorway was of massive proportions and framed by a handsome architrave. The exterior walls of the cella were relieved only by semi-circular, round-headed niches set in line with each intercolumnation; the rest was a stark expanse of beautifully dressed and laid masonry (Fig. 57). Above the peristyle was an entablature of stepped architrave, frieze and elaborate cornice, which broke into a majestic triangular pediment on the front and rear elevations. The Temple was set in its own Upper Temenos, the pilastered north-west wall of which has only recently been revealed by excavation. Seen from the terrace on top of the Temenos corridors, the temple would have been singularly impressive (Fig. 58), silhouetted against the sky, with a monumental flight of steps up to it from the Temenos below.

Fig. 57 The southern wall of the Temple of Zeus.

Internally there was a single plain chamber adorned only by low relief pilasters along the walls. A section of the south-eastern wall still stands to its full height (Fig. 59). These pilasters were probably furnished with gilded bronze capitals, providing the only architectural enrichment except for the *adyton*, or shrine, of which nothing now remains. A small doorway in the north wall admitted to the area towards the adjacent South Theatre. The simplicity of the interior allowed the superb quality of the masonry to speak for itself, producing an effect of controlled but great richness.

The temple was approached from the Temenos by a monumental flight of steps. The first stage of this rose in one flight to the roof level of the corridors, which thus became a vast terrace surrounding and overlooking the courtyard. A further flight took one onto the upper terrace on which the temple stood. Before the construction of the 'new' temple there does not appear to have been any direct communication between the Temenos and the hillside above. The lower flight, therefore, had to be

121

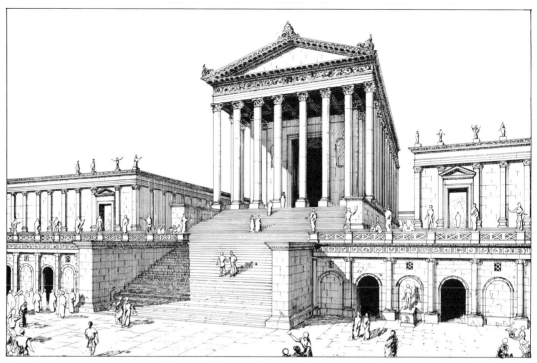

Fig. 58   A reconstruction of the Temple of Zeus at the end of the second century A.D.

Fig. 59   The ruins of the Temple of Zeus, a photograph taken by Corporal Phillips in 1867. The monument remains unchanged but the open hillside beyond is now covered by the new city of Jerash.

Fig. 60 The remains of the southern plinth of the monumental second-century staircase in the Temenos of Zeus, showing one of the first-century Ionic pilasters.

built against the wall of the south-western corridor, necessitating the lowering of its vault which carried the steps. This staircase was framed by high projecting pedestals, but these were not structurally integrated into the stonework of the wall. In the ruins of the staircase, traces can be seen of the tops of the arched openings which were buried behind them. The steps are not accurately aligned with the central axis of the temple; they are a foot to the right. Nor are they evenly placed against the corridor wall, for on the south side the pedestal stands beside one of the Ionic engaged half-columns (Fig. 60) whereas on the right it cuts straight up the middle of the half-column. The fine base moulding to the pedestal on the right is *in situ*, and the shape of the pedestal on the left is well preserved, with the front return showing. The handling of these architectural details is much more in tune with the temple than with that of the Temenos. Indeed, this very grand staircase was a later addition directly associated with the creation of the second-century temple. This being so, how was the earlier temple approached if it was in the same position as the present structure? One must perhaps consider whether, contrary to accepted belief, the first-century temple was not on the hill at all but within the Temenos itself.

Fig. 61 In the foreground, to the right of the tent, can be seen the foundations of an 'altar' (?) in the Temenos of Zeus, with a patch of the original paving just to the right of it (*see also Fig. 4*).

Recent clearance of the Temenos has revealed areas of the original paving, as well as the foundations and lowest courses of a structure approached by a flight of steps from the south. This is in the centre of the northern section of the Temenos (Fig. 61). It has been suggested that this is an altar platform set to one side of the main east/west axis of the complex, but it is also arguable that this may be the site of the first-century cultic altar-temple. If this is so, then it would lie centrally on the north/south axis established by the doorway already mentioned in the south-eastern wall of the Temenos.

The springing of a large-scale arch to the left of the reassembled interior wall (Fig. 54) indicates that there was a grand entrance here as well, as do the remains of a staircase rising from the Oval Piazza. However, the centre of this arch is not exactly aligned on the central axis of either the temple or the monumental staircase leading up to it: it is removed to the right by a foot or so. If one looks up from the foot of the steps, there is a persistent movement of the axis to the left as it mounts up the hill to conclude on the axis of the temple. All this speaks of an improvised arrangement employed to deal with the problem of integrating new structures with older ones. It was a daring scheme, for only a keen eye would spot this constant change, and in antiquity when all the buildings were standing to their full height, it may have been invisible.

The whole exercise was probably conceived to relate to the eastern colonnade of the Piazza (see page 80) which was geared to lead one's eye onto the principal entry. However, the Temenos and the staircase to the main entrance predate the creation of the Oval Piazza. Originally this staircase descended into the shallow depression below Camp Hill, but the lower flights were buried when the Piazza was laid out: these have recently been discovered during excavations.

The Sanctuary of Zeus presents enormous problems, and only a full archaeological excavation of the site will resolve them.

The temple on the hill was toppled by an earthquake sending the portico tumbling down the hillside where it has lain in disorder ever since (Fig. 57). All but one column of the peristyle were overturned, and the entire *adyton* end of the cella collapsed. During the Byzantine period the ruins were used as a quarry for building materials, as attested by identifiable elements having been discovered in the 'three churches' complex. The ruins thereafter remained exposed to the elements until 1925, when Professor Garstang undertook remedial and conservation work. Fig. 59 was taken by Corporal Phillips in 1867, and today little has changed. Garstang can, however, be thanked, for at his behest Horsfield placed the strong wooden stretcher across the doorway seen in Fig. 51, and held the north-eastern corner in place with wooden splints attached to a long wire hawser to prevent this most precarious section from toppling over. In 1981/2, this corner was dismantled and rebuilt, and is now in a more secure condition than it has been for centuries. At the same time three pillars of the peristyle were re-erected, but tragically they have been put up in the wrong place, their position having been wrongly calculated. The sections were reassembled before that area had been excavated and before a detailed 'reconstruction on paper' had been prepared; an instance of putting the cart before the horse. The conservation techniques employed for securing the columns are also at variance with accepted international practice. This sort of 'reconstruction' constitutes a major disaster, especially when one considers the exemplary work done at Pella by Brian Bowen working for the Department of Antiquities. As part of the Five Year Plan, the French Archaeological Institute will be, from April 1982, working in the Zeus Sanctuary. Eventually it is hoped to clear the fallen debris from the hillside and, where appropriate, to reinstate the majority of the peristyle correctly. When this is done, along with an investigation of the whole Sanctuary and possibly the reinstatement of the staircase, the complex will become one of the most striking monuments of Jerash.

To the west of the Temple of Zeus stands the larger of the two theatres in Jerash, the SOUTH THEATRE, which partly encroaches onto the upper limits of the

Sanctuary. This was started during the reign of Domitian, but there is evidence of an earlier theatre beneath the present structure. On its completion in the early second century, it was one of the most splendid civic monuments in the developing city and certainly the finest of its type in the whole province. Part of the cost was defrayed by generous donations from wealthy citizens such as Titus Flavius, son of Dionysus, who is recorded as having given a block of seats. This was the period when Trajan created his new Province of Arabia (A.D. 106), bringing Gerasa into the vortex of Provincial affairs so that the city's grandees willingly felt beholden to ensure that their city was as magnificent and celebrated as possible. To this impressive theatre would have come visitors, not only from the rest of the Province but also from the wider shores of the Empire, to witness great festivals. These visitors had to go away with the right impression of the city. Just such a festival was the one of the 'Sacred Guild of the ecumenical, victorious, crowned artists in the service of Dionysus and of our Lord', as an inscription relates. This was staged in the South Theatre; indeed a worthy setting.

The *cavea* of the *auditorium* (Fig. 6) was divided into two sections, with a wide terrace describing the full half-circle between them. The lower section, which was built into the hillside, was divided by steep flights of steps into four *cunei*, or blocks, each of which had fourteen rows of seats. The upper section was similarly divided into eight *cunei* with approximately fifteen rows. Although the *auditorium* has survived remarkably well, the top rows of seats are missing, and one cannot be sure of the exact original number. Even so, Kraeling was able to estimate that the theatre could have seated well over three thousand spectators. Each seat was numbered, starting with the lowest rows working from right to left. This lettering is very interesting and can be seen in the western *cuneus*. The lowest row of seats was on the top of a podium (Fig. 62) which had a wide, strongly moulded base and cornice with regularly spaced circular blind recesses in the wall. This podium was terminated at both ends by a pedestal on which a statue stood. Inscriptions in the theatre have enabled one to identify the statues and their donors; the statues are now in the Palestine Archaeological Museum in Jerusalem. The podium stood on two wide steps, on the upper of which the chairs of important dignitaries would have been set, looking out across the beautifully paved *orchestra*.

As was usual with most Roman theatres, the means of access to the seats was highly organised. Spectators having seats in the lower section were admitted into the *orchestra* through the high arched *vomitoria* on either side of the front of the stage. Those with seats in the flanking *cuneus* then mounted steps behind the statues at the ends of the podium, whilst those with seats in the middle crossed the *orchestra* and went up a steep set of steps which broke through the central point of the podium.

Those with seats in the upper section had to pass from the upper terrace of the Sanctuary of Zeus, round the back of the theatre, hard under the city wall, until

Fig. 62   The podium of the auditorium of the South Theatre.

they reached their appropriate *vomitoria* which admitted them onto the half-way terrace of the *cavea*. The upper section was also retained by a podium wall through which the *vomitoria* broke. On either side of these entrances narrow flights divided up a break in the upper podium, giving access to the stairways which divided the upper *cunei*. The upper *vomitoria* are well worth inspection not only for the engineering skill they display. The steep slope of the *auditorium* above is supported on a series of stepped arches (Fig. 63) of finely calculated masonry. This is the same arrangement as was used beneath the seats of the Hippodrome (see page 109). They are massively strong and afford exciting views back through the low doorways onto the almost fantasy architecture of the *scaenae frons*.

The front of the stage was divided into four sections with pedestals between them. Each section was decorated with a central pedimented niche flanked by arched niches. Steps at either end led up onto the stage which was partly sub-

127

Fig. 63 The stepped arch vaulting in one of the *vomitoria* of the South Theatre.

Fig. 64 The stage and rehabilitated first storey of the *scaenae frons* of the South Theatre.

vaulted and partly filled-in; it was here that remnants of an earlier structure, possibly the previous theatre, were found.

Across the stage rose the stage wall, or *scaenae frons* (Fig. 64). These elaborate architectural compositions are a common feature of Roman theatres, at times reaching magnificent proportions such as the one at Sabratha in Libya. They all have certain standard features, although the decorative design may vary from theatre to theatre. This *scaenae frons* has the obligatory three doors onto the stage from behind, with two large arched openings from the wings adjacent to, but slightly recessed behind, the orchestra *vomitoria*. The central doorway, called the *porta regia*, was set, like the two flanking it, in a half-oval recess formed by a projecting podium, on which stood a two-tier screen of columns. The front of each of these projections of the podium was recessed in the centre with a niche over them. The niches were framed by smaller columns carrying their own independent entablatures with scroll pediments. The doorways themselves were strongly emphasised by impost pilasters with finely carved capitals and a fully articulated entablature consisting of a stepped architrave, fluted frieze, an elaborately carved cornice and a bold triangular pediment (Fig. 22). It will be noted that the capitals of the impost pilasters are of the same type as those on the Hadrianic Arch and the South Gate, acanthus leaves rising in front of flutes. Above the main columns there was an entablature which followed exactly the line of the podium below, breaking forward over the pairs of pillars and sweeping back into the oval recesses. This entablature helped to establish the basic rhythm of the façade which on ground level was complicated by the deep recesses of the three doorways. It is probable that the whole arrangement was repeated on a second tier, giving the effect of a forest of pillars undulating across the curved and rectangular wall at two levels. The only difference between the two tiers being that above the doors there would have been niches. It is not known exactly how the façade was finished off at the top. Nonetheless, this was a striking design with a marked sense of 'movement'. The constant breaking forward of the entablature, the change from rectangular to curved space, the strong vertical and horizontal emphases, all amount to a piece of great visual excitement. The effect of one scale within another was the main counterpoint, whilst the bold, solid podium upon which the composition stood marked out the principal theme. Above, there rose a virtuoso series of harmonies and variations (Fig. 65). The effect today is rather lost because none of the top storey exists and much else is incomplete, but one can still sense the contrasts.

One of the first things George Horsfield did when he arrived in Jerash in 1925 was to begin conservation work in the theatre. Within a year the *orchestra* and the lower level *vomitoria* had been cleared, and the upper *vomitoria* partly so. Repairs were made to the side walls and the whole stage area revealed (Fig. 66). Since then, much has been undertaken by the Department of Antiquities in reinstating fallen

Fig. 65 A reconstruction of the *scaenae frons* of the South Theatre. Exactly how the upper part was treated is not known but it would have been along approximately these lines.

Fig. 66 Garstang's photograph of the excavations of the stage area of the South Theatre in 1927.

130

columns and in general repairs and consolidation. The majority of the *auditorium* is now in splendid condition and the stage has been paved. In recent years the whole area at the back of the *auditorium* has been cleared so that upper sections of the outer wall are now once again free-standing. The top rows of seats have been capped off with concrete, effectively securing the structure. All this has rendered the theatre both safe and majestic. There are, however, aspects of the work which are less happy. Large sections of the outer wall have been refaced, as part of the Petra/ Jerash Project, with harsh-looking new stone, so that it now appears quite new: it is also to a design for which there is no evidence. In the eastern corner of the *scaenae frons* (Fig. 22) ancient pieces have been reassembled, and the result is entirely authentic. One can hardly disapprove of the roughed-out sections which have been inserted into the three doorways to permit the restoration of the pediments and other features; a necessary employment to enable the character of the doors to be appreciated. But the insertion of new pillars and entablatures to the niches to the left of the *porta regia*, just so that the volute pediments can be put back into position, is less excusable. The capitals of these new pillars bear no resemblance to the originals. The rebuilding, however, of the rear wall behind the *scaenae frons* must be regretted, for we do not know what this wall was like and such suspect 'restorations' run the risk of endangering the validity of the whole structure; for how can one be sure what is genuine and what is not? Happily, the greater part of the theatre is completely genuine and captures most eloquently its ancient magnificence. In it, it is possible to catch in the imagination a faint echo of the 'victorious, crowned artists in the service of Dionysus' – perhaps some ancient, pagan St Cecilia Choir – who delighted audiences in the time of Trajan and charmed the ears of Hadrian.

Returning down the hill, one comes to what is perhaps the most famous and distinctive monument in Jerash, the OVAL PIAZZA (Fig. 4). This has frequently been referred to as the Forum; it was Burckhardt who first called it such, but there is no evidence to support this attribution. We do not know what function this marvellous space served. Nor is it strictly oval, rather it is like a lop-sided pear, for the ellipses are neither regular nor the same on both sides. The one on the east, starting from the entry of the Cardo, is an almost straight line before it turns tightly to approach the entrance to the Sanctuary of Zeus: the western ellipse has a more regular curve (Fig. 67). Their shapes are emphasised by a wide sidewalk, two metres wide, which ends in a neat kerb. The Piazza, which is well over eighty metres at its widest point, is beautifully paved with large slabs of stone laid in rows which follow the curves of the two colonnades (Fig. 68): the slabs of the sidewalks are laid in a more random way. In a subtle way the lines created by the paving concentrate the directional sense of the porticos whilst at the same time giving point to the altar which stood in the centre and from which the whole Piazza seems

Fig. 67 The east portico of the Oval Piazza.

to radiate. This paving, which is so wonderfully smooth and even, is one of the delights of Jerash; it is so orderly and sensible and yet so sensual.

The colonnades are of the Ionic Order, with the pillars standing on low blocks. They are evenly spaced except for two intercolumnations on the western side which are slightly wider: the architraves above are also fractionally higher, and it

Fig. 68   The concentric paving on the eastern side of the Oval Piazza.

is probable that at these points side streets were admitted into the piazza. As yet it has not been possible to determine how the South Theatre was approached from here.

The American Expedition made a significant discovery at the opening into the Cardo. Below pavement level they discovered the foundations of a triple archway which would have closed the street off from the Piazza. There is now little of this above ground except for a large L-shaped abutment in line with the portico on the western side of the Colonnade Street. In this abutment was an arch which admitted sideways into the space under the triple archway. There was a corresponding abutment on the eastern side of the street. The central opening was wider than the two which flanked it, and so it is reasonable to suppose that it was higher. In front of the two L-shaped abutments were free-standing columns on pedestals facing into the Piazza: it is possible that two similar pillars stood on either side of the central opening. On the street façade of this archway there were no such pillars, for the street colonnades were integrated into the fabric (Fig. 25). This means that the archway was the same width as the Cardo, a fact confirmed by the foundations, and was therefore a development later than the Oval Piazza. It should be remembered that this section of the Cardo was widened towards the end of the second century A.D. when the order was also changed from Ionic to Corinthian. The arch was also Corinthian.

This widening of the street necessitated the demolition of probably two columns from the eastern ellipse. The western reaches the sides of the arch directly in line with the southern arm of the L-shaped abutment. The eastern ellipse, however, does not arrive in line but finishes at a point just in front of the side of the arch, so that the entablature would have had to break back very awkwardly to meet the arch. The light and airy construction of the arch helped to hide this make-shift junction. Part of the abutment on the western side has been restored with the vousoirs of one of the arches laid out beside it. There was probably a previous archway relating to the original Ionic colonnade of the street, which was destroyed because it was not wide enough when the Cardo was widened.

When archaeological investigation of the site started in 1925, the Oval Piazza was still very much as Warren had found it and as Corporal Phillips had photographed it in 1867 (Fig. 15). Looking deeply into his photograph, one begins to realise how exhilarating it must have been to visit a ruined Roman city which had remained untouched for a thousand years: there is a romantic, spell-binding quality about it that sends shivers of anticipation down one's spine, and raises regrets that one had not been there at the time. When Horsfield arrived, the ruins were still only accessible on foot, so one of the first things he did was to lay down tracks which gave vehicular access to the South Theatre and up the Cardo as far as the South Tetrakionia. By 1930 his tracks were becoming well-used as the road north. An aerial photograph taken by Squadron-Leader Lester F. Humphrey of the RAF at this time (Fig. 69) shows clearly Horsfield's track dividing in the Piazza, one arm going off up the Colonnade Street (Fig. 16) and the other towards the South Theatre, which was then still in the process of being cleared. There are those who well remember travelling up this 'road' through the early awakenings of the ancient city.

ZONE II

The South Colonnade Street, the South Tetrakionia and its Circular Piazza, the South Decumanus, the South Bridge, the Central Colonnade Street, the Nymphaeum, the Propylaea Church and Propylaea Piazza, the Artemis Propylaea, the East Wall of the Artemis Temenos, the Artemis Temenos and the Temple of Artemis.

On entering the ancient Cardo from the Piazza, one is immediately conscious of how straight this famous colonnaded street is. Today this first section is known as the SOUTH COLONNADE STREET. The pillars on the western, left, side are more numerously preserved than those on the eastern side but there are neverthe-

Fig. 69 An aerial photograph of the Oval Piazza taken in 1930. The rectangular block in the middle of the picture is where the Tourist Restaurant on Camp Hill now is. The ruins of the Temple of Zeus and the South Theatre can be seen behind, at the top of the print.

less some extensive gaps in the portico, so the impression of an entire colonnaded street is not so strong. One has to try and visualise a complete colonnade on both sides creating a far greater sense of enclosure (Fig. 25), with a great deal of shade beneath the porticos and, indeed, across the street, which being aligned north/ south, would only have had the sun shining directly down it for a short period during the middle of each day.

The original paving of the street is a little less even than in the Piazza but it still makes for very easy walking. Running beneath it is a large surface water drain which is again in working order: it was cleaned out in 1980 by the Department of Antiquities, bringing to light a collection of the sort of small things which people drop in streets and which get swept down drains, such as coins and small pieces of personal jewellery; these bring a very human perspective to such grand thorough-fares. It is so easy when viewing grandiose schemes like these to forget that ordinary people used them in the course of their daily life.

The paving was revealed when Horsfield cleared this section of the street in 1925/6. When he started, it was still exactly as Corporal Phillips had photo-

Fig. 70 Corporal Phillips's photograph taken in 1867, of the South Colonnade Street.

graphed it in 1867; a romantic disarray of tumbled magnificence and evocative desolation (Fig. 70).

At the southern end of the street the gradient is steeper than further up, and it will be noted that the first half dozen or so pillars on the left are on a lower level than those further on. The height of the pillars remains the same so that for a long stretch the entablature is level. But the pillars all stand on small pedestals on portico level, with steps leading down between them to the sidewalk in the street. The bases of the pedestals are extended downwards in increasing depth to compensate for the continual fall in street level: likewise there is a compensating increase in the number of steps. When, however, the distance between the portico and the street levels gets too great, the whole portico is raised so that the next section of the colonnade is on a different level, more in relation to the street. This change in level meant that the entablature had to be carried on a bracket on the side of the next pillar. Just such a bracket can be seen on the western side of the street (Fig. 71).

This portico has been excavated recently by the Department of Arts of The Jordan University, under the direction of Dr Assem Barghouti, revealing a fine Roman mosaic floor of simple geometric pattern (Fig. 72). At the back of the portico/colonnade, a series of doorways with crisply carved stepped architraves has come to light, together with an internal portico *in antis* on the central axis of the main portico. Within this internal portico, doorways of some considerable pretentions are currently (1982) being excavated. Behind these, a few metres to the

136

Fig. 71   The South Colonnade Street today (*compare with Fig. 70*).

Fig. 72   A Roman mosaic floor recently revealed in the portico on the western side of the South Colonnade Street.

north-west, a section of a large-scale apse, set on the cross-axis of the doors, has been exposed. It is still too early to deduce the precise function of this evidently important building, but it has characteristics which might lead to its being identified as the Basilica of Roman Gerasa. The four pillars of the portico are larger than those of the street colonnade, and this alone makes it evident that the structure was of some significance. It is also an example of how a portico of a particular building could be used to enliven the visual perspective of the street scene (Fig. 25).

The building-up of the sidewalk to the level of the colonnade just to the right, and partly encroaching upon it, is Byzantine and may have been done to stabilise the pillars after their condition became unsafe following an earthquake. A similar raising of the sidewalk can be seen opposite, where a short flight of steps leads up to higher ground (Fig. 71). From here one can reach the Tourist Restaurant on the top of Camp Hill. Whilst one regrets that any modern building should stand on this prime archaeological site, at least this restaurant is low-level and unobtrusive, and provides a welcome and friendly facility for tourists. From its terrace there are delightful views down through the feathery pines into the Oval Piazza.

Shortly after this one comes to the crossing of the Cardo and the South Decumanus. The intersection, in its present form, takes place in a circular piazza nearly forty-four metres in diameter, in the centre of which stood the SOUTH TETRAKIONIA (Fig. 73). The date of the Circular Piazza is still under discussion. The Tetrakionia may be dated to the middle of the second century. At present only one of the podia is substantially intact; the other three are in varying degrees of ruin (Fig. 74). Although all four formed a single composition they are structurally independent, not even being tied together by a common stepped base as in the parallel monument in Palmyra. In this the pavement of the Piazza flows easily and uninterrupted through the monument. Each of the four 'towers' consisted of a square podium, four tall Corinthian columns standing on small pedestals, one at each corner of each podium, carrying a fully articulated entablature above. A statue was probably placed on the podium beneath the towering columns, Between the four podia can be seen a circular man-hole which provided access to the junction of the drains of the Cardo and the South Decumanus.

Each of the four podia is just over four metres square, and they are spaced about six metres apart. Each had a strongly shaped base moulding, above which the walls were relieved by a shell niche with pilasters and stepped hood, set between slightly projecting corner panels which formed corner plinths: the bases and cornices of these broke forward appropriately. Thus was established a vertical emphasis in what would otherwise have been a rather squat, horizontal element. Only greatly decayed sections of the columns of imported mottled marble remain, whilst nothing of the crowning entablature has been found. In its original state this

Fig. 73 A conjectural reconstruction of the South Tetrakionia in the middle of the Circular Piazza.

Fig. 74 The South Tetrakionia and Circular Piazza today.

monument must have been visually very exciting, with a constantly changing perspective through the sixteen columns as one moved round the Circular Piazza. It formed an effective break in the great length of the Cardo without impeding either the view or physical progress up the street (see page 84).

The façades of the four quadrant buildings of the CIRCULAR PIAZZA were probably identical, each having three doorways with a first floor window above. Set between these were high, engaged plinths which carried coupled free-standing columns with full entablature breaking forward over them. The street colonnades probably came to rest on square pillars with engaged half-columns on their inner sides; the entablatures were returned across the street portico to engage on either side of the quadrant buildings. In this way each façade was of five bays, the outer two being entrances to the street porticos and the inner three admitting to shops etc. As a group they formed a remarkable piece of integrated architectural planning, providing a tightly controlled rhythmic environment for the Tetrakionia. Little is now left of the buildings except on the north-west, and consequently the original feeling of enclosure has gone.

The podia of the Tetrakionia were first revealed when Horsfield levelled off the ground in the Piazza so that cars, having come up from the Oval Piazza, could turn round and return. This, of course, created interest in the area, and a small dig was mounted by the Yale University/British School Expedition in 1929. It was, however, the American Expedition which excavated the site, initially in 1930 and then between 1933 and 1934. The area behind the north-west quadrant provided the greatest interest because here were found three columns standing on a finely laid pavement on the same level as the western portico of the colonnade street, i.e. about a metre above the level of the Circular Piazza. Kraeling determined that these were the remains of a peristyle of a private house which had been demolished when the Piazza was laid out. The three shops behind each quadrant façade could be traced, but those in the north-west still had their walls standing to a substantial height. There was, however, much in-building during the Byzantine period, creating a fearsome complex of walls and small rooms. A considerable quantity of Byzantine pottery and coinage was found, as well as from the Ummayyad period. After the Moslem conquest the whole Piazza developed into a small village, with a mass of ill-made walls straggling over the whole area of pavement.

From the Circular Piazza today there is a good view westwards up the SOUTH DECUMANUS with a great many of its columns still standing for a considerable distance. The street rises up a gentle hill, and the bases of the columns, unlike those in the Cardo, are stepped one higher than its neighbour all the way up. The entablature is, however, sloping, and this gives a rather curious effect – as though it were sliding down hill. Little excavation has taken place behind the colonnades and so nothing is known of what lies beyond.

Eastwards, the South Decumanus descends steeply between its columns towards the River Chrysorhoas. Terminating the view is the minaret of a modern mosque. The line of the ancient street is crossed by the modern road with its none too endearing heavy traffic, before it comes out onto the SOUTH BRIDGE.

This was the southern of at least two, possibly three, bridges which crossed the stream: we certainly know of two but there may have been one aligned with the North Decumanus. Three arches are still standing (Fig. 75) but the wide one which leaps over the deep cut of the stream is now very slender, with only one row of vousoirs in place. The other two are slightly more substantial. The lower revetments have been carefully restored in new stone, and thus the original width can be gauged. This is the only surviving bridge from ancient Gerasa, and it is a pity that the modern city has been allowed to encroach so pressingly upon it. More serious is the invasion by modern development of the western bank: the multi-storey building now nearing completion is particularly offensive in this respect. It is not possible to return to the magnificent isolation in which Corporal Phillips photographed the bridge in 1867 (Fig. 76), but a more attractive environment and better access should be created for this important historical survival.

Corporal Phillips's photograph is important because it was taken before the Circassian settlement on the eastern bank and shows the whole site wide open to the sky, with the East Baths standing monumentally alone amid the ruins. Jerash at that time must have been a particularly thrilling place, with a unity and completeness which were both romantically and archaeologically invigorating.

From the Circular Piazza one enters the most important section of the Cardo, the CENTRAL COLONNADE STREET. When the Cardo was widened towards the end of the second century, this section was given even greater breadth than the southern leg. Even today it is a splendid thoroughfare, with almost all its western colonnade as far as the Artemis Propylaea still standing (Colour Plate 4a). The eastern side has fared less happily. The Byzantine building-up of the sidewalk will again be noted, but this time with the curious inclusion of a couple of niches with flanking miniature half-columns and strongly moulded hoods. This raising of the level amounts almost to an elevated sidewalk, for rough paving-blocks on the top of the debris in-fill have all but buried the pedestals on which the columns stand. The masonry blocks used for the purpose do not, except for a short section to the north, rest on the original sidewalk but are built directly onto the paving of the street. Part of the colonnade collapsed after an earthquake and was rebuilt, in places out of the original line, and here it may be that the footings needed to be strengthened, resulting in this awkward arrangement.

Beyond, the street resumes its original arrangement of a sidewalk leading to two or three steps which rise up to the pedestals and thus into the street portico. This soon changes, for on reaching the eight taller pillars of the Cathedral Gate –

Fig. 75 The Roman South Bridge today.

Fig. 76 Corporal Phillips's photograph of the South Bridge taken in 1867 before the eastern side of the valley had become settled as the new city of Jerash. The massive structure on the right is the East Baths (*see Fig. 137*).

Fig. 77   The Central Colonnade Street. The three taller pillars belong to the Nymphaeum.

believed to be the Propylaea of the original pagan temple of Dionysus – the portico level rises and the three steps protrude right out onto the sidewalk (Fig. 77). The spacing of these columns is curious. The central intercolumnation is, as one might expect, slightly wider than the others, but the four on the left are more widely spaced that the four on the right. Were it not for the colossal pillars of the Nymphaeum immediately next to them, this arrangement might look uncomfortable. At this stage, however, we shall move past this portico, for it will be dealt with in Zone IV (see page 177) when the Cathedral, to which it relates, is discussed. Instead, for the benefit of those who seek this feature in a Roman street, the ruts in the pavement made by chariot wheels should be noted at this point.

The NYMPHAEUM (Fig. 78) was one of the most lavish of all the civic amenities in Gerasa. It was completed circa A.D. 190. In purpose, a nymphaeum was a public water fountain, but in the Roman world these were often developed into grandiose displays of richly imaginative architecture. The one at Jerash is comparatively small but it was certainly one of the most elaborately ornamented. It was built into

143

the hillside and formed part of the retaining wall. The plan (Fig. 79) is a deep semi-circular recess eleven metres in diameter, flanked by a wall on either side, comprising a façade about twenty-two metres wide. Round the central recess were set seven niches on two storeys, semi-circular alternating with rectangular. Between these stood free-standing columnettes also on two storeys, over which the entablatures on both levels broke forward. The top row of niches was crowned with broken pediments over the semi-circular recesses. Giant Corinthian pilasters marked the extremities of the curve and carried the design round the corner onto the flanking walls, where there were semi-circular niches in two storeys, with a terminal pilaster on their far sides. Above the pediments in the deep recesses was a simple string course moulding which swept round in an unbroken line, thus stating clearly the basic semi-circular form of the recess. Above this rose a half-dome covering the whole composition. The entablatures on both levels were finely wrought, but on the upper level the architectural ornamentation was of the most florid and concentrated kind. The lower walls and niches were originally sheathed in *cipollino* marble, with its marvellous cool, cream-green striations, whilst above, the walls and niches were plastered and painted, as probably was the half-dome. Gilding was also probably used. The niches housed statues, with those on the lower level so engineered that they poured water into a large plastered basin which stretched the full width of the façade. This basin was enclosed on the street side by a plain and simple wall with moulded base and crown moulding, which acted visually as a podium for the fantasy architectural composition above. Through this wall seven holes with lion masks allowed the water to splash down into six shallow circular dishes set in the step, whilst the central hole poured its water into a huge red granite saucer, called a *laver*, standing on the pavement in front of the monument. One of the small dishes, the one immediately to the right of the *laver*, is charmingly carved with four squiggly fishes meeting head on, as though kissing, their eyes formed by holes through which the water could escape into the channel beneath (Fig. 80). This is one of the most delightful small details in Jerash.

In front of the basin wall are the stumps of four free-standing columns which do not have pedestals. Each is aligned with a corresponding giant pilaster on the façade; their scale is, however, different from the pilasters. Directly aligned with these are four colossal pillars on the line of the street colonnade; they are grouped in pairs with a wide central intercolumnation. Three of them are still standing to their full height with their magnificent capitals intact (Fig. 78). It is still a matter of debate as to how the Nymphaeum was roofed, if indeed it ever was. Kraeling argued that the central intercolumnation was spanned by a high arch corresponding to the one containing the half-dome behind. This would have been a startling and daring design and technically a remarkable feat, with a huge roof extending right back over the whole monument. This would have created a cavernous effect

Fig. 78 The Nymphaeum.

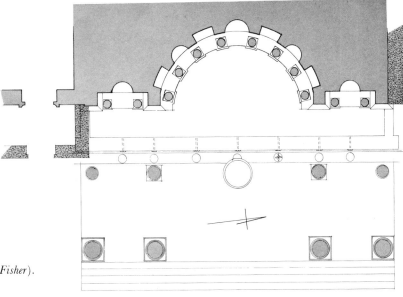

Fig. 79 Plan of the
Nymphaeum (*after C. S. Fisher*).

M ⌞ 1 2 3 4 5 6   Later additions

Fig. 81 A conjectural reconstruction of the Nymphaeum.

and one which plunged the drama of the façade into shadow.

And this, surely, is the point. The façade needed sunlight, either direct or refracted, to bring it to life. The richness of the *cipollino* marble and the painted upper part was contrasted with the airy network of columnettes, entablatures and

146

niches in glistening pale yellow limestone, and this would have required strong light to heighten its dramatic qualities. The possibility, therefore, that the Nymphaeum was never roofed except for the half-dome over the recess must be considered. The pairs of columns on the street front possibly carried independent entablatures which returned only on their outer extremities to meet their corresponding giant pilasters on the sides of the recess. The two larger pillars in front of the basin wall may have stood unconnected with the main façade, serving only as honorific columns surmounted by statues. The two smaller pillars in front of the outer limits of the basin may also have borne statues, standing, however, on extensions of the first level entablature of the main façade which here broke forward as an independent feature to support them. By this means a composition of scales and varying levels would have achieved an effect not unworthy of Second Style Pompeian wall-painting, in which illusionist architecture and interweaving perspectives took on a truly fantasy character. Perhaps here fantasy was translated into reality (Fig. 81).

To the right of the Nymphaeum can be seen the start of a narrow alley which originally climbed up steeply between the high retaining wall of the Artemis Terrace Forecourt on the right and the eminence on the left, until it reached the higher ground and the Stepped Street (see page 186). This has yet to be excavated.

To the right of this, a doorway has been reassembled from ancient pieces. The design has much in common with that of the Gate to the Cathedral (see page 177): to what this doorway led is at present not known.

Beyond, there is a long run of thirteen pillars backed by a line of shop fronts with a small rectangular exedra, with a portico *in antis* of two columns approximately in the middle. This is technically part of the Artemis Propylaea, which will be reviewed shortly. The high retaining wall behind has become very ruined, and the single doorways of the shops are in a fragmentary state. There is, therefore, none of the original feeling of enclosure which existed when the portico had its roof.

The crossing of the axes of the Cardo and the approach system to the Sanctuary of Artemis is now reached: probably the most important single architectural scheme in Jerash. Reference was made in Chapter Four (see page 86) to the axial approach system to the Temple, and in order to appreciate this orchestrated crescendo it is best to begin at the beginning; or at least as near the beginning as the present remains will permit. One should, therefore, turn east up four steps, and, pick one's way through piles of architectural fragments, into a courtyard which admits into the ruins of an apsidal-ended church. Pass right through this to a point on the far side of the apse from where one looks out over the modern city, with an abrupt drop to the modern road below.

The approach system to the Temple of Artemis started somewhere on the other side of the river, from where the route was carried across the Chrysorhoas on a

Fig. 82 The western abutment of the North Bridge.

Fig. 83 Plan of the Propylaea Church and the Propylaea Piazza (*after C. S. Fisher and R. Parapetti*).

massive bridge not dissimilar to the one already discussed (see page 141). The abutments of the NORTH BRIDGE are still visible from the road (Fig. 82). Having crossed the bridge, the route mounted a wide flight of steps and arrived at a triple gateway which gave access to a short colonnaded street. This street, and the small piazza which linked it to the Cardo, are a complex mass of ruins because during the Byzantine period the street was roofed over to form a basilical church, whilst the little piazza was built into to form an atrium. The scene is further complicated by the survival in the piazza of the first-century pavement as well as some of the late second century development; today elements of all three phases are to be seen.

The street/church is today referred to as the PROPYLAEA CHURCH (Fig. 83) because of its proximity to the Propylaea to the Temple of Artemis. The chronology should, however, be stated so that the three phases can be unravelled. At some date shortly after A.D. 50, when the new city was being laid out, a paved street was created which descended from the Cardo down the slope to the river; there may have been a predecessor to the present North Bridge. It was evidently an approach road to the early Artemis Sanctuary. In the second half of the second century, at the time when the central and southern Cardo were being widened, the approach system to the new temple was also made considerably grander. In the process the earlier road was buried under the short colonnade street and under a piazza raised upon four steps. In the Byzantine period, between A.D. 551–554, a series of earthquakes rocked Gerasa and did untold damage. It is believed that at this time the Artemis Propylaea collapsed, as well as the eastern section of the

148

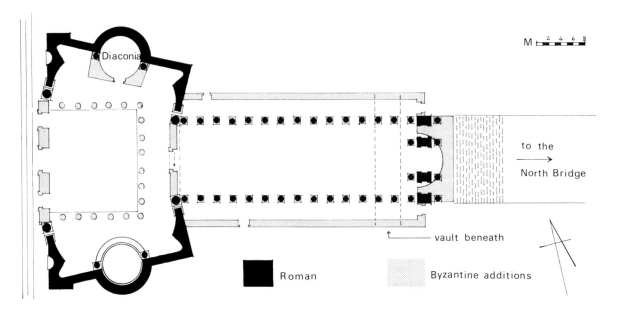

M ⊢—2——4——6——8⊣

Diaconia

to the
→
North Bridge

vault beneath

■ Roman   ▓ Byzantine additions

short colonnade street and the North Bridge. Just ten years later the western end of the street was repaired and a roof put over the whole length of it; the centre of the triple arch, or what was left of it, was torn down and a semi-circular apse erected in its place. A wall was built across the point where the street entered the small piazza, and the level of the piazza was lowered, revealing the paving of the first century street; into the piazza was built an atrium for the newly contrived church.

Little remains of the triple arch except for its end walls, but part of the architrave of the flanking openings can still be seen on the fronts facing into the street (or the church) (Figs. 28 & 84). From these it is evident that the flanking openings had straight lintels, whilst the central opening, just over three metres wide, was arched. An apse which was built into the space between them still stands to several courses.

Of the columns on pedestals which once adorned both sides of the street, eleven metres wide and nearly thirty-eight metres long, only those on the south side substantially remain (Fig. 83). These stood on two strong, deeply buried parallel walls, which ended at the triple arch. The eastern section was carried on a vaulted passage running north/south under the street, through which Mr Parapetti of the *Centro Scavi di Torino* believes a north/south side road passed (see page 93). The five eastern pillars of both colonnades were not reinstated when the church was constructed, resulting in the creation of a kind of transept arrangement across the eastern end in front of the apse. The western pillars on both sides became the division within the church between the nave and side aisles: these aisles having originally been the porticoed sidewalks of the street. The outer walls were rebuilt with rubble which was then plastered on both sides: not surprisingly very little of

149

Fig. 84 The Propylaea Church (*see also Fig. 28*).

this poor construction remains. A west wall was built across the entry into the erstwhile piazza. Two tall free-standing columns were left in place and the wall built up against them (Fig. 85); there was a single central door in this wall. Over the lintel was a flat relieving arch, which was still standing in the middle of the last century. It can be seen in Corporal Phillips's photograph (Fig. 89). The space between the pillars and the side walls was filled in with rubble and plastered over.

Fig. 85 The Propylaea Piazza. The first-century paving can be seen on the right, the Byzantine filling in on the left. The wall built up against the pillar on the left is all that remains of the west wall of the Byzantine Church which lay beyond.

Within the church the second-century street paving was relaid on the same level; it had probably been disturbed by the earthquake. The floor of the apse was raised about half a metre above the level of the church by using elements from the fallen arch and column pedestals. This apse contained at its centre the bishop's chair, flanked by two rows of seats for the priests and deacons. The altar was placed well forward in front of them, over a shallow basin let into the ground. This basin, or *thalassa*, is not an unusual feature and contained the water for washing ritual vessels and the celebrant's hands. The chancel and altar were contained behind a low stone screen wall constructed in a traditional way, carved panels

151

slotted into grooved base, posts and top rail. The chancel is set well within the line of the colonnades and of the extremities of the apse; this is an interesting example in Jerash of an arrangement favoured during the latter half of the sixth century. This late date is also evidenced by the poor quality of the construction and the way the building was botched together. True, it was decorated with rich mosaics to provide an appropriate setting for the increasingly lavish rituals of this period. But the basic structure was shoddy, and the glittering mosaics covered with a shining face a rapidly decaying fabric.

The atrium of the church, built into the small piazza, was no better constructed. This was a square open courtyard with colonnades of re-used pillars on three sides. Rough paving, rather like crazy paving, was placed on either side of the exposed first-century pavement to fill up the remaining space. A wall with three doors was built on top of the four steps which had previously led up to the raised platform level of the piazza. This meant that one had to mount four steps to get to the doors, through which there were four very steep steps down into the atrium: at best an awkward arrangement. The southern half of the piazza/atrium has not yet been cleared and is still a mountain of architectural debris. Substantial clearance has, however, taken place in the northern half, and it was here that an important discovery was made, initially by Horsfield, but examined and recorded later by the American Expedition. The exedra in the northern wall had been enclosed in the Byzantine period to create a circular chamber, in which was found a very fine mosaic which can be dated by its inscription to A.D. 565. The inscription mentions that this chamber was a *diaconia*, technically a room for the distribution of charity to the poor, but Kraeling has preferred one of the word's other meanings, that of a place in which offerings were received.

It was this *diaconia* mosaic and other circumstantial evidence which led Kraeling to argue the date of A.D. 565 for the construction of the whole Propylaea Church complex. In this the North Bridge was important because it was one of the only two or three means of communication across the river. Had the basilica been built when the bridge was still in commission, it would have cut off the access to the central part of the city where the Cathedral and other principal religious structures lay. This is unlikely to have happened. Kraeling proposed that the earthquakes of A.D. 551–554 probably brought down the North Bridge and ruined the short colonnade street. The street was thus rendered useless. It was then abandoned – until someone thought of turning it into a church. The *diaconia* mosaic date accords well with this supposition.

Interesting though the Propylaea Church and its atrium are, the real importance of the area lies in the late-second-century scheme which the Byzantine church replaced.

The colonnaded street was an approach up to the PROPYLAEA PIAZZA, one of the most original and imaginative shapes in all Syro-Roman architecture. Although not fully cleared and excavated, Mr Parapetti has been able to revise the plan published by Kraeling, showing it to have been an even more 'baroque' concept than had previously been believed. The colonnaded street stopped at a flight of four steps which gave into the raised piazza, the opening being eleven metres wide: the opening onto the Cardo opposite was nineteen metres wide, thus creating the shape of an isosceles trapezium (Fig. 83). The north and south side walls were not straight but, from the two monumental pillars which marked the entry into the street, cut back into rounded corners before swinging in tightly to encounter a pillar-framed exedra (the north one became the *diaconia*). On the other side of the exedras the walls swung away into another rounded corner before coming to an emphatic halt at two free-standing columns, one on either side of the wider opening from which four steps led down into the Cardo. It must have been an exciting experience to have come across the North Bridge and through the triple arch, down the short colonnade street and up into the bursting space of the raised piazza. All the time the scale and richness of architecture became grander and grander (Fig. 30). But nothing as compared with the magnificence and grandeur which lay ahead, viewed through the wider opening, the massive portico of the Propylaea to the Temple of Artemis, built by Attidius Cornelianus, Legate of Antoninus Pius, on the other side of the Cardo (Fig. 31).

The four giant columns of the ARTEMIS PROPYLAEA (Fig. 32) stand on pedestals and are nearly one and a half metres in diameter, which, even with the fairly flexible canons of classical proportions, means they must have been approximately sixteen metres high. Thus they towered over the porticos of the Cardo, the entablatures of which were caught by a bracket on the side of the outer two columns. The thirteen pillars north and south of the portico are, in fact, an integral part of the composition because they fronted the retaining wall behind, which ran the full length of the eastern side of the Sanctuary, a distance of one hundred and twenty metres. The street front of the Propylaea should, therefore, be looked upon as a run of thirteen pillars standing on pulvinated blocks, carrying an unbroken entablature which came to an abrupt halt with the towering mass of the central portico with its high pediment, only to pick up again with a further run of thirteen columns.

Today this effect is lost because the four giant pillars of the portico are truncated, negating the emphatic vertical interruption and the break in the horizontal line. Also, many of the northern thirteen columns are no longer standing.

The Propylaea portico, as distinct from the flanking street portico, is nineteen and a half metres wide, with a central intercolumnation rather wider than those on either side. These massive pillars carried a fully articulated entablature, of which

Fig. 86 The northern half of the façade of the Artemis Propylaea.

fragments can be seen arranged in heaps in the street. This entablature broke at the central intercolumnation, allowing the space to be spanned by an arch set within the crowning pediment (Fig. 31). This arch and the upper, sloping cornice of the pediment have been reassembled on the pavement of the street. This gives one a chance to inspect the elaboration of carved detail: close-to it may seem crudely done but one should remember that this carving was intended to be seen high above one's head where subtle nuances and delicate touches would be completely lost. What was needed in that bright sunlight was bold, explicit shapes which would stand out at a distance.

Behind these four pillars is a rough wall (Fig. 32) which was built some years ago to facilitate repairs to the gateway: this is at present (1982) being dismantled so that one will again have that marvellous vista through the whole edifice.

The portico was nearly fifteen metres deep and was set partly in a recess over four metres deep in the high retaining wall. On either side was a row of shops, with a rectangular exedra in the fourth place from the corners of the recess. These shops were two storeys high, with staircases at the back of each by which the room above could be reached – Rostovtzeff referred to the group as a 'veritable Burlington

154

Fig. 87 A reconstruction of the façade of the Artemis Propylaea (*compare with Fig. 86*).

Arcade'. Above each nicely finished doorway was a pilastered and entablatured window; examples can be seen in the walls to the left and right of the recess.

The great recess is marked by giant corner pilasters which are in line with the outer columns of the portico, from which plain side walls of finely dressed stone return to the main façade of the gate (Fig 86). This façade was an elaborate composition, with four free-standing columns on pedestals standing immediately in front of it (currently being reinstated), visually dividing it into three vertical sections: the inner pair were aligned with the inner columns of the portico. The central section contained the main doorway, a massive opening five metres wide and nine high, round which was a finely dressed stepped architrave. Due to the great span the lintel appears to have been a series of vousoirs rather than a single piece, over which was a relieving arch to take the weight of the internal pediment above. In the flanking sections were smaller doors with stepped architraves, over which were pulvinated friezes of briskly carved leaves supporting an elaborately decorated cornice. When Horsfield and Ricci cleared and repaired the gateway between 1928 and 1931, these side doorways had to a great extent collapsed (Fig. 90) and, being unable to find the missing cornice, a blocked-out substitute was inserted which illustrates the general shape but does not deceive the viewer: the architrave lintel and pulvinated frieze are original. Above each side doorway was a deep arched shell niche of great elaboration. Each was framed with low relief, plain pilasters standing on a miniature podium, and having block capitals from which

155

Fig. 88   The inner, staircase, façade of the Artemis Propylaea.

sprang a richly carved hood moulding. On either side was a further plain pilaster, in front of which was set a slender columnette standing on the small podium which at these points broke forward to carry them. A full entablature covered the whole composition, breaking forward over the columnettes as did the low pediment above. The architrave of this entablature appears to have been stepped, whilst the frieze was lavishly carved like the cornice, with immense scroll *acroteria* on the outer corners of the pediment.

Over all three sections extended a deeply carved and drilled acanthus rinceau frieze, fallen pieces of which can be seen in the street below. This frieze carried a richly carved cornice: this whole entablature broke forward above the four columns against the façade wall. Over this rose an internal pediment under the roof of the entire Propylaea. In the tympanum over the central doorway was the

Fig. 89 Corporal Phillips's photograph of the inner façade of the Artemis Propylaea (*compare with Fig. 88*). Not only was the great staircase completely buried in 1867, but the relieving arch over the door into the Propylaea Church, seen through the central gate of the Propylaea, was still standing; this has since fallen. The hillside beyond is now covered by the new city of Jerash.

dedicatory inscription, most of which has been found. In antiquity it must have been a magnificent sight (Fig. 87), full of 'movement' and variety, all regulated in a design of the strictest discipline. Each element and piece of carving was eloquent but kept firmly in its place, with plenty of plain surface to act as a foil so that the total effect was one of balance and control.

Through the doorways one is confronted by a monumental flight of steps set between high flanking walls of excellent plain masonry. The inner, west, façade (Fig. 88) is virtually a repetition of that within the portico, except that the free-standing columns are omitted and replaced with strong, beautifully pro-portioned pilasters. The main acanthus rinceau frieze is also replaced by simpler, slightly bellied flutes, whilst the pulvinated friezes and cornices over the side doorways are also omitted. In some ways the logic of the design is better demon-strated on this side, where there is less of a sense of ruin and where the detailing is more restrained.

Fig. 90 Horsfield's clearance of the great staircase; the depth of the in-fill will be noted.

Fig. 91 The great staircase today, with one of the votive altars which was found *in situ*.

In the flanking walls are two small doors, one on each side of the first flight, which gave access to the rooms above the shops on either side of the portico recess.

The clearance and conservation of the Propylaea was a huge undertaking which was entrusted, initially, to P. A. Ricci in the absence of George Horsfield, who had been made Director of the Jordanian Department of Antiquities. When he arrived, the Propylaea was much as Corporal Phillips had photographed it in 1867 (Fig. 89), with the walls in a dangerous condition. George Horsfield had already cleared the gate and the steps in 1925, carving his way through a deep deposit of sand and time, to reveal the mounting staircase (Fig. 90). Apart from effecting repairs to the side doorways, he took down the walls flanking the steps, which were in an uncertain condition, and rebuilt them exactly as before. Ricci had to retire due to ill health in 1929, a fate which overtook his successor, Lieutenant Commander A. G. Buchanan in 1930. Horsfield took over the work again himself, and by the spring of 1931 had relaid the great staircase and restored the gate to its present state.

It is, therefore, up Horsfield's splendid staircase that one now mounts (Fig. 91). It is a marvellous experience, and it is one of the few places in Jerash where one can come near to the original feeling of architectural enclosure. There are seven flights of seven steps which lead up to the ALTAR TERRACE.

The foundations of the Altar (Fig. 33) have been revealed, although what the character of the superstructure was like is unknown. From here the Terrace turned back along the sides of the staircase to the top of the Propylaea, creating a U-shaped courtyard. It has been suggested that on the top of the side walls of the staircase there was a portico, but no trace of this has been found. Certainly there is a terrace three metres wide above the side walls, behind which the arms of the U-shaped terrace extend at a slightly higher level.

Behind the Altar three flights of steps, over one hundred and twenty metres wide, stretching the full width of the Sanctuary, formed an approach to the magnificent east wall of the Temenos. Today only the central section of these steps has been restored. At the top one has a view of the temple, but in antiquity one was not afforded this view, for the temple was still hidden within its Temenos.

Very little now remains of this TEMENOS EAST WALL except for the stumps of four or five columns standing on their pedestals. Originally there was a long colonnade of twenty-two columns terminating in rectangular exedras over which there were probably towers (Fig. 92). The Propylaea to the Temple of Jupiter at Baalbek was remarkably similar architecturally, and the parallels are interesting. In the plain wall behind this colonnade was the main entrance into the Temenos, set on the central axis of both the stairs and the Temple of Artemis.

One now entered the sacred enclosure, a vast space, one hundred and sixty-one metres deep on the axis of the Temple and one hundred and twenty-one metres on

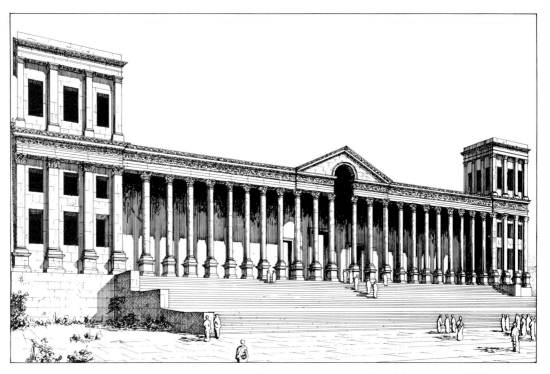

Fig. 92 A reconstruction of the eastern wall of the Temenos of the Sanctuary of Artemis. Little of this huge structure now remains.

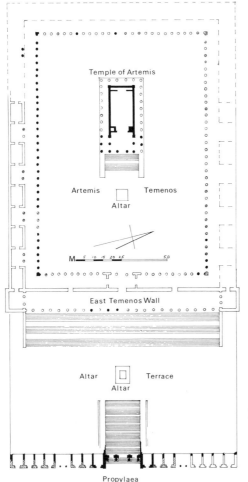

Temple of Artemis

Artemis   Temenos

Altar

M 5 10 15 20 25   50

East Temenos Wall

Altar   Terrace

Altar

Propylaea

Fig. 93 Plan of the Sanctuary of Artemis.

the cross axis. Deep porticos (Fig. 93) surrounded the whole area; the north and south sides each had thirty-six columns, the east and west twenty-six each. At the corners there was a square column with half-columns set on the sides facing down the two respective colonnades (Fig. 94). All colonnades stood on a stylobate, or ground level wall, which looked like a continuous step, and they were seven and a half metres high. Behind the north and south porticos were a series of rooms and rectangular exedras with twin-pillared entrances. Very little of these chambers now remains except for a few low walls. The porticos on the north and south sides were seven metres deep; the east, backing onto the East Temenos Wall was a little wider.

Today there is none of the original sense of enclosure. The bright sunlight shines across the huge flat area with little shade, and there is no feeling of secrecy. The colonnade on the south side is the best preserved (Fig. 95). The Department of Antiquities has recently cleared its western end, and the effect is quite startling, for the upper parts of the columns which have been exposed for centuries are now weathered to a marvellous silvery grey, whilst the lower parts, so recently exposed, still retain their creamy-white colour (Colour Plate 3). The western colonnade is still buried in the hillside.

On the central east/west axis of the open courtyard stands the TEMPLE OF ARTEMIS (Fig. 96), the *raison d'être* for the long system of approaches, or *Via Sacra*. Second only to the Oval Piazza, it is the city's most famous monument. Although ruined, it is magnificent and commands the broad expanse of the Temenos with authority: when there, one cannot help looking at it. It does not stand in the middle of the Temenos: it is set back with, as C. S. Fisher points out, almost twice as much space in front of it as behind.

The design of the Temple may be orthodox, showing no great innovative strokes such as in the *Via Sacra*; its construction, however, was of the highest quality. It stood on a high podium, over twenty-two metres wide and forty metres long, with boldly moulded base and crowning cornice features. On the entrance front this podium was thrust forward nearly fourteen metres on the north and south sides to frame a staircase of two flights of seven steps which approached the temple door. Originally there were eleven columns to each long side, including the portico, each thirteen metres high and standing on squared blocks, and six across the east and west fronts. The portico was three intercolumnations deep, but the third took the form of a solid wing projecting forward from the sides of the cella, ending in a three-sided pilaster: these were matched by corner pilasters at the back angles of the building. The main door probably had exactly the same proportions as the central door in the Propylaea. From the debris it has been determined that this doorway was spanned by a flat arch, or lintel made up of vousoirs. Strangely, there was no architrave round it. The doorway was flanked by niches, with pilaster

Fig. 94 A corner pillar in the Temenos of Artemis, with the Temple beyond.

Fig. 95 The ruins of the southern portico of the Artemis Temenos. The pale colour of the lower parts of the columns indicates the depth to which they had been buried.

frames, entablature and pediment standing on low-relief plinths. The design and execution of these niches is curiously naif, and has echoes of Nabatean work, although such a connection at this date would be surprising.

Of the original twelve columns of the portico only one is missing, and the remainder stand as majestic as they ever did. Today they have weathered to an extraordinary dark peach, or bronze colour, and are marvellous when seen against the dark blue of the sky (Colour Plate 1). The carving of the capitals is wonderfully rich, and has retained its edge and crispness over all the centuries. This has led Mr Parapetti to suggest that the entablature over the peristyle was never erected, 'since had it crashed down it would have broken off much delicate ornament'.* This argument is further supported by the fact that, whilst several blocks from the architrave have been identified, re-worked and re-used in the Byzantine churches (this is especially evident in St Theodore's), no sections of the frieze or cornice have been found either in the debris or as re-used material. None of the other pillars of the peristyle remain standing, and the superbly laid masonry of the cella is exposed to view. Originally the peristyle had been designed to carry a full entablature with a pediment over the eastern and western ends. If the temple was completed, it would have been a singularly handsome structure (Fig. 97), standing creamy white against the shining sky.

Below the cella and the walkway round the peristyle is a multi-compartmental crypt with barrel vault, which can be entered through doors in the north and south walls of the cella. These crypts rise in height from very low below the portico, through a higher section under the eastern part of the cella, to the greatest height under the western part. This change in height is reflected within the cella. Half-way down the interior two steps took the floor to a higher level before encountering a centrally placed flight of steps which led up into a deep recess in the western wall (Fig. 98). This recess was the shrine, or *adytum*, which contained the image of Artemis. A segmental arch spans the *adytum*, with a semi-circular relieving arch over it: both still stand, the relieving arch looking rather curious and lost without a job to do. Round the walls a series of shallow rectangular niches was set high up. The interior is still choked with much rubble but the lines of the cella can be followed. The walls look very bare, and there is a conspicuous lack of any carved ornament. Dowel holes liberally scattered all over these surfaces indicate that the interior was sheathed in marble. None of this now survives; it was probably robbed-out during the Byzantine period to adorn the walls of the Cathedral and other Christian churches which were then springing up all over the city. The Temple certainly fell out of use during the fifth century, when the Temenos was also probably robbed of all its paving – none has been found – and the whole area

* R. Parapetti, *Annual of the Department of Antiquities*, 1980.

Fig. 96   The Temple of Artemis.

was turned into a pottery factory with kilns and worksheds. One large kiln, at the foot of the steps in front of the Temple, has recently (1980) been excavated by R. Pierobon for the *Centro Scavi di Torino* who discovered late-Byzantine sherds in the lower levels and Ummayyad above, indicating that pottery manufacture and some economic activity in community life was still going on, at least in that quarter of Jerash, right into Moslem times.

Later, the Moslems fortified the Temple, constructing from fallen masonry the baulk work on the podium. This was the citadel which King Baldwin II besieged and captured.

Below the present level of the Temenos, traces have been found of an earlier development of this sacred site. These remains are not yet fully understood, but they indicate that before the magnificent second-century developments there existed here a smaller shrine to the patron deity of the city.

Artemis was interesting, for although she was a rather late arrival in the power circle on Mount Olympus (Homer was pretty contemptuous of her in the *Iliad*) she developed into a popular and celebrated deity. She is usually thought of as the huntress (Diana in the Roman pantheon) but her proper sphere covered a much wider field than that. Earth, particularly the uncultivated parts, forests and hills, came under her care, as did women, especially at childbirth and at death. Indeed, she was a 'Lion unto women'. Later she became famous as a city-goddess, the role in which we find her here. She was a daughter of Zeus, sister of Apollo and was venerated as a bringer of fertility to man and beast. She is also often identified with the Artemis of Ephesus, but the two cults had quite different origins.

Today, she and the other ancient gods and goddesses are gone and their houses empty and roofless. But there is still a magic about her place as the wind creeps in and whispers through the silent, sun-warmed columns. Its murmuring is like an echo of some long-lost incantation, like praises seeking a departed deity.

ZONE III

The Atrium Mosque, the West Baths, the North Tetrapylon, the North Colonnade Street, the North Gate, the North Piazza and the North Theatre.

North along the Colonnade Street from the Propylaea, the Cardo is crossed by a modern service road which leads up to the Jerash office of the Department of Antiquities, a white, rather fanciful building, high on the terrace above, which has quite a history of its own. On the right shortly past the Propylaea Piazza, excavations in 1981 exposed the first ancient mosque to come to light in Jerash. It is of the Ummayyad period and is an important addition to our knowledge of Gerasa at that time. Even though the population of the city had shrunk by the time of the Moslem invasion, it is very likely that there were as many mosques in the city as there had been churches. This mosque was built into the atrium of a Roman structure – hence the name, the ATRIUM MOSQUE – with the mihrab being a re-used niche of the Antonine Period. The evidence from this excavation has yet to be fully sifted, but its importance is obvious.

Beyond the service road is a huge ruin standing forlornly by itself; high, wide arches erupt out of a fantastic pile of rubble which spreads itself with reckless abandon over a large area. These are the remains of the WEST BATHS. This complex has never been cleared or excavated, but its general plan was established by Mr A. StJ. Harrison, architect to the British Mandate Government in Palestine. No date can yet be ascribed with certainty to this enormous structure.

At the centre was a large hall divided into three bays by heavy, unadorned pilasters which probably supported some kind of vaulted ceiling; Kraeling

Fig. 97 A reconstruction of the Temple of Artemis, assuming that the temple was completed.

suggested a barrel vault. From its shape and its relationship to other chambers, we can be fairly sure that this was the *frigidarium*, or cold bath, in which case the central space could have been taken up with a large rectangular swimming-pool. In the centre of the west wall, an opening led into a recess off a square chamber, with another recess opposite on the western side. Over the square was placed a dome, probably a saucer on pendentives. This was in all probability the *caldarium*, or hot bath, an identification supported by the existence of flues in the walls. Other rooms must have served as *apodyteria*, or changing-rooms, and possibly a *tepidarium*, or warm bath. There are two side pavilions, the southern of which has its excellent domed ceiling still in place: these pavilions may have served as rooms for lectures and discourses, for which accommodation was frequently provided in such establishments. For the Baths were more than just places in which to sweat off the day's anxiety or to enjoy a swim; they were as much centres of social and didactic life. The position of the pavilions close to the two presumed entrances on the eastern side would have segregated them from the hubbub and hilarity of the bathing areas, making them appropriate for a more serious turn of mind.

A peristyle was placed on the western side, which turned round to enclose the

Fig. 98   The interior of the Temple of Artemis.

caldarium wing. Only fragments of this now remain (Fig. 99); isolated pillars popping up in an uncoordinated way from the rubble-strewn ground. The Baths conform to the standard Roman type, although they are much more modest than those in Rome, or, if one wants a provincial example, than the superb Hadrianic Baths at Leptis Magna.

The Colonnade Street continues northwards, soon to be crossed by the North Decumanus. This junction is marked by the NORTH TETRAPYLON. There was good reason why this piece of street architecture was built. When, between A.D. 150 and 180, the central section of the Cardo was widened and recast in the Corinthian order, the section north of the North Tetrapylon was left at the original width and in the Ionic order. Likewise, the western part of the North Decumanus did not approach the junction exactly at right angles; it is a few points off to the south to bring it directly in line with the North-west Gate in the city wall. The eastern section, as far as we know, for it has never been excavated, did stand at right angles and went past the side of the West Baths, and may have crossed the river by a bridge of which there is now no trace.

This awkward junction was masked by what Buckingham called a 'rotunda': what is, in effect, a four-way arch. The structure was a square building with a large circular domed space in the middle, with four wide archways, each five and a half metres wide, leading out into the converging streets (Fig. 100). Each façade was treated differently. The façade facing south was embellished with pilasters at the corners of the opening, with capitals of the familiar acanthus and flutes design. The street colonnades were not aligned with these but were set in line with free-standing columns on either side of the arch: the indications are that the entablatures were not carried over onto the Tetrapylon but ended on the last pillar of the colonnades. On the north side there was an identical pair of pilasters framing the arched opening, and also free-standing columns on pedestals. The street colonnades, of the Ionic order, started after the next intercolumnation, but how their entablatures were joined, if at all, to the Gate is not certain. The last pillar of these colonnades stood just on the centres of the pilasters and their fronting free-standing columns.

The west façade was more elaborate because the pilasters of the opening were repeated as a feature on the extremities of the front. Between these pairs of two pilasters was a semi-circular niche. The Ionic colonnades of the street to the west were, however, aligned on the outer pilasters. Again it is debatable whether the entablatures were structurally joined to the Tetrapylon on this side. The eastern façade was altogether more complicated, and, being very ruined, it is not possible now to be certain of the design. The pilasters at the opening were certainly repeated, but immediately left and right of them are the remains of sizeable plinths with moulded bases and crowns: these probably carried niches framed with

Fig. 99 The ruins of the West Baths. Through the archway there still remains a finely preserved interior dome.

columnettes.

A full entablature went round on all four sides, with a stepped architrave, lotus-leaf frieze and a cornice; fragments of these are to be seen lying about on the ground. Quite what the superstructure was like we do not know but each façade may have carried a pediment, which would have effectively masked the exterior of the dome over the central space.

This central space was also handsomely decorated (Fig. 101). The walls of the four openings were deep but they led to quadrants across which was a moulding forming a kind of high dado, under which was a neat base moulding returned at its ends upon itself. Over this was a very shallow segmental niche standing on a projecting base, which certainly carried framing columnettes supporting an entablature and pediment which broke forward in the usual way. There is nothing to indicate how the dome was treated internally.

This fine monument, one of the most refined in Jerash, has never been fully studied and, although it has been cleared and conserved, there is much to be done in the approaches to it, particularly to the west. Even now one has to squeeze up a set of steps to gain the present ground level from which the Ionic columns of the south side of the Decumanus emerge half-way up their height. It is an enchanting

169

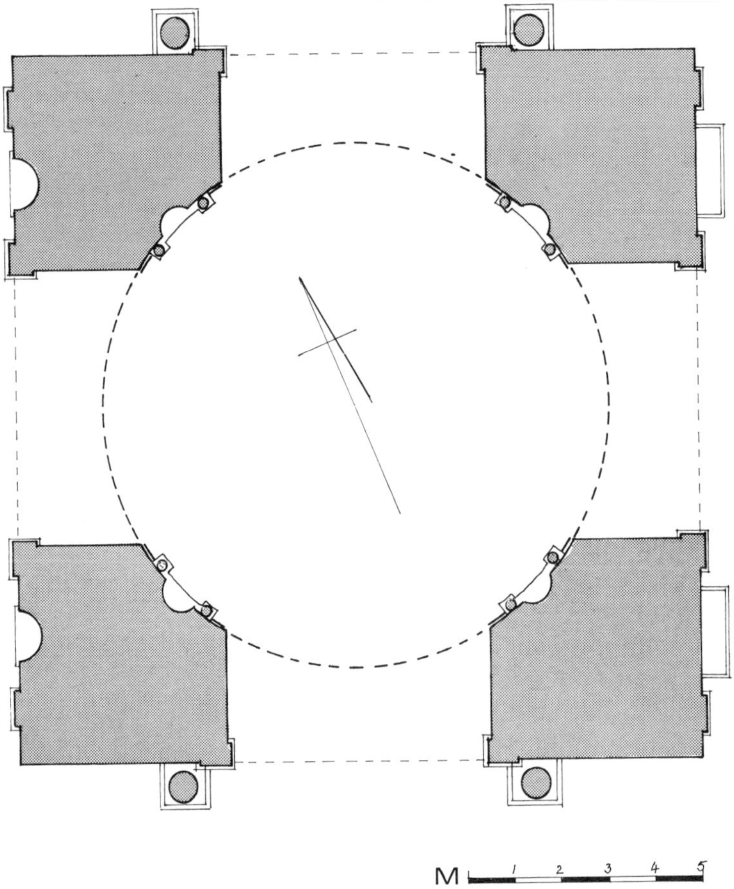

Fig. 100 Plan of the North Tetrapylon.

M |___ 1 ___ 2 ___ 3 ___ 4 ___ 5

Fig. 101 The North Tetrapylon, looking west.

spot, like being in some eighteenth-century painting of romantic ruins. But the fill on which one is standing hides a street of columns, and this must eventually become a prime area for archaeology.

From the North Tetrapylon one enters one of the quietest and most intimate sections of the Cardo, the NORTH COLONNADE STREET (Fig. 102 and Colour Plate 2). It is not much frequented by visitors, and possibly in consequence has a dream-like charm and sense of picturesqueness which is delightfully romantic. It has been cleared of debris, and much of the original paving has been revealed. It is of the original first-century width and Ionic order except for four slightly taller Corinthian columns which mark some building of importance. It is not quite an eighteenth-century view, it is too tidy, but there is a sense of rural peace which would have delighted William Pars. After so much towering splendour and grandiose architectural display, the scale here is more human and the feeling more domestic. Surprisingly, it is now more attractive than when Corporal Phillips photographed it in 1867, for then it was a desolation unsoftened by gentler touches (Fig. 103).

At the end of the street stands the ruined NORTH GATE. An inscription which

originally stood over the arch informs us that it was built in A.D. 115 by C. Claudius Severus, Legate of Trajan, who was responsible for building the road from Gerasa to Pella. It lacks sophistication in the handling of its architectural detail, even though the plan is ingenious. Indeed, the main interest of the Gate lies in this plan (Fig. 104) which can be traced with ease. The road from Pella arrives at the Gate at an angle of 18° off the axis of the Cardo. It was desired that the Gate should face square onto this road and at the same time be full square at the end of the street. In consequence the plan is wedge-shaped, with the two façades lying at an angle of 18° to each other. Basically both are the same design but, due to the curious way the angle is accommodated, the outer façade is longer than the inner. The design is, therefore, expanded, and the niches which flank the single archway are made wider and more widely spaced within the engaged half-columns. Also, due to the angle, the passageway of the arch is 'squint', leading to a rather uncomfortable setting of the arch, particularly on the outer side. There are examples of gates or scenic arches turning corners in other cities in the Roman east, most notably at Palmyra where the Monumental Arch is a work of the most dazzling ingenuity and brilliance. The North Gate at Jerash is markedly less than brilliant, and Detweiler

171

Fig. 102 The North Colonnade Street, which retains the original width and Ionic character of the first-century Cardo.

Fig. 103 Corporal Phillips's photograph of the North Colonnade Street, taken in 1867.

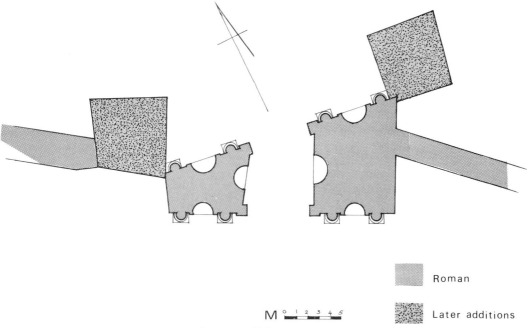

Roman

M ⌞0 ⌞1 ⌞2 ⌞3 ⌞4 ⌞5

Later additions

Fig. 104   Plan of the North Gate (*after A. H. Detweiler*).

is probably not far from the mark when he suggests that it was the work of an engineer rather than of an architect. Certainly it is finely engineered, with excellent foundations and a remarkable drainage system built into the structure.

The Gate replaced an earlier one which Detweiler believed stood a few metres to the south and was set on the main axis of the street. It is evident that the city wall was rebuilt along a different line, so that it could engage the new Gate more effectively. This gave rise to the north salient, which is a distinctive disturbance in the easy run of the city defences. The two bastions which stand on either side of the Gate, and partly built against it, are either Byzantine or of the Crusader period, and are very poorly made.

The area west of the North Colonnade Street is still under cultivation as far as the western half of the North Decumanus. This street leads up from the North Tetrapylon, across the sides of the fields, to a totally unexcavated area known as the NORTH PIAZZA (Fig. 105). What purpose this area served is unknown, but it is surely related to the North Theatre which lies just south of it. Although both Schumacher and Krencker attempted a plan of the piazza, its true lines will only be revealed by excavation.

Two porticos of stately Corinthian columns faced each other across the open space, but how the western and eastern sides were treated we do not know. The south portico (Fig. 106) probably backed onto the rear of the *scaenae frons* of the North Theatre. This is a tantalising area which needs not only archaeological work

Fig. 105 The unexcavated North Piazza.

Fig. 106 The monumental pillars of the North Piazza.

Fig. 107 The North Theatre, sometimes called the Odeon. Only the upper
cunei are exposed, there being half as much again still buried in the centre.

but also conservation because some of the pillars are in a precarious state.

To the south lies the NORTH THEATRE, sometimes called the Odeon (Fig.
107). This is still in a ruined condition even though Horsfield did effect repairs to
the upper level in 1925. The theatre was probably entered by long corridors
leading off the piazza on either side of the stage. These led also onto the stage and
into the *orchestra*, and then through vaulted passageways beneath the *auditorium*.
Vomitoria in turn led off this, giving access to the seats. The *cavea* was divided into
four *cunei* on the lower level and eight on the upper. The podium wall of the upper
section was decorated with groups of three round-headed niches between each exit
from a *vomitorium*. These exits had lintels on which the stepped architrave framed
the opening. Behind these rectangular openings, one of which can be seen on the
right of Fig. 107, the *vomitoria* were step-vaulted as in the South Theatre. The lower
part of the *cavea* is still buried along with the *orchestra* and stage. The *scaenae frons* has
long since fallen, but the stump is of sufficient thickness to support a two-storey
superstructure which was probably decorated in a manner not dissimilar to that in
the South Theatre. The remains of this are probably to be found beneath the fill
now choking the *orchestra*.

175

Under the Five Year Plan, this area of the ancient city, from the North Colonnade Street westwards to the North-west Gate, has been allocated to British, Australian and American expeditions. These teams will work closely in conjunction, yet in separate sections. This may well prove to be a fine piece of international co-operation which will certainly change the character of this area beyond recognition. Instead of being a rural back-water, it will become a hive of activity which will, in time, provide Jerash with a major new centre of attraction and historical interest.

ZONE IV

The Cathedral Gate, the Cathedral, the Fountain Court, the Glass Court, the Sarapion Passage, the Stepped Street, the Baths of Placcus, the Basilica of St Theodore, the Church of SS. Cosmas and Damian, the Church of St John the Baptist, the Church of St George, the Synagogue Church, the Church of Bishop Genesius, the Church of SS. Peter and Paul, and the Mortuary Church.

The Early Christian monuments of Jerash are a subject for study in themselves, full of interest and fascination. The Propylaea Church has already been mentioned (see pages 148–52) so now it is to the remaining ecclesiastical buildings that we turn.

South of the Nymphaeum stands a row of eight columns on pedestals which are higher than those further down the street. Although they continue the line of the street colonnade, they form a separate portico to the precinct which lies on the hillside behind. To emphasise this, the steps which rise to them are thrust out onto the sidewalk, and the central intercolumnation is wider than those on either side (Fig. 77). A curious feature of this portico, however, is that the intercolumnations of the pillars on the south are wider than those on the north. The southern pillar is in line with the end wall of the structure behind, but the northernmost pillar is placed considerably in from the end of the corresponding wall at the north end. Originally all eight may have been evenly spaced, except for the central intercolumnation, but when the Nymphaeum was built in A.D. 190, it was found necessary to dismantle the northern four and rebuild them closer together so that they did not obstruct the grand new work. Whatever the reason, the appearance is unbalanced. This portico marked the entrance to a temple complex which is believed to have been that of Dionysus.

Behind the pillars is a wall with doorways in it, two to the south and three to the north, but inspection will immediately show that this wall is a later addition, built in front of an earlier wall in which there were finely framed doorways, two to each side. These are the original shop doors of the second-century façade. The later walls will be seen to have been built of re-used blocks, with little regard for the architectural details with which they are carved. At some date before the area was finally deserted, the two rooms on the north were occupied by a blacksmith who had his workshop in the front part and stored his charcoal in the back. When the American Expedition excavated this area in 1929, they found enough charcoal to fill two or three sacks.

It is with the central opening and its very elaborate doorway that we are particularly concerned (Fig. 108). This was the Propylaea doorway to the vanished temple of Dionysus (?). During the fourth century the dilapidated and probably disused temple was taken over by the growing Christian population and redeveloped into the Cathedral we see today. The old propylaea was then adapted and partly rebuilt as the CATHEDRAL GATEWAY.

The mid-second-century A.D. carving on this Gate is rich and luxuriant (Fig. 23). The doorway was flanked by columns on pedestals, over which the entablature and pediment broke forward in the style of a 'Syrian' niche. These pillars were tucked into small rectangular recesses, on the forward returns of which were massive square pilasters marking the corners. Their bases are still *in situ* but their capitals have been placed on the forward corners of the later additions (Fig. 108): admirable though it is that they are displayed close to their original position, it does tend to give the impression that they are part of the later Byzantine structures.

Through the Gateway is a monumental flight of steps, with four tall Corinthian columns standing on the lower steps, two each on different levels but with their capitals at the same height. High walls of badly weathered stone flank this stairway in a similar, though smaller, manner to that behind the Artemis Propylaea. These steps and flanking walls are an early Byzantine rebuild, for beneath the steps are the foundations of an earlier flight on a slightly easier gradient: probably the line of ascent to the pagan temple. These earlier steps even pre-date the Gateway. It was probably an earthquake in the middle of the fourth century which wrecked the classical arrangement, necessitating the rebuilding of the flanking walls and the relaying of the steps. In this reconstruction old material was used, robbed from disused older buildings. All the elements of the Christian arrangement were found when the stairs were cleared, making it possible to reconstruct, on paper at least, the appearance of this approach to the Cathedral (Fig. 109). The flanking walls had a crown moulding, part of which can be seen on the north side at the top of the steps. On this stood a colonnade of Ionic pillars carrying a stepped architrave; remnants of all these are now lying arranged on the upper terrace. One truncated column was found *in situ*. Both colonnades were joined together by a large room or rooms carried on a bridge supported by the four columns on the

Fig. 108   The Cathedral Gate and Staircase. Before the Christian era, this was the Propylaea to a pagan temple, possibly that of Dionysus.

stairs. Over the head of the staircase was a high arch springing from square pillars. At the foot of the staircase are two narrow flights of steps, which are later additions to provide access to the rooms over the shops, presumably built after any internal staircase within the shops had either fallen or otherwise gone out of use.

The sense of enclosure cannot now be experienced because none of the super-structure is standing (Fig. 110). It is evident that the Cathedral staircase was

178

Fig. 109 A reconstruction of the Cathedral Staircase as it was in the fifth century.

Fig. 110 The Cathedral Staircase today.

wrecked by another earthquake which effectively rendered it impassable. All its elements were found in the debris just where they had fallen. So often, however, it is the little human touches which bring such ruins alive, and these stairs are no exception for buried among them were the contents of a jewel box dropped by someone fleeing as the area began to topple.

The wall at the top of the steps is the east end of the Cathedral. To be greeted by a blank wall after such a grandiose approach may be thought an anticlimax: logically one would have expected a grand doorway leading into the basilica or its atrium. But this is the east end of the church and the main doorway from the atrium is on the west. The sense of axial approach as understood by the Hellenistic and Syro-Roman world, in which architecture conducted one from place to place in a carefully organised programme, seems not to have been a factor in Byzantine planning, so in Jerash one cannot say that this abrupt visual halt would have worried the Gerasenes. However, the opportunity was taken to place a shrine at the head of the stairs and so provide some sort of focal point for the ascent. During the excavations of this area the remains of this shrine were found. It had been placed in the centre of the wall and consisted of a fine shell niche, possibly of Hadrianic origin and so re-used material, flanked by pilasters over which there must have been some kind of entablature. Painted in red letters along the band beneath the shell are the words *Michael, Holy Mary, Gabriel*: there are also indistinct traces of red paint on the curved wall of the niche forming the outline of a figure; this red paint was much clearer when the niche was first brought to light, and it is thought likely that it was the base for a gilded background. Plug-holes indicate the positions of lamps and a grill across the face of the niche. Kraeling has argued a date no earlier than the second quarter of the fifth century for this shrine, a period when the cult of the Virgin was becoming widespread. It is interesting that the Archangels Michael and Gabriel appear together frequently as guardians of entrances to churches.

To reach the interior of the basilica and its atrium, worshippers had to turn either left or right at the shrine and then westwards down covered passageways which ran along the outside of the north and south of the church (Fig. 111). The north passage can be divided into two sections, a wide eastern part which Kraeling postulates was the women's narthex, spanned by six irregularly spaced arches supporting the roof, and a narrower western section which admitted at its western end into the atrium. The south passage was even narrower for all its length, and was possibly the men's narthex until its western end was appropriated to a side chapel built at a later date.

The principal entrances to the CATHEDRAL were through three doorways in the western wall, which divided the basilica from its atrium. Unfortunately we do not know to whom the Cathedral was dedicated, and even its date is based on deduction: Kraeling put this at A.D. 365, making it the earliest surviving Christian monument in Jerash. Nor is there any explicit evidence that this was actually the cathedral of Gerasa.

Today it is sadly ruined. Of the two Corinthian colonnades which divided the aisles from the nave, only three columns on the south side are still standing, two of which are without their capitals. Even in antiquity it was despoiled on more than one occasion. A considerable number of architectural members were found during the clearance of the site, and these have been stacked along the lines of the two colonnades, militating yet further against any visual appreciation of the site (Fig. 112). With careful exploration, however, the plan can be followed, for the side walls are still standing to their lower courses and the curve of the apse is clearly visible.

In addition to the three western doorways there were three doors each from the north and south passages into the body of the church. At the eastern ends of the aisles there were also doors into the two rooms which flanked the apse. The walls in which these doors are set were originally revetted with thin veneers of marble or coloured limestone: fragments of dark red and green marbles have been found in the apse. Twelve re-used second-century Corinthian columns on each side of the nave separated it from the aisles, and these carried a stepped architrave also robbed from some earlier structure. Above this rose high walls which were ablaze with glittering glass mosaics. The four eastern bays were screened off in the usual way to create a chancel where stood the altar, most likely under a baldachino (Fig. 34). In the centre of the apse would have been the *cathedra*, flanked by two curved rows of seats for the other cathedral clergy. Very little of this now remains, but the lines of the screen between the pillars and across the nave can be traced.

The nave was paved with stone flags but only a small section of this now remains against the chancel screen, where the pulpit or *ambo* projected out into the nave. In the aisles, however, the flooring is still intact and is of a pale pink limestone. Sockets on the edge of this paving close to the walls indicate the position where benches were set for the use of the elderly or sick: evidence of the old adage 'the old and the sick go to the wall'.

The Cathedral was badly damaged even before it was finally abandoned. The five western bays were destroyed, either by natural collapse or by an earth tremor, and no attempt was made to reinstate them. Instead, a new, very shoddy and makeshift wall was built across the nave and aisles. In essence it was a patch-up which reduced the basilica to the usable remaining eastern part: the footings of this wall can still be seen.

In front of this new west wall was built a portico, with the columns standing on a stylobate. A shallow trench has exposed this a few inches below the surface. This stylobate rests, by strange chance, on the base moulding of the podium of the

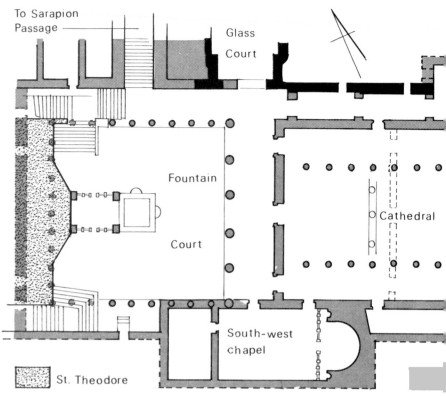

To Sarapion Passage

Glass Court

Fountain

Court

Cathedral

South-west chapel

St. Theodore

Fig. 111 Plan of the Cathedral Staircase, the Cathedral and the Fountain Court (*after C. S. Fisher*).

pagan temple which preceded the basilica on this site.

The Cathedral atrium which lies immediately west of the basilica is known as the FOUNTAIN COURT, and it has as complex and fascinating a history as any other monument in Jerash. Ancient sources, including Pliny, mention a number of shrines dedicated to Dionysus where on the occasion of his festival water from a fountain was turned to wine. It has been suggested that this 'miracle' also occurred at the Sanctuary of Dionysus at Gerasa: Diodorus relates that the miracle also took place at Teos, where the Christians took over the whole site in the fourth century. Epiphanius also records that in the fourth century water was changed to wine at the fountain 'in the martyrion'* at Gerasa at the Feast of the Miracle of Cana. This can only be the fountain in the centre of the Cathedral atrium. Is it possible, therefore, that, as at Teos, the Christians at Gerasa took over a well-established 'miracle' and converted the whole concept into a Christian celebration. Early Christians frequently took over ancient, deeply rooted cults, rituals and practices, and gave them religious respectability by wrapping them in a new Christian purpose so that they continued to serve as devotional activities.

* Epiphanius, *Panarion*

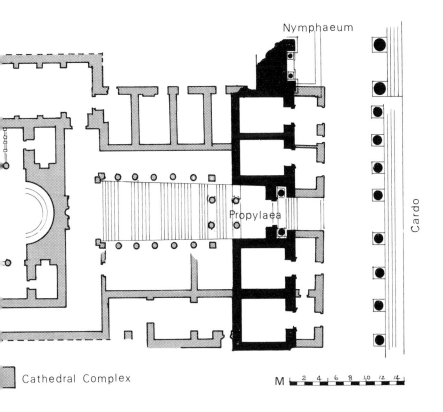

Nymphaeum

Propylaea

Cardo

Cathedral Complex

M

This fountain stood in the centre of the atrium. To the east of it was a row of six tall second-century columns standing on octagonal blocks, which formed the entrance portico to the Cathedral: one of these is still standing. The pavement under this portico was divided into panels, into which were set a pattern of red limestone octagons and smaller white limestone squares. Much of this is still intact (Fig. 113). The other three sides of the atrium were originally furnished with lower, Ionic colonnades paved with mosaics, but these were in the· main demolished when the Basilica of St Theodore was built.

The Fountain Court was paved with small, rectangular blocks, much of it robbed from earlier buildings. The low walls of the Fountain were made of fine pink sandstone, except for the western side where re-used geometric ceiling coffers were inserted. Whether this anomaly is part of the original arrangement or a later adaptation connected with St Theodore is uncertain. Two basins were attached to the walls of the Fountain, one each on the northern and eastern sides. The water for the Fountain was brought from the great reservoir at Birketein (see page 213) by way of a conduit along the east side of the Artemis Temenos, after which it divided, providing water for both the Nymphaeum and the Fountain Court. On reaching the Court, the water was conveyed to the Fountain through a lead pipe

Fig. 112 Interior of the Cathedral today (*compare with Fig. 34*).

lying under the diagonally laid paving stones. This was discovered by the American party but, tragically, no sooner had it been found than it was stolen.

Apart from the reorganisation of the atrium necessitated by the building of St Theodore to the west, the atrium was further disarranged by the construction of the south-west chapel during the sixth century. This not only blocked the western end of the south passageway but intruded on the southern Corinthian pillar of the porch and resulted in the demolition of three of the Ionic columns of the south portico of the atrium. It had its own tiny, very plain atrium, approached from within the chapel through a small off-centre doorway. The chancel occupied the whole of the apsidal end, across which there was placed the conventional screen. The doorway from the portico is now choked with sand and rubble, whilst the interior is full of fallen masonry and wildly overgrown. This is partly intentional, for when the Americans excavated this chapel they found a mosaic floor, and until it can be properly conserved it is better that it is recorded and then reburied. There are many cases of this happening in Jerash, and although it is a wise precaution one is impatient for the day when all the splendid mosaics within the city have been consolidated.

Opposite the north side of the Cathedral porch is the GLASS COURT. The

184

Fig. 113 The Fountain Court with the ruins of the Cathedral beyond.

walls are Roman, the court having served as a space between two properties of the classical period. It was, however, adapted to serve as a dependency of the Cathedral at the same time as the basilica was built. The original floor level of this small court was a little below that of the Fountain Court, and so steps were built to provide access. At the same time the wide opening giving into the atrium was made narrower. The chief interest of the Glass Court lay in its mosaics, which were laid when these adaptations were made. They are very fine – Kraeling dates them to the first half of the fourth century – but in the main they have been reburied to await consolidation and preservation.

To the left of the Glass Court is an opening in which there is a flight of steps leading up to a doorway (Fig 114). This is called the SARAPION PASSAGE after the inscription found here relating the name of Sarapion, son of Apollonius, who provided the money for an *andron* for the Temple of Artemis. It is still uncertain

185

Fig. 114 One of the stairways up from the Fountain Court. The left-hand flight leads to the Basilica of St Theodore, the right to the Sarapion Passage.

what is meant by an *andron*, but it seems likely that this adjunct to the Temple stood hereabouts, connecting perhaps in some way the Temple of Dionysus with that of the patron deity. The Passage led from the north portico of the Fountain Court to connect with a room which opened onto a street running down the south side of the Artemis Sanctuary to the Nymphaeum. The doorway is a triple opening, and it is assumed that through the sides access would have been gained to the roof of the north portico, from where one could look down into the Fountain Court. The northern side of the door frame has some good detailing.

At the top of the Passage, through a doorway which still carries its lintel, is a reconstructed vault under the south side of the Artemis Temenos, which now serves as a mosaic museum. Running west in front of the Museum is the STEPPED STREET (Fig. 115) which went down a natural depression between the Artemis Sanctuary and the Cathedral complex in the direction of the Nymphaeum. Only the western section has so far been excavated, although there are plans for its clearance eastwards as far as the Colonnade Street.

Tucked into the angle formed by the Sarapion Passage and the Stepped Street is an extensive complex of rooms which were excavated by the American Expedition in 1931. It is now much filled in and the layout is no longer clear. This was a public Baths built by Bishop Placcus in A.D. 454/55, according to an inscription found in its atrium.

It must be admitted that these BATHS OF PLACCUS are a meagre affair when

Fig. 115 The Stepped Street. On the left lay the Baths of Placcus.

compared with the two hugely grand establishments of the Roman period. But it is interesting that the idea of the Baths should have survived at all into the Byzantine period, with all the principal compartments such as *frigidarium*, *tepidarium*, *caldarium* (in this case *caldaria* for there were two hot rooms), *apodyteria* etc., still appearing on the plan. There were also an entrance portico onto the Stepped Street, an atrium and latrines. That these Baths should have been founded and erected by a bishop, close to, and indeed connected with, the principal ecclesiastical complex is noteworthy. As C. S. Fisher points out, 'They form a natural adjunct to the highly developed *domus ecclesiae*. . . .'* The Church was at the centre of life, and all activities revolved round it. The great ecclesiastical establishments often had a huge complex of buildings connected with the Church proper but which were not consecrated to liturgical use, such as schools, hospitals, hostels etc., which served the community. This centred virtually all activity into the

* C. S. Fisher, ex Kraeling's *Gerasa*.

187

Fig. 116 A conjectural reconstruction of the Fountain Court in its final form.

physical orbit of the Church: in this way early Christianity sought to regulate the secular as well as religious life of the faithful. It is not unnatural, therefore, that the Church should take under its wing the concept of the Baths.

The BASILICA OF ST THEODORE was constructed between A.D. 494 and 496, and its eastern apse was built out into the Fountain Court, necessitating the removal of the entire western portico of the atrium and the western ends of those on the north and south. The actual Fountain was linked to the end wall of the apse by a pair of arches forming a small porch set before the wall of the Fountain, which was then given a canopy. On either side of the apse stairways descended into the courtyard (Fig. 114). It is the remains of this final arrangement (Fig. 116) which we see today.

Gone are the north and south porticos, and only the stumps of the Cathedral porch remain except for its southern pillar. There is now no trace of the canopy over the Fountain, and the screen which enclosed its attached porch is only indicated by grooves in the paving-stones. Nonetheless, the polygonal apse of St. Theodore still thrusts forward like the bow of a great ship, its plain, well-made walls capped by a bold string-course cornice, giving an impression of great strength (Fig. 117). Above, on the upper level, the two rows of columns of the

Fig. 117   The Basilica of St Theodore from the Fountain Court.

interior fall back in a steep and dramatic perspective. The lie of the land plays an important part in the arrangement of this complex, for the Cathedral stood on a terrace above the Cardo, whilst St Theodore stood on yet another terrace higher still. Like the Cathedral, St Theodore was approached through north and south lateral passageways from the east (Fig. 118), in addition to the three main entrances through an atrium to the west: present-day visitors usually reach the basilica via the north steps in the Fountain Court (Fig. 114) and the north passageway.

These passageways appear to have been supplementary to the principal eastern entrances, which were through small lateral rooms on either side of the apse. The basilica is slightly smaller than the Cathedral but the style is more developed. It was started under Bishop Aeneas in A.D. 494. The nave is divided from the aisles by

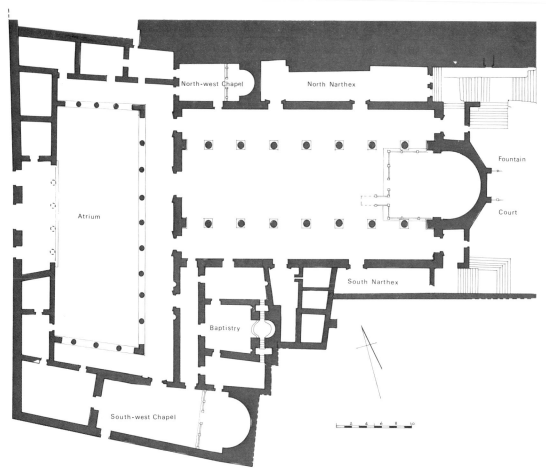

Fig. 118 Plan of St Theodore's and its dependent buildings (*after A. G. Buchanan and C. S. Fisher*).

colonnades of seven Corinthian columns, which carried arches over which plain walls rose to an open timber roof. The floor of both the nave and aisles was laid with coloured limestone flags arranged in simple geometric patterns, a little of which survives. The chancel extended one and a half bays into the body of the church and was screened off in the conventional way; traces of this can be seen together with the siting of the *ambo* projecting into the nave. The eastern end was a deep apse, in which there were the usual two rows of seats flanking the central chair. The altar under its canopy was set directly under the arch fronting the semi-dome of the apse. In its heyday, St Theodore's Church must have been magnificent, particularly because of its mosaics which encrusted the high walls above the colonnades and in the semi-dome, and because of the marble cladding of its walls (Fig. 36).

The western end had three doors, a central one into the nave and one each into the aisles, all communicating directly into the atrium. The lintel of the central doorway is a re-used section of the peristyle architrave of the Temple of Artemis (see page 163); further sections can be identified elsewhere in the atrium. There were also three doors on the north side, the eastern two admitting into the north passageway which, as in the Cathedral, may have been a narthex. The remaining door to the west led into a small apsidal chapel, which had a good mosaic floor of an elaborate geometric pattern. The south aisle wall had four doors in it which admitted into a series of rooms, three of which had mosaic floors. The western three of these formed a Baptistry with a pool-font fitted very neatly into the apse of the central room. The pool was approached down narrow sets of steps from the two flanking rooms. This arrangement was a later adaptation of a previous chapel whose floor was lower. This floor was raised at the time of the adaptation, leaving the pool-font at the original level. West of the Baptistry was a corridor, paved with mosaics and walled with veneers of marble or limestone, which led to a large chapel or small subsidiary church known as the South-west Chapel.

All these dependent buildings are now overgrown, with much of the detail which excavation laid bare now blurred or completely hidden. The Baptistry in particular is in a tragic condition. It is one thing to re-cover mosaics so as to preserve them, quite another to allow the ruins to fall into still greater neglect.

To the west of the basilica and the Baptistry wing was a long atrium with colonnaded porticos on the north, east and south sides, all of which had mosaic floors. Some of the Ionic columns are believed to have been removed here from the west portico of the Fountain Court when that was dismantled to accommodate the apse of St Theodore. There were three doors in the western wall leading into the north/south street outside. The wide central doorway still stands but the side doors were blocked up at a later date (Fig. 119). The basilica and its dependencies were evidently ruined by an earthquake, for when it was excavated in 1928 all the elements of the structure were found exactly where they had fallen. After this destruction the church was abandoned, and the ruins of the atrium were taken over by squatters who built-in extraneous walls.

Beyond the rooms behind the north colonnade of the atrium lay a complex mass of buildings containing rooms of all shapes and sizes. These were excavated towards the end of 1931 and proved to be what Kraeling termed the 'Clergy House'; accommodation for the resident priests attached to St Theodore. They are historically interesting but of no great importance architecturally, nor of any particular beauty. They have to a great extent been re-covered.

Ruined and denuded of its former magnificence though it is, the whole complex of the Cathedral, the Fountain Court and St Theodore's is one of the greatest interest and significance. Not only do the buildings cover a long period but, as Kraeling has pointed out, 'in disposition the completed group corresponds closely to the original disposition of the buildings round the Holy Sepulchre in Jerusalem.

Fig. 119   The atrium of St Theodore's. Note that the doors on either side of the central opening have been blocked up.

The portico on the street and the great stairway at Gerasa correspond with the propylaea and the eastern atrium at Jerusalem; the Cathedral with the Martyrium of Constantine; the Fountain Court with the Second Atrium and the Calvary, and St Theodore with the Anastasis. Even the two baptistries in the two places occupy approximately the same position . . . the resemblance between the two dispositions is so close as to leave no doubt that in its final form the Gerasa plan was deliberately modelled on the Jerusalem pattern, and that it now shows better than any other extant group of structures what the buildings in Jerusalem once looked like.'

It is well to remember that the level ground outside the atrium of St Theodore's was the site of a major excavation which extended as far north as the wall of the Artemis Temenos and south past the limits of the basilica. Having completed work on the churches, attention was turned to clearing the Temenos of the Temple of Artemis, but there was such a huge volume of infill that a dumping area had to be designated before any earth could be moved. Such dumps have to be carefully sited because random or careless dumping runs the risk of burying even deeper some hidden structure which might in time prove to be of great significance. A 'careful survey' was therefore made, and it was decided that the area west of the atrium of St Theodore would be the best site. Just to be sure that nothing of importance lay below this shallow depression, the area was excavated. With the exception of a temple structure, termed Temple 'C', nothing of real significance was found.

Temple 'C' may be dated to the middle of the second century, although no inscriptions were found on site relating to it. Fisher and Kraeling have raised the possibility that it was an Heroön, a shrine raised to the memory of dead heroes, for its plan and layout are remarkably similar to the Heroön at Calydon in Aetolia. The funerary associations of Temple 'C' helped to support this contention. The rest of the remains proved to be a complex of minor structures of a principally domestic type. All the information from the excavation was meticulously recorded and published in the *Annual of the American Schools of Oriental Research*, 1931. Thus despite the fact that the site was then covered with the infill from part of the Artemis Temenos, we have full knowledge of what is there, and this is available to future scholars. It was an important excavation nonetheless because of the light it shed on the development of pottery types and on the early history of that vicinity.

Almost due west lie the 'Three Churches' of SS. Cosmas and Damian, St John the Baptist, and St George. All three were built between A.D. 529–533 as an integrated triple block (Fig. 120) and shared a common western atrium. The CHURCH OF SS. COSMAS AND DAMIAN is the northern of the three, dedicated to twin brothers who although born in Arabia studied medicine together in Syria and became famous doctors. Their charity was famous and extended to never charging a fee to any of their patients. During the religious persecution in Cilicia in the early fourth century they were martyred and became, after St Luke, the patron saints of physicians. Their church in Jerash was constructed on basilical lines, with a wide central nave flanked by north and south aisles, and a wide apse at the eastern end. The divisions between the three parts were, however, not pillars but solid piers which would have given a much more massive and muscular appearance to the interior. Other than perhaps for capitals for the piers and a cornice, there would have been little in the way of architectural decorative treatment. Very little now remains of the structure: the piers are but stumps, there are no signs of the row of seats in the apse, and only the base of the chancel screen. There are traces in the wall of the north aisle of a pillared recess which probably formed some kind of narthex. The west wall still stands to a certain height, with three doorways in it giving into the nave and side aisles: whilst two further doors in the wall of the south aisle opened into the adjacent Church of St John the Baptist. The aisles also terminated in doorways, the one in the north aisle into a plain square room, the other in the south aisle into a small tripartite Baptistry shared with St John's. It was a simple arrangement with an almost basic spatial concept.

Nonetheless, the interior would have been very fine, decorated with painted plaster on the walls and glittering glass mosaics in the semi-dome over the apse. It is the mosaic on the floor which today is the chief glory. As one approaches along the north side, one has a fine view down onto this (Fig. 121). The mosaics (see also page 99) extended across the interior but the aisles were treated in a much

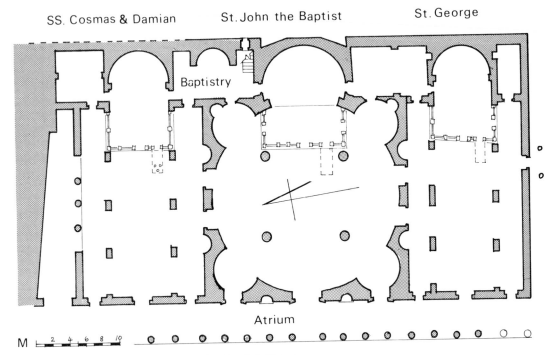

SS. Cosmas & Damian   St. John the Baptist   St. George

Baptistry

M |—2—4—6—8—10|

Atrium

Fig. 120 Plan of the 'Three Churches' (*after C. S. Fisher*).

Fig. 121 The mosaic floor of SS. Cosmas and Damian; the finest preserved mosaic pavement in Jerash.

simpler way to the nave, with a continuous panel of a repetitive small-scale motif on a plain ground held within a border in which swastikas alternated with squares containing a cross or a knot design. Between the piers were panels of varying geometric designs. The cross and swastika border was then repeated to contain the design of the nave mosaic. This consisted of a mathematical progression of squares and diamonds: the diamonds, which were larger than the squares, contained a dazzling array of geometric patterns, whilst the squares held pictures of birds, fowl and animals with smaller squares set between them in which were 'box perspectives' (Fig. 40).

Of particular interest is the panel which lies in front of the chancel screen. In the centre of this is a long inscription contained in a separately framed panel called a *tabula ansata*, which relates the dedication of the church in early A.D. 533, under the patronage of Bishop Paul. On either side of this are portraits of the donors, Theodore and his wife Georgia (Fig. 122). He stands on the left, dressed in his official vestments as a *paramonarius*, or one who was in charge of a church structure, holding in his right hand, stretched across his body, an incense-burner. Georgia stands on the right, under where the *ambo* would have stood on three slender columnettes, with her hands upraised in adoration. Her cloak is tied with a sash and brooch, whilst round her neck is a necklace; earrings and a hairnet augment her attire.

There are additional donor portraits and inscriptions in the first row of diamonds, the one on the north being John, son of Astricius, next a text which records the gift of the Tribune by Dagistheus, one of Justinian's generals, and lastly, after a geometric vine-trellis diamond, is Calloeonistus with his thick mop of hair and knee-length boots. He is shown, as is John, son of Astricius, carrying a basket symbolising the act of giving.

The remaining squares depict a fascinating array of both domestic and wild animals, which are endearingly portrayed with much vitality. The geometric designs of the diamonds are bewildering in their variety and the brilliance of their colouring. Of all the mosaics in the churches of Jerash, this seems to have been the only one to survive the iconoclastic fury evoked by the decree of Caliph Yazid II (A.D. 720–724) which ordered the destruction of all human and animal images and pictures in Moslem lands. It is possible that by that date the church had long since ceased to function, probably because it had already collapsed and become full of debris which obscured the offending figurative subjects.

The survival of this mosaic is a happy chance, for it is a splendid expanse of finely controlled and executed design which, as Kraeling rightly points out, 'gives the best opportunity of judging the original effect of the ensemble in such a pavement'.

To the south, through two doors in the south aisle, lay the circular CHURCH OF

Fig. 122   The donors of the SS. Cosmas and Damian mosaic: Theodore (*left*) and his wife, Georgia (*right*).

ST JOHN THE BAPTIST. The plan of this (Fig. 120) is obviously based on that of the cathedral at Bosra, although on a much smaller scale: the cathedral at Bosra was only built twenty years before St John's was started. The circle was set in a square, with four deep horseshoe exedras at the corners, and a spacious apse at the eastern side. Four re-used second-century Corinthian columns formed a square at the centre of the circle and almost certainly carried a lantern, through the windows of which the church was lighted; there may have been an additional window over the west doorway. There were semi-domes over the exedras and the apse, and these were decorated with glass mosaics. The walls were sheathed in veneers of marble. As usual there were three doorways on the western side, a big central one (Fig. 123) which still has its massive vousoirs, and the two side ones which admit into the two western exedras. The chancel screen extended out from the apse up to the eastern pair of centre columns. In front of the screen, beneath the lantern, was a mosaic inscription which related that the church was erected under Bishop Paul and was paid for with benefactions by Theodore, foster-son of Thomas.

Apart from the singular interest of the *martyrium* plan which is unique in Jerash, it is the floor mosaics which provide the principal feature of the church today. It is much damaged, with only some substantial fragments surviving. Some of these, including the representations of cities (see page 99) and the exotic candalabrum from one of the exedras, have been removed to the Museum. Some fragments of the acanthus rinceau and ribbon border (Fig. 39), which followed the line of the wall right round the church, are still in place and have been consolidated to prevent

196

Fig. 123 The circular interior of the Church of St John the Baptist.

further damage (Fig. 124). However, it was the pictorial mosaics which provided
the main interest. In them, set in the segments round the central square, were
representations of cities or places of religious veneration. They were linked
together by a river scene (see page 99). There are many parts of this mosaic
missing and others mutilated beyond recognition, but Alexandria (now in the
Museum) with its name written over it can be seen (Fig. 38), whilst Pharos,
Canopus and Memphis have been identified. Of particular interest in respect of St
John's itself was the picture (also in the Museum) of the Shrine of St John and St

197

Fig. 124 A section of the acanthus rinceau and ribbon border in St John's.

Cyrus at Menuthis (identified by Crowfoot), which shows a square building surmounted by an octagonal lantern (Fig. 125) probably very much like the one that would have crowned this church. Apart from its great interest, this picture has a charming, almost domestic, touch in the way the fine linen curtains have been knotted: there was no such thing as curtain track and so they were tied in this way to admit more light and air, a phenomenon one can still see not infrequently.

Behind the north-east exedra was a small Baptistry which also could be entered from the south aisle of SS. Cosmas and Damian. This was originally a small chapel but later converted into a baptistry when the pool-font was let into the floor and a flight of steps built up the internal south wall to connect with a bridge which spanned the street running along the outside of the east wall. The baptistry floor was paved with red and white marble, with a large cross within a circle laid in front of the pool-font. This baptistry is now in a rather sad and neglected state but could quite easily be put in good order.

Another room on the corresponding side of St John's apse, approached through the south-east exedra, also gave access to the basilical church to the south. This was the CHURCH OF ST GEORGE. In plan and internal arrangement (Fig. 120) it is very similar to SS. Cosmas and Damian, although it is a fraction smaller. Here again it is the mosaic floor which is the main point of interest. This has suffered

Fig. 125   The 'St John and St Cyrus' pictorial mosaic from St John's.

badly both from the effects of time and the hand of man. The design of the nave mosaic was a sophisticated composition of elongated hexagons and octagons tied together by a web of strands which knot into swastikas in groups of four round the octagons (Fig. 126). This refined and infinitely pleasing design has suffered serious damage, but there are plans for its conservation. It suffered at the hands of the iconoclasts, for in each octagon and hexagon there were originally figurative representations. These were smashed out but were patched in plain tesserae: it was a rather clumsy repair job, for the inserted tesserae were larger than the original ones, and no attempt was made to reinstate the geometric pattern where this was damaged. It is, however, an interesting example of iconoclastic damage.

By the time of the Moslem conquests the two other churches were probably out of commission, and it has been suggested that for a while St George's served as the Cathedral of Gerasa. This would have been after the destruction of the mother church by earthquake. St George's itself had to be repaired at intervals. Subsidence of the south wall caused havoc with the mosaic floor in the south aisle. The mosaics in both aisles are unrelated schematically to that in the nave, and consisted of a more orthodox square and diamond pattern along the lines of SS. Cosmas and Damian (Fig. 127). Here again one sees the patching-up of the squares after the iconoclasts had gone.

199

Fig. 126   The nave mosaic of the Church of St George.

All three churches had the same atrium, the east colonnade of which is the only one to survive (Fig. 128). It was paved with a simple mosaic floor, of which only a fragment remains. The pillars are a motley assortment of varying sizes, having been robbed from older structures, like most of the building materials of the churches themselves.

On high ground due north of the three churches, overlooking the Temple of Artemis, is the SYNAGOGUE CHURCH. There was on this site a building, the atrium of which may be dated to the third or fourth century. This was probably a synagogue which was in use for a long period before being turned into a church between A.D. 530 and 531. This change of use made a nonsense of the plan (Fig. 129), for the atrium was at the east rather than at the west. This was quite reasonable for a synagogue, for these were oriented on the Temple at Jerusalem; in Jordan this would have been towards the west, and so the atrium was rightly to the east. When converted into a church the basic plan remained the same but the orientation had to be switched round. In the change the west colonnade of the atrium was demolished to make way for an apse. The chancel thus lay over the vestibule of the earlier synagogue, covering in the process a mosaic floor depicting incidents in the Flood: a procession of animals two by two. Further mosaics from the synagogue were covered when the church floor was laid; these earlier mosaics are now very fragmentary, including one giving the name of benefactors who paid

200

Fig. 127 The north aisle mosaic of St George's. A good example of repair work after iconoclastic defacement of images in the squares. Note the larger tesserae used to patch the broken panels.

for the repair of the synagogue at an unknown date. The church was paved with a geometric pattern mosaic similar to that in SS. Cosmas and Damian. In the western end, where in the synagogue would have been housed the Ark of the Covenant, there was created a porch covering a single door into the body of the church.

The pulvinated pedestals, on which stand the pillars not only of the nave but of the atrium (Fig. 130), are curious but not unknown in Jerash and other cities in Galilee: the order was Corinthian. The church was dedicated in A.D. 531 during the episcopate of Bishop Paul, a period of great church-building in Jerash, which coincided with a phase of Jewish persecution in line with Justinian's anti-Jewish repressions. It has been argued that the area about the Synagogue Church was the Jewish quarter of the ancient city. Due to its exposed situation it has suffered badly; also the slope of the hillside to the south has been responsible for the disappearance of the wall on that side of the building. Nonetheless, the lines of the structure can be followed quite easily.

South of the Synagogue Church and west of the three churches lie the ruins of BISHOP GENESIUS'S CHURCH. This was the last church to be built, as far as we know, in Jerash. It was constructed in A.D. 611, just before the Persian invasion, by Bishop Genesius. This date is given in an inscription in the mosaic floor.

The plan of the church is straightforward but there are some interesting

Fig. 128 The eastern side of the atrium of the 'Three Churches'.

developments displayed in it (Fig. 131). The apse stands unattended by lateral chambers, whilst the chancel is treated as a separate architectural entity within the overall design. The structure is basilical, with colonnades dividing the nave from the side aisles. However, these colonnades stopped on reaching the chancel arch. In place of them there was an arch on either side of the chancel before the curve of the apse was reached. These arches led into north and south side chapels, each furnished with a small niche in their eastern walls. The screen of these chapels runs in line with that of the chancel, which does not break forward into the body of the church in front of the apse: this is the only instance in Jerash of an arrangement which was to become common practice in Greek churches.

Although the western end has never been completely cleared, the apse at the eastern end presents one of the clearest examples of the arrangement of a chancel existing in Jerash. Clearly visible are the two rows of seats for the clergy, with a central flight of steps leading up to the bishop's chair. The altar was placed immediately in front of this within the apse, an unusual development for it is

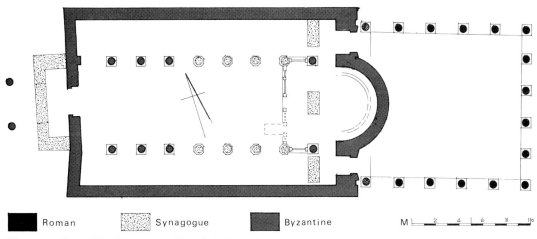

Roman   Synagogue   Byzantine   M

Fig. 129   Plan of the Synagogue Church (*after C. S. Fisher*).

Fig. 130   The ruins of the Synagogue Church.

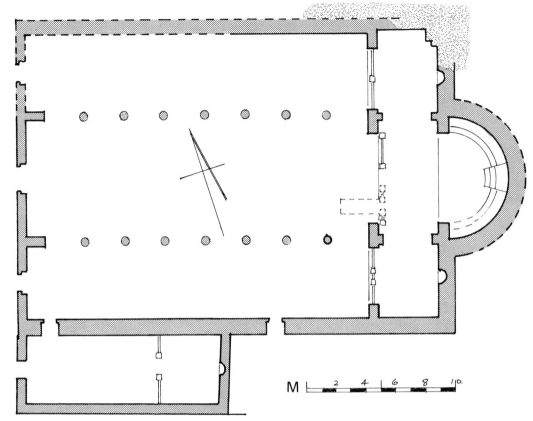

Fig. 131   Plan of Bishop Genesius's Church (*after C. S. Fisher*).

Fig. 132   The ruins of Bishop Genesius's Church.

commonly located further forward. In front of this, below the chancel arch, are the remains of the screen's foundations. The *ambo* was in its usual place south of the central axis, protruding into the nave. The eastern end of the church indicates, as Crowfoot pointed out, the increasingly elaborate ritual of the Church for which accommodation had to be made. Bishop Genesius's Church is important because it is clearly pointing in the direction of most Orthodox churches today.

The walls of the apse were probably sheathed in marble, whilst the full width of the chancel was paved with mosaics. Both the nave and the aisles were similarly laid, but little now survives. The north chapel was paved with coloured stone, and this is still visible. The mosaic in the south chapel is also visible, regrettably because it is now disintegrating into a distressing condition. It is a simple design, with a Greek key border containing a diaper field on which are diamond shapes, with an amphora holding the centre of the panel.

Southwards, following the line of the city wall which is close at hand, is the CHURCH OF SS. PETER AND PAUL. This formed the principal structure in a complex of buildings which may have included the nearby Mortuary Church. Little of the complex has been uncovered, and only the eastern section of the colonnaded atrium has been revealed. From this the church was entered through the usual three doors into an orthodox basilica (Fig. 133). Colonnades of re-used second-century columns divided the interior into a central nave and two aisles, all three terminating at eastern apses. The walls were plastered and painted, except in the apse where there was marble sheathing.

An inscription in the mosaic floor of the nave relates that the church was dedicated to SS. Peter and Paul, and the name of the founder, Anastasius, who is believed to have been the successor to the See of Gerasa after Bishop Paul. No date is given but the construction may be dated to A.D. 540.

It is the internal arrangement which is of interest, with its two complete rows of apsidal seats and centrally placed chair. Immediately in front of this stood a Calvary, the base block of which, with its three rectangular slots, was found in place and is still on site (Fig. 134). In front of this, in the middle of the chancel, stood the altar. The line of the screen is set well back towards the apses in the side aisles, but it breaks forward to a full two bays into the nave. There were no gates through this screen in the aisles, only one in a central position before the altar. The east end of both aisles is treated architecturally as a side chapel, but there is no physical communion between them and the aisles proper. Instead they became lateral extensions of the chancel. Here again there was a moving towards the liturgical layout which was to be seen fully developed at Bishop Genesius's Church.

This church contained an important series of floor mosaics which covered the main body of the nave and both aisles. These have been re-covered. Even so there

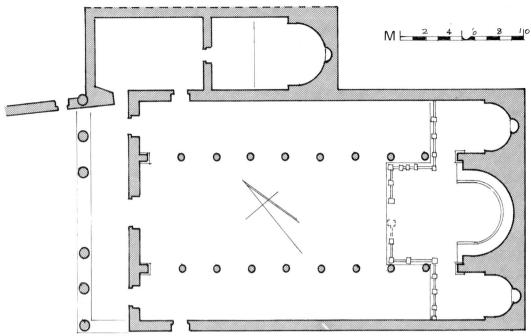

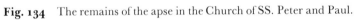

Fig. 133 Plan of the Church of SS. Peter and Paul (*after C. S. Fisher*).

Fig. 134 The remains of the apse in the Church of SS. Peter and Paul.

are clear analogies here with the mosaics in St John the Baptist, and it is considered that, although slightly later in date, they are by the same team of craftsmen. The principal comparison lies in the portrayal of cities and the rich acanthus rinceau border.

The MORTUARY CHURCH lies a short distance to the south. It has deteriorated since excavation in 1929 and is now full of rubble, earth and a tangle of undergrowth (Fig. 135). Its lines can be made out, with the curve of the apse adorned with a tall niche and a stretch of its south wall. This was called a 'single hall' church, i.e. one without aisles. It was built into the hillside on which stands the city wall, and has thus been protected to some extent from the elements.

Beneath the accumulated rubble are the remains of a fascinating mosaic floor, in which geometric patterning assumes a new dimension somewhat akin to strapwork. It is fearfully mutilated – partly by iconoclasts and partly by time – but is nonetheless very fine.

Gerald Lankester Harding was a man who loved Jerash and wished to be buried there. A simple white stone bearing his name marks the place near SS. Peter and Paul. His death on 11th February, 1979, was a tragic loss to Jordanian archaeology and epigraphy, for no one had done more to care for its monuments and antiquities, and to draw international attention to them. He had been responsible for an enormous amount of excavation through his position as Director of the Department of Antiquities, and it was he who initiated the *Annual* of the Department which is still a major archaeological publication. He worked with some of the greatest names in archaeology, not least with Pére Roland de Vaux with whom he excavated the Scroll Caves at Qumran. He was a prolific writer and became widely respected for his scholarship. His book *The Antiquities of Jordan* introduced him to the wide general public through its readable and thoroughly scholarly handling of such an enormous subject. After his retirement, with great tact, he went to live in Lebanon but returned to Jordan in 1976 and spent his last years in the land he loved so deeply.

ZONE V

The Watergate and the Valley Garden, the East Baths, and the Procopius Church. The Reservoir and Festival Theatre at Birketein, and the Tomb of Germanus.

Where the South Wall crosses the River Chrysorhoas it descends the sides of the wadi very steeply. At this point the river splashes over a waterfall, and it was over this that the WATERGATE was built. This consisted of two towers set obliquely to the stream so that the water was forced into a narrow chanel before going over the

Fig. 135 The Mortuary Church.

falls. Not much of this now remains, although stretches of the wall on the eastern side are still evident.

Below the falls the river meanders through a lushly green valley encircled by voluptuous trees and planted with orchards (Fig. 136). The ruins of a Turkish (?) house with its graceful arch add a point of interest in a way that a Gothick folly might diversify an English landscape park: Brown would certainly have thought that this site had 'capabilities'. This is referred to as the VALLEY GARDEN, and there are proposals to create here a place for quiet recreation not only for tourists but for the whole city.

As though stranded in the middle of the bustling new city stand the colossal EAST BATHS (Fig. 137). These were considerably larger than the West Baths already discussed. The present ruins are only a fragment of the original complex. The early third century has been suggested (see page 51) for their construction. The plan was laid out on the same principle as the huge orthodox structures of Rome: by any standard this was a large and majestic building. Most of it is now covered by the new city, and traffic screeches round close to the towering walls of finely laid masonry and lofty arches. Occasionally some other fragment of the

Fig. 136 The Valley Garden. In the shadow of the trees is a cliff over which the river Chrysorhoas falls.

vanished complex can be seen erupting strangely, almost violently, from the crumbling walls of a deserted property nearby.

High on the hillside of the southern part of the new city lie the scanty remains of the PROCOPIUS CHURCH. An inscription in the mosaic floor in front of the chancel screen relates that the work was supervised by Procopius under the patronage of Bishop Paul and a deacon and *paramonarius* called Saul. The dedication is not given but the date A.D. 526–527 is shown, making this the earliest sixth-century church in Gerasa. What strikes one is the close similarity of its basilical plan (Fig. 138) to that of SS. Peter and Paul: indeed, there are only twelve or thirteen years between them. The three apsidal ends are substantially the same, as is the arrangement of the chancel screen, except that here there were gates through from the aisles. Excavation revealed not only the colonnades of the nave but also the seating in the apse, which conforms to the orthodox pattern. The apse retained traces of plaster painted to look like veined red marble. This has been buried again and lies under the embankment supporting the road above. Little of the basilica is now to be seen, with only the stumps of three columns of the north colonnade showing; the positions of the rest are marked by their pedestals (Fig. 139).

Fig. 137 The colossal East Baths, now located in the centre of the new city of Jerash.

This church had an exceptionally magnificent mosaic floor which was amongst the finest in Jerash. Even though it was mutilated by the iconoclasts and subsequently repaired, it is a dazzling collection of designs. Little of the nave floor remains, except for a fragment of the strongly formed acanthus rinceau border and the inscription *tabula ansata*. Between the pillars there were geometric panels, with no two of the same design. Knot and coil 'strapwork' predominated. In the north aisle the design was a complicated geometric progression in which octagons contained figurative representations (smashed out by the iconoclasts) and elongated hexagons are tied together in a closely knit interplay of strands; there are analogies here with St George's (see page 199). A rondel of almost Celtic complexity was placed one-third the way up the design.

The north and south chancel chapels had a single composition mosaic filling the entire apse; they are like fine oriental carpets. The one in the north chapel was a geometric design of diamonds tied together by interlocking straps: this is perhaps the best preserved of them all, partly due to its protected position and partly the fact that there were never any figurative elements in it. There is a finely drawn meander border almost entirely intact. The south chapel had a less elaborate pattern, a guilloche border containing a diaper in which are set alternating rosettes and diamond-shaped fleurons. A circular medallion was placed on the central axis and was surrounded by a meander border: this is now damaged, as is the south-western section of the main field.

The south aisle had probably the grandest and most energetic design; a series of large octagons on their points, each surrounded by squares leading off into diamonds before linking up with the next repetition of this scheme. Each octagon, square and diamond contained inventive exercises in knot-work, all calculated with great precision. There are here strong similarities with the mosaic floor of the now lost church of the Prophets, Apostles and Martyrs.

It is well that this rich collection of mosaics is being kept buried, but when its conservation can be undertaken it will provide an additional attraction to the eastern half of Jerash, along with the East Walls set in their 'green belt'.

A short distance north of the city lies Birketein, which in Arabic means 'double pool'. It is set in a fertile valley amid gently rolling hill country; a place of trees, sunlight and quiet (colour plate 4b). In ancient times this area was a popular place for a suburban villa, quite apart from its religious attraction. It was approached by a processional way leading from the North Gate. In antiquity the hillsides were probably well-covered with forests and delightfully cool after the heat of the city. The area is still very attractive, and much planting has further enhanced its amenities: it also has some important antiquities which are well worth visiting.

It was at Birketein that the notorious Festivals of Maiuma were celebrated. This is the only site where an inscription tells with certainty that the precinct and structures were designed for these celebrations. Elsewhere it has always been a process of deduction. Birketein is, therefore, of singular importance. The Maiuma was probably of Phoenician origin and was a nautical festival which involved, amongst other activities, the ritual submersion of naked women. By the third century, however, the festivities seem to have degenerated into rather promiscuous affairs resulting in the eventual prohibition of the event. The Festival was particu-larly condemned by the early Christians. Nonetheless, in A.D. 396, Honorius and Arcadius repealed the prohibition on condition that the Festival was conducted along morally proper lines and that "it followed chaste customs". The sensuality of warm, sunlit water seems, however, to have been irresistible, for in A.D. 399 it was again banned. It is interesting that, in A.D. 535, Christian Gerasa revived the pagan festival but in an acceptable new guise. As with the Dionysus wine miracle, so does the Church seem to have converted the Maiuma into a Christian 'harvest festival', for, as McCown has pointed out, it 'closely resembles many features of medieval and modern harvest-home and Thanksgiving festivals in Europe and America.'*

* C. C. McCown, *Journal of the Palestine Oriental Society*, 1936.

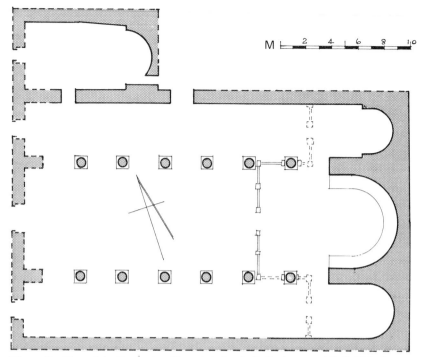

Fig. 138   Plan of the Procopius Church (*after A. G. Buchanan and C. S. Fisher*).

Fig. 139   The ruins of the Procopius Church.

Fig. 140   The great double reservoir at Birketein. It was here that the notorious Maiumas Festivals took place.

The great pool (Fig. 140) is rectangular and divided into two parts by a barrier wall. It is forty-three and a half metres wide, eighty-eight and a half metres long and some three metres deep. Originally, a colonnade, which can be dated to A.D. 209, ran along the western side framing the ancient processional way (Map 4). This was one of the main reservoirs for ancient Gerasa; indeed the Nymphaeum and the Fountain Court are known to have been supplied from here.

At the south-west corner of the pool stood the FESTIVAL THEATRE, built into the side of the fir-clad hill. It was not very big but was well made, having a large *cavea* probably almost double the size of what now remains. This faced the stage across a semi-circular *orchestra*. This *auditorium* was approached through vaulted passageways north and south, which also gave access to the stage. These passageways debouched into the orchestra by way of a fine arch (Fig. 141): access to the four lower level *cunei* was up steps on either side facing the stage, with an additional flight in the centre of the podium wall. There is no trace of any *vomitoria* but these may have been, if they existed, created only for the now vanished upper level.

213

Tomb of Germanus

Festival Theatre

Gate

Map 4 Birketein. There are now few remains of the Gate or of the colonnade along the west side of the double reservoir.

Fig. 141   The Festival Theatre at Birketein.

The *scaenae frons* was not furnished with the usual triple entries, for the back of it stood high above the processional way. The theatre was excavated in 1931 by the American Expedition and is still in good condition: mercifully it has not been over-restored. Its setting is delightful.

A short way up the valley beyond the pool, along a track through woods, stands the ruin of the TOMB OF GERMANUS. This was built along the lines of a 'Temple Tomb', with a square cella entered from beneath a portico of four pillars on its western side. The carving of the capitals to these pillars is in keeping with the Antonine period, that suggested by McCown for its construction. It has never been excavated and now lies in a tumbled mass of masonry down the gentle slope (Fig. 142). Three of the pillars of the portico are still standing, carrying their entablature. But all is ruin, romantic and moral, with the sarcophagus toppled, lidless and

215

Fig. 142   The ruins of the Tomb of Germanus: *sic transit gloriae mundi.*

empty to the sky. Virtually all of its elements are still there lying where they fell, embowered in thistles and the wiry grasses of the high hills. It would be not too great a job to reinstate this elegant structure. Germanus, son of Molpon, was a centurion probably of an auxiliary cohort, who paid for the rebuilding of the Temple of Zeus Epicarpius (the fruit-bearer) which is known to have stood near Birketein.

Germanus was evidently both pious and public-spirited, and it is well that his tomb is at Birketein, for here there is that intangible, quiet, feeling of the present past. By thinking of him, a man who knew the streets and sanctuaries of Gerasa in their glory, we can perhaps recapture in present-day Jerash some of the vanished sense of splendour and thrill, as we thread our way through the silent testaments of history and know those selfsame streets and sanctuaries.

216

Glossary of Architectural Terms

Adyton   The inner sanctuary, holy of holies, reached from the cella of a temple or shrine.

Agora   Large open place of public assembly.

Apse   Demi-domed semicircular or polygonal termination, usually to a chancel or chapel.

Architrave   The lowest of the three main divisions of an Entablature; also, the moulded frame surrounding a door or window.

Atrium   A courtyard, usually open air, completely or in part surrounded by a pillared, covered portico.

Cavea   Semicircular auditorium of a theatre.

Cella   The main body or room of a temple.

Cornice   The top, projecting, section of an Entablature.

Cunei   Blocks of seats in an auditorium.

Entablature   The upper part of an Order, placed usually above and connecting columns, consisting of Cornice, Frieze and Architrave.

Exedra   An open, rectangular or semicircular recess.

Frieze   The middle division of an Entablature, usually decorated but sometimes left plain.

Intercolumnation   The space between two adjacent columns.

Nymphaeum   Literally, a temple of the Nymphs, but applied to pleasurable places containing flowers, statues and, most particularly, fountains and pools of water.

Orchestra   The paved, usually semicircular area between the stage and the auditorium of a Roman theatre.

Pediment   The low-pitched gable end to a classical building, delineated on all three sides by the cornice.

Peristyle   The colonnade round the inside of a courtyard or room, but also used to describe the 'peripteral' colonnade round the outside of a structure.

Pilaster   A shallow rectangular face of a column attached to a wall and projecting only slightly from it.

Podium   A platform on which a temple or other building stood.

Propylaea   A stately entrance to a temple precinct or palace.

Scaenae frons   The wall at the back of the stage in a theatre, containing the principal entrances onto the stage.

Temenos   A sacred enclosure or precinct.

Tesserae   Small cubes of glass, stone, ceramics or marble used in mosaics.

Tetrakionia   A structure consisting of four pavilions, usually with, or supported by, columns.

Tetrapylon   Correctly, a four-way gate, but more loosely a tall structure, containing four gateways, intended to demarcate or decorate.

Vomitoria   Passages for entrance and exit, usually applied in the context of a theatre or ampitheatre.

Selected Bibliography

Avi-Yonah, M., and Stern, E., *Encyclopedia of Archaeological Excavations in the Holy Land*, Oxford, 1978

Bietenhard, H., *Die Dekapolis von Pompeius bis Trajan*, Frankfurt, 1963

Brunnöw, R. E., and Domaszewski, A., *Die Provincia Arabia*, Strasburg, 1904–9

Buckingham, J. S., *Travels in Palestine, through the Countries of Bashan and Gilead*, London, 1821

Burckhardt, J. L., *Travels in Syria and the Holy Land*, London, 1822.

Butler, H. C., *Ancient Architecture in Syria*, Princeton, 1907

Conder, C. R., *The Survey of Eastern Palestine*, London, 1883

——*Tent Work in Palestine*, London, 1879

Greek Anthology, The, translation by W. R. Paton, London, 1916

Greenhalgh, P., *Pompey, the Roman Alexander*, London, 1980

Hammond, N. G. L., *Alexander the Great*, London, 1981

Harding, G. L., *The Antiquities of Jordan*, Lutterworth, 1974

Hengel, M., *Judaism and Hellenism: Studies in their Encounter in Palestine during the Early Hellenistic Period*, Philadelphia, 1974

Holland, J., *Imperium Romanum*, London, 1979

Irby, C. L., and Mangles, J., *Travels in Egypt and Nubia, Syria and the Holy Land*, London, 1832

Jones, A. H. M., *The Later Roman Empire*, Oxford, 1964

—— *The Cities of the Eastern Roman Provinces*, Oxford, 1971

Josephus, *Jewish Antiquities*, ed Ralph Marcus, London, 1937

——*Jewish Wars*, ed H. Thackeray, London, 1927

Kempinski, A., and Avi-Yonah, M., *Archaeologia Mundi* Geneva, 1979

Kraeling, C. H., *Gerasa: City of the Decapolis*, New Haven, 1938

Krautheimer, R., *Early Christian and Byzantine Architecture*, Harmondsworth, 1965

Laborde, Léon de, *Voyage de la Syrie*, Paris, 1837

Lyttelton, M., *Baroque Architecture in Classical Antiquity*, London, 1974

Merrill, S., *East of the Jordan*, London, 1881

McCown, C. C., *The Ladder of Progress in Palestine*, London, 1943

Parker, S. T., 'The Decapolis Reviewed', *JBL*, Los Angeles, 1975

BIBLIOGRAPHY

Pliny (The Elder), *Natural History*, ed H. Rackham, London, 1942

Pliny (The Younger), *Letters and Panegyricus*, ed Betty Radice, London, 1969

Robinson, E., *Later Biblical Researches in Palestine*, London, 1857

Rostovtzeff, M., *Caravan Cities*, Oxford, 1932

—— *Social and Economic History of the Roman Empire*, Oxford, 1926

Rowe, A., *The Topography and History of Beth-Shan*, Philadelphia, 1930

Schumacher, G., *Abila of the Decapolis*, London, 1889

—— *Pella of the Decapolis*, London, 1888

—— *Northern Ajlun 'Within the Decapolis'*, London, 1890

—— *Across the Jordan*, London, 1889

Seetzen, U. J., *A Brief Account of the Countries adjoining the Lake of Tiberias, the Jordan and the Dead Sea*, London, 1810

—— *Reisen durch Syrien, Palästina, Phönicien, die Transjordan-Länder, Arabia Petraea und Unter-Aegypten*, ed Kruse, Berlin, 1854

Seyrig, H., *Temples, cultes, souvenirs historiques de la Décapolis*, Syria, 1959

Smith, R. H., *Pella of the Decapolis*, Wooster, Ohio, 1973

Spijkerman, A., *The Coins of the Decapolis and Province of Arabia*, Jerusalem, 1978

Strabo, *Geography*, ed H. L. Jones, London, 1932

Warren, C., 'Expedition to East of Jordan', *PEFQS*, London, 1869

and articles and reports in the *Palestine Exploration Quarterly* and *Quarterly Statements*, *Revue Biblique*, *Bulletin of the American Schools of Oriental Research*, the *Annual of the Jordanian Department of Antiquities*, the *Journal of the Palestine Oriental Society* and the *Journal of Biblical Literature* and other journals of learned Societies.

Index

References to illustrations are given in italic figures

Abila, city of, *14*, 15, 19, 20, 27, 28, 30, 48, *49*, 57, 61,
  64
  acropolis, Tell Abil, 19, 48
  hypogea, 48
  Quweilbeh, 19, 48, *49*
  ruins of, 48
Abila of Lysanias, city of, 15, 16
Adra, city of, 15, 16
Alexander the Great, 11–13, 18–21
Altar Terrace, 91, *91*, 159, *160*
American Expedition, 76, 106, 109, 133, 140, 152,
  177, 184, 186, 215
American Palestine Exploration Society, 73,
  74
American School of Archaeology, 73, 76
American Schools of Oriental Research, 76
Amman, city of, 19, 33–5, *34*, 63, 64, 71, 75
Ammon, Kingdom of, *10*, 11, 18, 19, 23, 33
Antioch, city of, 15, 19, 26, 29, 63
Antiochus IV, 22, 26, 28, 114
Antoninus Pius, Emperor, 33, 49, 50, 153
Arabia/Arabians, 15, 25, 193; *see also* Nabateans
'Arabian God', the, 35, 36; *see also* Nabateans
Araq el Amir, 23–7, *24*
Arbila, city of, 16; *see also* Irbid, city of
Aretas IV, 35
Artemis, deity, 36, 50, 163, 165
Artemis, Sanctuary of, *83*, 85, 147, 148, 159, *160*, 186
  Approach system to, *see* Via Sacra
  Temenos of, 89, 91–3, 159–64, *160*, *162*, 183, 186,
    192, 193
  Temple of Artemis, 33–6, 50, 56, 61, *62*, 64, 65,
    68, 86–92, *90*, *91*, 147, 153, 159–67, *160*, *162*,
    164, *166*, *167*, 185, 191, 200
Association for Promoting the Discovery of the
  Interior Parts of Africa, 63
Atria/Atrium, 87, 94, *96*, 99, 148–52, *149*, *151*, 165,
  182, 184–92, *190*, *192*, 200, *202*, 205
Atrium Mosque, the, 165
Augustus, Emperor, 21, 30

Baalbek, sanctuaries of, 61, 92, 159
Bacon, Prof B. W., 76
Baily, the Rev W., 72, *72*
Barghouti, Dr Assem, 136
Baths, East, *see* East Baths
Baths of Placcus, 186–8, *187*
Baths, West, *see* West Baths

Beisan/Beth-shan, 19, 57, 67; *see also* Scythopolis
Beit Ras, town of, 19, 48, 61, 64; *see also* Capitolias
Bennett, Mrs Crystal-M., 33, 56
Biblical, 13, 59, 60, 63, 68, 74
  New Testament, 13, 31
  Old Testament, 21
Birketein, 50, 68, 183, 211–16, *213–16*
  Festival Theatre, 51, 68, 213–15, *214*, *215*
  Reservoirs, 213, *213*, *214*
  Tomb of Germanus, 68, 215, 216, *216*
Birtles, Serjeant, 72, *72*, 73
Bishop Genesius's Church, *see* Churches
Bosra, city of, 17, 32, 37, 99, 196
Bowen, Brian, 125
Bridge Street, the, 87–9, *88*, 93, 148, 149, *149*, 152,
  153
  redevelopment of, *see* Propylaea Church
British Institute at Amman, 33
British School of Archaeology, Jerusalem, 73, 75, 76,
  140
Brünnow and Domaszewski, 75
Buckingham, J. S., 16, 63–7, 71, 79, 168
Burckhart, J. L., 63–7, 71, 131
Butler, H. C., 26, 47
Byzantine, 13, 24, 25, 52–7, 87, 93–101, 119, 125,
  140, 148, 173, 180
  building methods, 56, 93–101, 119, 125, 150, 152,
    163, 177, 180, 190, 191, 205
  Court, 52, 93

Camp Hill, 35, *38*, 80, 114, 119, 125, *135*, 138
Canatha, city of, *14*, 15, 16, 20, 27, 30, 32, 47
  Byzantine Period, 55
  Hellenistic Period, 47
  Roman Period, 47
  ruins of, 47, 55
  see also Kanawat, city of
Capitolias, city of, *14*, 15, 16, 19, 20, 27, 48, 49, 54,
  60, 61
  acropolis, 49
  hypogea, 48
  St Peter of, 54
  See of, 49, 54
Cardo, the, 37, *38*, 50, *50*, 80, 82, *83*, 84–6, 88, 89, 92,
  93, 131–4, 138, 140, 141, 147, 148, 153, 165,
  168, 171, 189; *see also* Colonnade Street, the
  redevelopment of, 37, 50, 85, 134, 168
Cathedral, the, 35, 36, *83*, 92, 94–6, *95*, 143, 152,

INDEX

163, 177, 178, *178*, 180–85, *182*, *184*, *185*, 186,
188, *188*, 189–92
  Gate to, 77, *79*, 92, 94, 141, 147, 176–80, *178*, *179*,
  182, 192
  'Mary' niche, 180
  Narthex, 94, 180, *182*
  South-west chapel, *182*, 184
  Steps to, 92, 94, 177–80, *178*, *179*, *182*, 192
  Terrace east of, 92, 94, 177–80, *179*, *182*, 192
Centro Scavi di Torino per il Medio Oriente e l'Asia, 88,
  149, 164
Christian, early communities, 31, 32, 40, 41, 52, 53,
  177, 182, 211
  Roman attitude to, 52–5
Chrysorhoas, river, 112, 141, *142*, 147, 152, 168, 207
Churches:
  Bishop Genesius's, *83*, 201–5, *204*
  Mortuary, the, *83*, 207, *208*
  Procopius, the, *83*, 209–11, *212*
  Prophets, Apostles and Martyrs, of the, *83*, 96, *97*,
    99, 211
  Propylaea, the, *83*, 87, *87*, 88, 147–52, *149*, *150*,
    151, *157*, 176
  St George, *83*, 94, 99, *100*, 101, 193, *194*, 198–200,
    200–2, 210
  St John the Baptist, *83*, 94, *98*, 99, 193, *194*, 195–8,
    197–9, *202*, 207
  St Theodore, 56, *83*, 95–7, *96*, *97*, 163, *182*, 183,
    184, *186*, 188–92, *189*, *190*, 191, 192, *192*
  SS Cosmas and Damian, 55, *83*, 94, 99, *100*, 101,
    193–5, *194*, *196*, 198, 199, 201, *202*
  SS Peter and Paul, *83*, 205–7, *206*, 209
  Synagogue, the, *83*, 200, *203*
Circassians, 75, 141
Circular Piazza, the, 50, *50*, 52, *83*, 84, 86, 138–40,
  139, 141; *see also* South Tetrakionia
Citadel at Amman, *see* Philadelphia, Qal'ah, el
City Plan, 36, 65, 77, *79*, 80, *83*, 92, 93, 101, 149
City Walls, 36, *83*, *111*, 112, 113, 119, 168, 173, 207,
  211
Clergy Houses, the, 191
Coele-Syria, 11, 12, 15, 16, 18, 23, 29
Coins/numismatics, 17, 29, 30, 35
Colonnade Street, the, 37, *38*, 61, 64, *66*, 67, 80, *81*,
  83, 84, *86*, 133–41, *136*, *137*, 141–7, 165, 168,
  170, *172*, 173, 176, 186
  Central section of, *83*, 141–7, *143*, 168
  North section of, *83*, 170, *172*, 173, 176
  South section of, *83*, 134–41, *136*, *137*
  redevelopment of, 37, 50, 85, 134; *see also* Cardo,
    the
Colonnade Streets, 33, 37, 42, 46, 84
Conder, Lieutenant, 74, 75
Constantine the Great, 52, 53, 96
Constantinople, city of, 52, 59, 60, 75, 93, 107
Councils of the Church, 53, 54, 56
Crowfoot, J. W., 35, 76, 198, 205

Damascus, city of, 12, 14, *14*, 15, 20, 27, 32, 46, 57,
  60
Darius of Persia, 12

Dead Sea, the, 10, 12, *14*, 71, 72, 74
Decapolis, the, 11, 13, 17–22, 26, 28, 29, 31, 32, 46,
  48, 49, 57, 59, 65, 75
  cities of, 14, *14*, 15, 16, 19, 26–31, 40, 41, 46, 47,
    49, 52, 57, 58, 67; *see also* Canatha, Capitolias,
    Damascus, Dium, Gadara, Gerasa, Hippos,
    Pella, Philadelphia, Raphana, Scythopolis,
    cities of
  corporate character, 11, 13, 15–19, 29
  Region of, 14, *14*, 15–17, 26, 28, 29, 60
  visitors to, 59–76
Decumani, 82, 84, 93
  North Decumanus, *83*, 85, 141, 168, 169, 173
  South Decumanus, *83*, 84, 85, 93, 138, 140, 141
Department of Antiquities, 25, 73, 75, 103, 125, 129,
  135, 159, 161, 165, 207
Dera'a, city of, 47
Detweiler, A. H., 106, 107, *109*, 171, 173
Diaconia, the, 152, 153; *see also* Mosaics
Dion, city of, *see* Dium, city of
Dionysus, Temple of, 35, 36, 50, *79*, 92, 94, 143, 176,
  177, *178*, 181, *182*, 186
Dium, city of, *14*, 15, 16, 19, 26–9, 32, 37, 47
Domus ecclesiae, 54–6, 94, 96, 185, 187, 188
Donations, 35, 36, 50, 56, 114, 115, 126, 185, 195,
  196, 200
Drains, 50, 135, 173
Dusares, deity, 35, 36, 46

Earthquakes, 58, 114, 125, 138, 141, *142*, 148, 151,
  180, 182, 191, 199
East Baths, 51, 141, 208, *210*
Edom/Edomite, *10*, 12
Egypt/Egyptian, 12, 29, 77
Emperor's Divine Majesty, 52, 53
Epiphanius, historian, 16, 40, 41, 53, 182
Eusebius, historian, 16, 31, 32, 40

Fahl, Battle of, 57
Festivals:
  Guild, at Gerasa, 37, 126, 131
  Maiumas, 211
  Miracle at Cana, 182, 211
First Revolt, the, 30–32, 35, 36, 40–42
Fisher, Dr C. S., 76, *97*, *145*, 161, *182*, 187, *190*, 193,
  194, *203*, *204*, *206*
Five Year Plan, 103, 125, 176
Fortifications:
  at Abila, 48
  at Canatha, 47
  at Gadara, 42
  at Gerasa, 36, *83*, *111*, 112–14, 119, 173, 207, 208,
    211
  at Hippos, 46
  at Pella, 40
  at Philadelphia, 33
Fountain Court, the, 182–6, *182*, *185*, *186*, 188, *188*,
  189–92, *189*, *190*, 213
French Biblical School and School of Archaeology,
  73
French Institute in Amman, 25, 125

Gadara, city of, 11, *14*, 15, 16, 19, 20, 29, 30, 42–6, 60–63, 66
   cultural centre, as a, 42, 46
   hot springs, near, 44, 45, 61, 67; *see also* Hammah, el
   poets, 45, 46, 58
   ruins of, 42, 43, *43*, 55, *55*
   tombs, 43, 66–7
   West Theatre, the, 43, 44, *44*
Gadora, city of, 16
Galilee, district of, 26, 32, 201
Galilee, Sea of, *10*, 13, 14, 42, 46, *55*, 60, 74
Gamala, city of, 60
Garstang, Prof John, *66*, *69*, 75, 76, *76*, *107*, 115, *115*, 125, *130*, *158*
Georgia, wife of Theodore, 101, 195, *196*
Gerasa, city of, 11, 13, *14*, 15, 16, 19, 26, 27, 30–39, 43, 49–53, 60, 68, 94–103, 126, 141, 143, 171
   Bishops of, 53, 186, 189, 195, 196, 201, 202, 205, 209
   building programmes, 31, 49, 51, 56, 57, 201
   city plan, *see* City Plan
   city walls, *see* City Walls
   domestic buildings, 36, 140
   history of:
      Byzantine Period, 53–7, 92–101, 176
      Hellenistic Period, 35, 80, 114, 119
      Moslem Period, 57, 58, 164, 165, 195, 199
      Roman Period, 35–8, 49–52, 88, 101, 115
   Nabatean community, 35, 36
   proposed expansion, 38, 105, 113
   residential quarter, 86
Germanus, centurion, 50, 216
German Evangelical Mission, 42, 54
German Orient Company, 73
Gilead, *10*, 11, 103
Glass Court, the, *182*, 184, 185
Glass Mosaics, 57, 95, 96, 99, 181, 190, 196
'Great Mother' cult, 52
Greek culture, 17, 20–22, 42–6
Greenhalgh, P., 29

Hadrian, Emperor, 33, 37, 41, 49, 51, 53, 104, 113, 131
   visit to Gerasa, 37, 38, 113
Hadrianic Arch, the, 38, 65, 77, *78*, *83*, 104–9, *104*, *106*, *108*, 112–14, 129
Hammah, el, hot spring, 45, 67
Hammond, Prof Nicholas, 12
Hanour, Edward, 72, *72*
Harding, G. L., 77, 207
Hasmonean dynasty, 13, 17, 27, 28
Heliopolis, city of, 15, 16
Hellenism/Hellenistic:
   cultural character, 20–23, 26, 27, 42, 43, 45, 46
   impact of, 13, 20–23, 26–8
   origins of the Decapolis, 11, 13, 17–20, 30, 32
   polis – city concept, 13, 19–23, 26–31, 49
Hennessy, Dr Basil, 41
Hera, deity, 35, 36
Heresies, 16, 40, 53, 54

Heroön, the, 193
High Place, 115
Hippodrome, the, 57, *83*, 105, 107–11, *109*, *110*, 127
Hippos, city of, *14*, 15, 19, 27–30, 46, 60
   Byzantine Period, 46, 55
   Fiq, 46
   Hellenistic Period, 46
   Qal'at Husn, 19
   Roman Period, 46
   Ruins of, 55
   See of, 55
Holland, Jack, 52
Holy Land, the, 59, 63, 65, 68, 73, 93, 101
Holy Sepulchre, Church of, 58, 191
Horsfield, George, 106–9, 125, 129, 134, 135, 140, 152, 155, *158*, 159, 175
Humphrey, L. F., 134
Hyrcanus Tobiah, 23–6
Hyrcanus, John, 27

Iconoclasm, 195, 199, *201*, 207
Idumea, state of, 12, 26
Ina, city of, 15, 16
Inscriptions, 35–8, 46, 50, 62, 75, 100, 106, 108, 112, 119, 126, 157, 170, 185, 186, 205, 209
Irbid, city of, 16, 47, 64
Irby and Mangles, 24, 42, 65–8, 71, 77
Isis, deity, 50, 52
Islam, 57, 60, 63; *see also* Moslems
Ituraeans, the, 27, 29, 47

James, F., 41, 54
Jannaean Revolt, the, 27, 28, 114
Jerash, city of, 11, 19, 48, 56, 57, 59, 61–8, *69*, 71–3, 75, 76, 79–217, *83*
   environs, 103
   modern city, *83*, 103, ·112, *122*, 141, *142*, 147, *157*, 208, 209
   Tourist Centre, 111, 112
   Tourist Restaurant, 35, *135*, 138
Jerusalem, city of, *10*, 12, 13, 22, 23, 25–9, 31, 32, 40, 41, 53, 57, 59, 71, 75, *84*, 126, 191, 192, 200
Jews, the, 21–3, 26, 27, 29–31, 42
   communities in the Decapolis, 31, 32, 42, 201
Jones, A. H. M., 21, 47
Jordan, River/Valley, *10*, *14*, 36, 38, 41, 42, 57, 67
Jordan University, 136
Josephus, historian, 11, 15, 25, 27–32, 41, 42
Judah/Judea/Judaic, *10*, 13, *14*, 22, 23, 27–31, 46

Kanawat, town of, 47; *see also* Canatha, city of
Kraeling, Prof Carl H., 16, 35, 50, 76, *84*, 88, 101, 106, 114, 126, 140, 144, 152, 153, 164, 180, 181, 185, 191, 193, 195
Krautheimer, R., 56, 93, 94
Kruger, Dr E., 42

de Laborde, Léon, 68, *70*
Labrousse, A., *120*
Lapp, Nancy L., 24
Lapp, Dr Paul, 24, 25

INDEX

Lux, Dr Ute, 42
Lyttelton, Dr Margaret, 79, 84, 89, 92, 107

Maccabees, 22, 26, 27
Maccabeus, Judas, 26, 27
McCown, C. C., 36, 50, 76, 105, 211, 215
Macedonian settlements, 12, 13, 18, 19, 21–3
Mecca/Medina, cities of, 57, 58
Merrill, Selah, 73, 74
Military, 17, 29, 31, 36, 41, 47, 51
Mithras, deity, 52
Moab, Kingdom of, *10*, 11
Monumental Steps, the, *83*, 89, *90*, 91, *91*, 92, *156*,
   157, *157*, *158*, 159, *160*
Mortuary Church, the, *see* Churches
Mosaics, 57, 95, *95*, 96, *98*, 99, 100, *100*, 101, 136,
   137, 152, 184, 190, 191, 193, *194*, 195–201, *196*,
   198, *199*, *200*, *201*, 205, 207, 210, 211
   'Alexandria' mosaic, *98*, 197
   Diaconia mosaic, 152
   'St John and St Cyrus' mosaic, 197, 198, *199*
Moslems, 57, 140, 164, 165; *see also* Islam
Müller, E. B., 107, 109
Museum, at Jerash, 186, 196, 197

Nabateans, the, 17, 25, 32, 35, 36, 46, 47, 115
   deities, 35, 36
   trade routes, 32, 35, 36
Narthex, 94, 180, *182*, 190, 191, 193
Nemesis, temple of, 50
North Bridge, the, *83*, 86, 87, 89, 93, 147, 148, *148*,
   152, 153
   Archway on, 87, *87*, 89, 148, 149, *149*
North Gate, the, 37, *83*, 85, 170–3, *173*, 211
North Piazza, the, *83*, 173, *174*, 175
North Tetrapylon, the, 50, 51, *83*, 85, 168, 170, *170*,
   171, 173
North Theatre, the, 50, *83*, 173, 175, *175*
Northey, the Rev A. E., 73
North-west Gate, the, 112, 168, 176
Nymphaeum, the, 50, *83*, 86, 92, 143–7, *143*, *145*,
   146, 176, 183, 186, 213

Odeon, the: at Amman, 33, 35
   at Jerash, 175, *175*
Ovadiah, Asher, 46
Oval Forum, the, *see* Oval Piazza
Oval Piazza, the, 35, 37, *38*, 50, 58, 62, 68, *69*, 80, *81*,
   82, *82*, *83* 114, 124, *124*, 125, 131–5, *132*, *133*,
   135, 138, 140, 161
   Archway to Cardo, 80, *81*, 82, 84, 133, 134
   central altar, 131
   paving of, 80, *81*, 131, 132, *132*, *133*

Pakidas, deity, 35
Palestina Secunda, 54, 55
Palestina Tertia, 33, 55
Palestine, *10*, 12, 16–23, 26, 27, 30, 36, 41, 55, 57,
   59, 71, 94, 96, 107, 165
Palestine Association, 63, 71
Palestine Exploration Fund, 71–5

Palmyra, city of, 11, 47, 61, 67, 68, 77, 84, 85, 138, 171
Parapetti, Roberto, 88, 93, 149, 153, 163
Parker, Dr S. T., 15, 16
Parthians, the, 27, 30, 47
Pella, city of, 11, 13, *14*, 15, 16, 19, 20, 26–32, 37,
   38–41, *40*, 47, 57, 60, 67, 68, 71, 125, 171
   Bishops of, 54
   Christians at, 31, 32, 40, 41, 53, 54
   history of:
      Byzantine Period, 53, 54
      Hellenistic Period, 38, 40
      Roman Period, 40, 41
   identification of, 71
   ruins of, 40, *40*, 54
   suburbs, 40
   Tell el Hosn, 38, 40
Persians, the, 12, 13, 19, 28, 46, 57, 107, 201
Petra, city of, 11, 17, 37, 64, 67, 77, 84
Petra/Jerash Project, 103, 111, 112, 131
Philadelphia, city of, *14*, 15, 16, 19, 27, 30, 32, *34*, 37,
   43, 56, 63, 114
   Bishops of, 56
   History of:
      Byzantine Period, 33, 55–6
      Hellenistic Period, 33
      Roman Period, 33–5
   Qal'ah, el, 33, 56
   ruins of, 33, *34*, 35, 43
Phillips, Corporal, *34*, *69*, 72, *72*, 73, *122*, 125, 134,
   135, *136*, 141, *142*, 150, *157*, 159, 170, *172*
Photographs, archival, 33, *34*, *66*, *69*, 71, 72, *72*, 73,
   76, 107, 115, *115*, *122*, 130, 134, *136*, 141, *142*,
   150, *157*, *158*, 170, *172*
Pierobon, R., 164
Pilgrims, 58
Pliny the Elder, 14–16, 21, 182
Pliny the Younger, 53
Pompeian Era, 17, 29
Pompey the Great, 13, 17, 28–30, 35, 42, 46–8
Pottery, 37, 112, 140, 164
Procopius Church, the, *see* Churches
Prophets, Apostles and Martyrs Church, *see*
   Churches
Propylaea, the Artemis, 50, 65, 86, 89, *90*, 92, 108,
   141, 147, 148, 153–61, *154–8*, *160*, 161, 165, 177
Propylaea Church, the, *see* Churches
Propylaea Piazza, the, *83*, 86–90, *88–90*, 93, 147–53,
   149, *151*, 165
   redevelopment of, 87, 93, 148–52, *150*, *151*; *see also*
      Propylaea Church
Province of Arabia, 17, 32, 37, 126
Province of Syria, 17, 29, 30, 32
Ptolemaic Empire, the, 19, 20–23, 77
Ptolemy, Claudius, the Geographer, 15, 16, 19

Rabbath Ammon, city of, 19, 33
Raphana, city of, 15, 16, 20, 47
Ricci, P. A., 155, 159
Robinson, the Rev E., 68, 69, *70*, 71
Rome/Roman, 17, 21, 25, 26, 28–32, 45, 51–3, 57,
   77, 82, 107, 168, 208

INDEX

Rostovtzeff, Prof M., 26, 76, 105
Royal Engineers, Corps of, 71, 74
Ruqqad, river, 57

Saana, city of, 15, 16
St Apollinare Nuovo, Ravenna, 96
St George's Church, *see* Churches
St John the Baptist's Church, *see* Churches
St Sabina, Rome, 96
St Theodore's Basilica, *see* Churches
SS Cosmas and Damian's Church, *see* Churches
SS Peter and Paul's Church, *see* Churches
Salamis, Battle of, 12
Salt, es-, city of, 71, 72
Samaria, city of, 13, 23, 29
Samoulis, city of, 15, 16
Sarapion Passage, the, 36, *182*, 185, 186, *186*
Sassanians, the, 51, 52
Schumacher, G., 44, 45, 75, 173
Scythopolis, city of, 11, *14*, 15, 19, 26–31, 41–3, 57, 67
    Bishops of, 54
    History of:
        Byzantine Period, 54
        Hellenistic Period, 41
        Roman Period, 41
    ruins of, 41–3, 54, 67
    Tell el Husn, 41
    See of, 54
Seetzen, U. J., 59–64, 67, 68, 71
Seleucid Empire, the, 18–21, 26–9
Simon bar Giora, 32
Smith, G. A., 16
Smith, Dr Robert H., 19, 20, 28, 31, 41
South Bridge, the, *83*, 141, *142*
South Gate, the, 77, 82, *83*, 105, 109, 111–14, *113*, 129
South Street, the, 82, *83*, 114
South Tetrakionia, the, 50, *50*, 58, 62, *83*, 84, 85, 134, 138–40, *139*; *see also* Circular Piazza
South Theatre, the, 36, 37, *39*, 43, *69*, 77, *78*, *83*, 109, 121, 126–31, *127*, *128*, *130*, 133, 134, *135*, 175
South-west Gate, the, 50
Spijkerman, Father A., 17, 19, 22, 32
Stephanos Byzantios, 13
Stepped Street, the, *83*, 141, *142*
Stinespring, W. F., 73
Strabo, historian, 15, 17, 37, 45, 46
Surveys: Eastern, 74, 75
        Western, 71, 74
Sydney University, 41
Synagogue, Church, the, *see* Churches
Synkellos, Georgios, 28
Syria, 12, 17–20, 22, 27, 28, 30, 32, 47, 48, 55, 63, 64, 75, 77, 85, 94, 107, 193

Tabaqat Fahl, 38, 40, *40*, 47, 57, 67, 71; *see also* Pella, city of
Temenos East Wall, the, 89, 91, 159, *160*, 161
Tetrapolis, the, 15

Theodore, *paramonarius*, 101, 195, *196*
Tiberias, city of, 46, 60
Titus, son of Vespasian, 32, 41, 42
Tobiad family, 23, 26; *see also* Hyrcanus
Town planning, 79–85, 92, 93, 101, 180
Trade/trade routes, 30, 32, 35–7, 46, 47, 51, 52, 54, 56
Trajan, Emperor, 15, 17, 32, 33, 37, 48, 49, 51, 53, 126, 131, 171
Trajanic Era, 17, 48
Transjordan, *10*, 12, 13, *16*, 18, 20–27, 31–3, 55, 57–9, 63, 71, 74, 75, 94, 96, 99, 200

Ummayyad Period, 57, 140, 164, 165
Umm Qeis, 19, *43*, *44*, *55*, 60, 61, 64, 65
University of Pennsylvania Museum, 41, 54

Valley Garden, the, *83*, 208, *209*
Via Nova, 17, 33, 37
Via Sacra, Gerasa, 85–8, 91, 93, 147–9, 152, 159, 161
Vomitoria:
    at Gadara, 44
    at Gerasa, 109, 126, 127, *128*, 129, 175, 213
    at Scythopolis, 42

Wadi Jalud, 41; *see also* Scythopolis
Wadi Jirm, 38, 40, *40*; *see also* Pella
Wadi Kefrain, 23
Wadi Quweilbeh, 48, *49*; *see also* Abila
Wadi Syr, es-, 23
Walid, Khalid ibn al, 57
Warren, Captain C., 71–3, 72, 134
Watergate, the, *83*, 207, 208, *209*
West Baths, the, 50, *83*, 93, 165–9, *169*, 208
Wilson, Captain, C., 71
Wooster College, Ohio, 41, 54

Yadin, Prof Y., 17
Yale University, 76, 140
Yaqusah, Battle of, 57
Yarmouk, river, 15, 44, 57, 65
Yazid II, Caliph, 195
'Younger Goddess', temple of, 50

Zayadine, Dr Fawzi, 115
Zeus Epicarpius, temple of, 50, 216
Zeus Helios Sarapis, temple of, 50
Zeus Olympius, deity, 36, 50, 114, 165
Zeus, Sanctuary of, 35–7, 80, *83*, 114–24, *116*, 125–7, 131
    Temenos of Zeus, 37, *39*, 80, *81*, 82, 112, 115–25, *116–19*, *122–4*
        Altar platform, 115, *116*, 124, *124*
        Corridors, 115, *116*, 117, 119, 120
        Monumental steps, *116*, 120–23, *122*, *123*, 125, 126
        South doorway, *116*, 119, *119*, 124
        Vaults, 115, *116*, 117, *117*
    Temple of Zeus, 35, 36, 50, *66*, 80, 82, *83*, 114, 115, *115*, *116*, 119–22, *120–22*, 125, 126, *135*